Women, Camp, and Popular Culture

D1526816

Katrin Horn

Women, Camp, and Popular Culture

Serious Excess

Katrin Horn
American Studies
FAU Erlangen-Nürnberg
Erlangen, Germany

ISBN 978-3-319-87885-0   ISBN 978-3-319-64846-0   (eBook)
DOI 10.1007/978-3-319-64846-0

Cover design by Fatima Jamadar

Printed on acid-free paper

This Palgrave Macmillan imprint is published by Springer Nature
The registered company is Springer International Publishing AG
The registered company address is: Gewerbestrasse 11, 6330 Cham, Switzerland

Für meine Eltern

ACKNOWLEDGEMENTS

Writing a book is hardly a party for one and so I share the glitter and glory of this endeavor with several people and institutions without whose encouragement and support my interest in camp might have led to an overly long Tumblr post, but certainly not to this book. I am grateful to my editor at Palgrave, Lina Aboujieb, for believing in this project, her assistant Karina Jakupsdottir for her support in preparation of the manuscript, and the anonymous reviewer for their encouraging words and helpful suggestions for alterations. For their financial support, I owe gratitude to the Bavarian American Academy, the Office for Gender and Diversity at FAU Erlangen, and Universität Bayern e.V. For providing my 'safe space' in academia while their insightful feedback nonetheless encouraged me to work that much harder, I am grateful to the members of the American Studies Colloquium at FAU Erlangen-Nürnberg, especially Andrew Gross, Karin Hoepker, and Carmen Dexl. Ana Popović deserves praise for her helpful feedback on the manuscript. Lastly, even in a musical-inspired utopian dream sequence I could not have imagined a more supportive supervisor than Antje Kley without whom this project most likely would have not seen completion.

For their challenging questions, which made me rethink my approach and clarify my arguments, I want to thank my students at FAU Erlangen-Nürnberg, University of Bayreuth, and JMU Würzburg. I was furthermore fortunate enough to present my work in (different stages of) progress at conferences and summer schools, in lecture series and classes nationally and internationally. For everyone who invited me: thank you for allowing me to test my theories on live audiences. I want to thank especially Fabio Cleto for his heartening words in the very early stages of this project, Dana Heller for her encouragement and support, Linda Mizejewski for sharing her research on Kathy Griffin with me before publication, and Maria San Filippo for allowing me to present my research in her seminar at Harvard and for her encouragement and help in writing my book proposal.

While writing my dissertation and then turning it into this book took up much of my time over the past years, it did not take up all of it. The remaining hours needed to be filled too, and so I would not want to forget Raina, Dana, and Nancy who turned my research stay into a three-month story of falling in love with Boston; Alex and Betti who provided long-distance support and much-needed distraction; and Bohne who was a friend in the darkest hours and gayest (quite literally) moments.

Finally, none of this would have been possible without my family's constant support. My mother continues to be an inspiration in strength, perseverance, and dedication. And my whole family—as distant from the humanities as they are—perpetually surprised me by seeing the merit in spending five years on reading, watching, and writing camp, even when I doubted it myself.

Completely doubt-free I can say I made my best decision long before I read my first notes on camp or ever contemplated academia, and that the past years have proven just how lucky I am. No words can adequately express how (excessively, seriously) grateful I am to my wife Marie for her patience, for her confidence, and for building a life with me while I was busy obsessing about popular culture. If I had a vintage car to drive into the sunset to the soundtrack of cheesy love songs, I wouldn't want to do it with anyone but you.

Katrin Horn

CONTENTS

CHAPTER 1

Beyond Gay Men and After the Closet: Camp's New Politics and Pleasures

Few other music events garner as much global attention as the Eurovision Song Contest (ESC), an annual music-meets-politics-meets-TV-extravaganza watched by over 100 million people worldwide, in which a constantly growing number of "European" countries (including Australia) compete against each other with tragic ballads, elaborate dance sequences, and sparkling costumes for the honor of being the show's next host country and thus a chance to put themselves into Europe's media spotlight. Overt political statements are forbidden, yet perceived "voting blocs" among neighboring countries as well as cultural divides between the supposedly progressive West and a more conservative East (and South) have led to heated debates about what exactly the contest and the respective contestants stand for (politically), what the winners and losers might *mean* outside the three-hour telecast. Naturally, such debates only increase whenever an act perceived as controversial wins. Such was the case in 2014 when the Austrian entry, Conchita Wurst (Thomas Neuwirth) a bearded drag artist, received the most points out of 26 competing countries who voted by jury, popular vote, or any combination thereof. Conchita Wurst and her Bond anthem inspired "Rise like a Phoenix" (including Bond themed fantasies of revenge) were henceforth heralded as proof of an increasingly tolerant Europe (Hoff), as the final breaching of "neighborhood voting" (among audiences, not juries) (Dambeck), and as Eurovision's "newly serious side" in contrast to what Richard Osborne describes as the show's standard camp sensibility.

© The Author(s) 2017
K. Horn, *Women, Camp, and Popular Culture,*
DOI 10.1007/978-3-319-64846-0_1

While all three interpretations of the event seem debatable, I take issue particularly with the latter, as Osborne's claim shows a fundamental misunderstanding not only of the ESC, but also of camp. He might focus on an event whose reach to the US is still rather limited (despite encouraging tweets sent to Conchita Wurst by popular US—and camp—idols Cher and Lady Gaga, and LOGO's recent decision to broadcast the event for US audiences). Yet, like others describing cultural phenomena around the globe as camp, he largely draws on a US history of the term's use and relies on references to US scholars. As such, his misconceptions are symptomatic of the recent popular discourse about camp more generally—including a neglect of women and of the serious.

Relying mostly on Susan Sontag's "Notes on Camp" (1964), Osborne proposes a definition of camp that is less than just a-political. In his estimation camp amounts to little more than mere surface fun comparable to trash appreciation, which leads him to single out the French entry, Twin Twin with "Mustache," as supposedly typical of Eurovision camp. The act in question consists of three (ostensibly) straight men in colorful outfits singing about beards as the one missing piece to the puzzle of a fulfilling life. On the other hand, Conchita Wurst stands out among her fellow competitors for Osborne for not "revelling in bad taste; [... but rather] trying to expand our notions of good taste," and thereby distancing herself from Eurovision camp via the sincerity of her intentions. While there is a fundamental difference between the two acts, despite their similarly over-the-top aesthetics and the shared context of production, it is neither that Conchita Wurst is the exception at the ESC, nor that she offers the meaningful alternative to an otherwise profane exhibition of camp exuberance—quite the contrary, in fact. Even considering the arguments of Sontag's inaugural study of camp's presence in the cultural consciousness of the 1960s, "trying to expand our notions of good taste" (Osborne) is exactly camp's main goal. Following a large canon of queer investigations of camp which came after, responded to, and were critical of "Notes on Camp," the reversal of aesthetic judgments—that is, the introduction of an alternative (queer) basis for value, beauty, and artistic merit—produces more than a-political play with superficial signs and styles. Rather, the inversion of standards of taste at the heart of camp affords its audiences and its producers the ability to invert their (social) standing as outsiders, as freaks, or "the other," and thus to address and establish new communities of taste.

Another aspect, which is ignored in Osborne's (and similar) discussion(s), dates even further back than Sontag's semi-scholarly bullet points of camp characteristics and is found in Christopher Isherwood's novel *World in the Evening*. His protagonist insists on sincerity as the basis of camp appreciation:

> You can't camp about something you don't take seriously; you're not making fun *of* it, you're making fun *out* of it. You're expressing what's basically serious to you in terms of fun and artifice and elegance. (110, emphases added)

In this respect, a drag queen with a beard, surrounded by animated flames, who sings about the rise of the ostracized, and dedicates his victory to the vision of a pan-European gay rights movements, is not the *opposite*, but the *epitome* of camp.

Osborne—and most others who have written about Conchita Wurst's victory—further misconstrue both camp's and the ESC's legacy in terms of its practitioners. No article connects Austria's win to that of Serbia's in 2007, when a woman in a loose tuxedo, with dark glasses and short hair, belted out a dramatic ballad in her native language and beat the Ukrainian frontrunner, reasonably well-known drag-techno act Verka Serduchka. For "Molitva" ("Prayer") Marija Šerifović was accompanied by a group of high-femme background singers clad in fitted, curve accentuating tuxedos, high heels, and long hair, whose clasping hands, at the end, formed hearts connecting all the women on stage, including the butch-coded lead singer. Annamari Vänskä reads this clash between high drama and almost childlike gesture against the backdrop of androgyny and ambiguous sexuality as *lesbian* camp—otherwise it has been thoroughly disregarded in discussions of the ESC's queer history.

Osborne's neglect of this female contribution to ESC's camp legacy and denial of this legacy's survivalist and progressive potential reflect not only a bias in treatments of the ESC, but importantly also in writing about camp more generally. After a rise in theory-focused monographs and readers on camp in the 1990s inspired by the new status and demands of queer theory, and later treatments of pop-cultural phenomena like *Buffy the Vampire Slayer* (1997–2003) and *Xena: Warrior Princess* (1995–2001) as feminist and queer texts, scholarly interest in camp has significantly waned after 2000. At the same time, essays and comments in popular magazines and online—like

Osborne's—increasingly use the term in a depoliticized manner and in exclusive connection to gay male consumers.

This book presents an argument against both misconstructions as it illustrates camp's continued relevance in popular culture as an "area of consent and resistance" (Hall 239), particularly in the reception by queer audiences and with a focus on contributions by and meanings for female producers and consumers. By focusing on examples of popular media produced after 2000 the following chapters show how an acknowledgment of camp strategies allows for a more complex evaluation of the representation of women and sexual minorities that refuses the dichotomy of supposedly "positive" (strong, independent, diverse, etc.) and "negative" (weak, stupid, reactionary, stereotypical, etc.) depictions, which serves as the litmus test within a hegemony of visibility. This representational binary often "reproduces the very marginalization of lesbians and gay men that the text[s] might be trying to undermine" by inviting tolerance from audiences with heteronormative values, which ultimately positions them as subjects in a position of (discursive) power vis-à-vis queer objects (Peele 2). Instead, this book takes into consideration intertextual references and deconstructive ideas to think about representation in terms of a specifically "queer visibility" which aims, as Rosemary Hennessy has argued, "not to include queers in the cultural dominant but to continually pressure and disclose the heteronormative" (36). For such a project, camp is singularly valuable as it draws on and imagines queer communities via its reliance on a canon of alternative media consumption that enhances its affective component, while bearing witness to the historic gaps and disruptions within media's heteronormative framework. Through the denaturalizing and parodic effect of its stylistic excess, camp furthermore adds a critical edge and distance to its engagement with tropes and motives of contemporary media. Thus, camp presents a way of dealing with popular culture that goes beyond either total assimilation or complete opposition, and thereby offers an answer to the question of how queer subjects can participate in the mainstream media landscape without having to lose or deny their identity (Creekmur and Doty 1–2).

These arguments are presented via exemplary readings of three distinct pop-cultural phenomena that are discussed both in a chronological order and in the order of their audience numbers and thus presence in mainstream media, varying from films that target a niche audience, to a sitcom on national TV, and finally an international pop star. The texts in question, *D.E.B.S.* (2003, Dir. Angela Robinson) and *But I'm a Cheerleader* (1999, Dir. Jamie Babbitt), *30 Rock* (2006–2013, NBC, created by Tina Fey), and Lady Gaga are also chosen to represent three key media of popular culture—film, TV, and popular music—to illuminate camp's significance across media boundaries. Additionally, this approach accounts for the media-specificity of the intersection between camp's queer and metareferential effects, and for the affective strategies possible in different media contexts (e.g., seriality vs. liveness). The choice of primary texts thus reflects camp's multivalence and mutability in different cultural and media contexts.

As pointed out above, camp—at its most basic level—is the inversion of taste in favor of the neglected, the other, the marginalized. From this playful shift in aesthetic judgments camp derives its broader potential "as a way of making cultural, social and sexual critique under guise of harmless humour" (Pearson 570). My notion of what constitutes critique is informed by Judith Butler, who—with reference to Raymond Williams and Michel Foucault—argues that critique is not a question of finding fault and passing judgment. Instead critique should be understood as a "practice that not only suspends judgment [...], but offers a new practice of values based on that very suspension" ("Critique"), and I would add in the specific context of camp, the pleasure derived from it. Due to this inherent connection of critique and pleasure, of distance and affect,—what I call *detached attachment*—I am interested in "mainstream" media rather than subcultural products whose distance from normative modes of representation and transgressive intent is immediately recognizable.[1] This selection of texts results furthermore from camp's dependency on normative cultural texts to achieve its parodying effect, which makes its analysis in this very context much more fruitful. As David Bergman maintains, "camp exists in tension with popular culture, commercial culture, or consumerist culture" (4–5).[2] Finally, camp, like any form of critique or strategy of queering, reaches a much wider audience in popular culture. Focusing on mainstream pop culture thus means expanding the discussion about queerness, camp, and critique, and limiting it at the same time, as a critique in mainstream culture will inevitably be less radical in terms of gender variance (trans issues are only referred to in passing) and intersectionality (queer characters of color with substantial screen time are almost unknown entities in popular culture, similar to a "minority" feminism) than its articulation is less commercially oriented discourses and media might be. However, I agree with Lori Burns and Mélisse Lafrance that to refuse to engage with commercial products "simply because of its ties to capital is to dismiss the media through which most people gain most of their cultural literacy" (xii). Put differently, the acknowledgment that popular culture cannot be radical in the sense of being anti-capitalist should not exclude the notion that it is still capable of transporting other forms of resistance within the limitations of a capitalistic framework and market logic.

To clarify camp's critical potential, Chap. 2 offers a summary of camp's history and theory to explain how it has evolved and what it means today. At its core, camp is defined as a parodic device that uses irony, exaggeration, theatricality, incongruity, and humor to question the pretext's status as "original" or "natural." This approach is informed both by "classic" discussions of camp as an originally gay-coded strategy, such as Jack Babuscio's and Richard Dyer's, and by later texts which open camp to feminist and queer readings, in particular Pamela Robertson's and Fabio Cleto's. For certain additional aspects of camp, such as parody and gendered excess, Linda Hutcheon, Helene A. Shugart and Catherine Egley Waggoner provide useful definitions. The summary also stresses camp's connection to metareferentiality—how texts draw awareness to their mediated status, foregrounding their own constructedness and thus the discursive, rather than the "natural" quality of their represented contents.

Chapters 3–5 then examine camp in three different variations, namely: with a focus on traditions of lesbian representations in post-New Queer Cinema; with an eye to postfeminist discourses in American TV; and, finally, as the continuation of pop music's queer legacy in a changed cultural and media context. I cast such a wide net, rather than focus on a narrower selection of texts, to stress first how camp is an always relational, secondary phenomenon—a form of parody, a coping mechanism—that is hence constantly adapting and evolving depending on contexts of production and reception, and changing in accordance with shifting paradigms of identity, sex, and gender. Second, such a transmedial, and to a certain extent diachronic, approach illustrates how mutation, change, and adaptation to changing cultural, technical, and representational circumstances do not equal compromise when it comes to camp's capability to engage with pop-cultural texts in a manner that allows for simultaneous emotional investment and critical distance. All three examples can be placed within a lineage of established camp (con) texts—gay cinema, feminist sitcoms, and pop diva—yet bring something decisively new to the table, both in terms of style and in their awareness and recognition of contemporary subject matters: *But I'm a Cheerleader*, among other things, takes on "re-education camps"; *30 Rock* dedicates several episodes to topical issues such as hiring practices in the TV industry, the "having it all" debate, and the exploitation of women's bodies for entertainment purposes; while Lady Gaga's artistic output presents her as equally invested in political questions (such as the overturn of the military policy of "Don't Ask, Don't Tell") and in technological advancements and their influence on the reception of stars.

The examples thus span a broad thematic field. Nonetheless, two films, one series, and one pop star comprise a relatively small sample of primary texts from over ten years of popular culture. This choice of corpus is indebted to Henry Jenkins', Tara McPherson's and Jane Shattuc's argument that in popular cultural studies "attention to the particular takes on special importance," because comprehending "the particularity of popular culture alters our glib assumptions that it is formulaic, that it always repeats the same messages, that it always tells the same stories and serves the same interests" (15). To accentuate these particularities, all the chapters connect their respective case studies to a canon of intertexts and embed them within a larger cultural and commercial context. Chapter 3—dedicated to two feature films with a lesbian focus—shows that even an increase in visibility can become the target of camp parody through an intervention into the construction of clichés and the reliance on stereotypes—particularly if those follow an exploitative logic rather than provide new modes of identification. Two films produced after the heyday of New Queer Cinema, *D.E.B.S.* and *But I'm a Cheerleader*, are presented as paradigmatic for a new "Great Dyke Rewrite," a phrase coined by queer film scholar B. Ruby Rich to describe a shift in lesbian and queer women's engagement with popular culture (25). I position these two films as romantic comedies that break the genre pattern of this heteronormative filmic convention to provide a specifically queer happy ending through stylistic and narrative deviations. Furthermore, the films use tropes of lesbian representation from both Hollywood cinema and the more recent "lesbian chic" in a manner that exposes them as clichéd, yet still invests them with cinematic pleasure. Hence, the films are read as consequences of and reactions to two opposing cultural events: the questioning of representational traditions in the avant-garde films of New Queer Cinema on the one hand; and the commodification of lesbian sexuality in mainstream media on the other. Both developments are discussed in terms of their influence on, and complication of, visibility as well as their connection to earlier modes of lesbian representability. Chapter 3 thus explores how these gaudy romantic comedies cast old stereotypes—the queer villain, the homoerotic boarding school environment—in new contexts of hyper-visibility and hyper-stylization to allow for the joyful consumption of these "guilty pleasures," even as they stress the discriminatory history and problematic presence of lesbian stories in Hollywood cinema.

Chapter 4 discusses the NBC sitcom *30 Rock*, created by and starring *Saturday Night Live* alumna Tina Fey, as both partaking in and criticizing the postfeminist media environment that has shaped recent discussions of feminism in popular discourses. Referred to as a "sensibility" (Gill) that functions as the undercurrent of diverse media from romantic comedies to makeover shows and self-help books, postfeminism presents a particularly robust object of critique as opposition is always already embraced, only to be simultaneously discarded as dated. The chapter introduces postfeminist media's central issues and contradictions—feminist ideals of communal achievements of equality and self-determination versus neoliberal demands of self-policing and individual responsibility—and their incorporation into other contemporary TV series perceived as camp(y). The representational politics of *30 Rock* are further contextualized within the legacy of feminist sitcoms and their sidekick–lead pairings—going back to *The Mary Tyler Moore Show* (1970–1977)—which have been a source of female excess and queerness that several scholars have interpreted as instances of feminist camp. *30 Rock* reinvents the dynamic between its main female characters and blurs the lines between quality sitcom and sketch comedy. The subsequent constant "laying bare of the devices" and a female lead–comic sidekick constellation, which inverses hierarchies of opinion and lifestyle typical of earlier feminist sitcoms, result in the show's capability to critique postfeminism without judging and to partake without agreeing. Camp here presents an intervention into postfeminism's reliance on "knowing winks" and irony used to sell a new kind of "retro-sexism," a rejection of its primacy of heteronormativity, and a critical commentary on its glorification of "natural" femininity.

Chapter 5 explores how the supposed saturation with "gay" and/or "over the top" imagery in popular music does not prevent a meaningful engagement with camp due to the latter's ability to take a turn for the darker and the grotesque in its effort to disrupt normative modes of representation. The chapter is therefore dedicated to Lady Gaga's oeuvre, with particular attention paid to her concert tour *The Monster Ball*, and analyzes its metacommentary, queer intertextuality, and aesthetic surplus to account for her work's success on both critical and affective levels. The chapter stresses how the mastering of "new media" (online videos, cross-media branding) on the one hand, and "old masters" (Andy Warhol, Madonna, *Thelma & Louise*, Kenneth Anger) on the other, serves to establish Lady Gaga as both mega and meta pop star, and thus a prime example for the potential intensification of critical appeal through commercial success. Her stress on the performativity of identity (through costume, gesture, voice, etc.) further demonstrates how critical sincerity and affective authenticity can be achieved independent from personal "realness." The chapter traces how camp features in her defamiliarization of star discourses and representations of gender and sexuality, and how it thus intervenes in the assimilation of gay images and of the commodification of sexualized female bodies, and instead creates space for queer affects and affinities.

Overall, *Women, Camp, and Popular Culture* establishes camp as a detached attachment that enables the participation in and enthusiasm for mass culture at the same time as it stresses its shortcomings, dangers, and limitations. It is therefore read as subversive and dismantling—of normative discourses—as well as creative and encouraging—of interpretative communities and affective investment. Enabling a distancing proximity, camp's critical potential equally stems from its sincerity towards that which dominant discourses have neglected, ridiculed, or rejected, and manifests itself in its resistance to seemingly self-evident (but never politically neutral) meanings, and its ability to renegotiate cultural affiliations and differences. Hence, camp's reliance on partially reactionary or misogynistic images should be acknowledged not as a dependence on hegemonic texts, but as crucial to its critique. It serves as a constant reminder of how powerful and ubiquitous dominant discourses and text are, while simultaneously pointing at their gaps and incongruities, whereby it undermines their claim to totality and truth. The book's central objects, camp and pop(ular culture), are consequently understood as mutually dependent and partially overlapping, but never absolutely congruent or absorbed; even as pop culture offers camp's most fruitful grounds—its fodder and critical foil—camp remains a distinct and specific strategy to engage with a pop culture's faults rather than as a default reaction to pop.

The following chapters show where and how camp is employed in US popular culture in our new millennium as a strategy to complicate as much as enhance the pleasure we take in popular culture. Underlying these considerations are the central claims that the focus on style and surface typical for camp is not equivalent to a limitation to the superficial. Quite the contrary, considering the impact of images, styles, and pop-cultural texts, in short "the frivolous," on contemporary discourses of (normative) gender and (accepted) sexualities, camp's embrace of the excessive and humorous enables rather than restricts sincerity and affective intensity. And if we accept that to critique is "to make harder those acts which are now too easy," as Foucault argues (171), then camp offers exactly that by pointing to popular culture's ideological issues and deficiencies, thus making it harder to be complacent with repressive and exclusionary tropes of representation. To fully grasp camp's brand of critique, however, we need to consider also the reversal of Foucault's dictum; to think conversely not only about that which culture makes too easy, but also those acts which are made harder by dominant discourses, namely to find alternative and affirmative pleasures and sources of identification in mainstream media. Building on a definition of camp at the intersection of its history as in-group communication and its rediscovery as deconstructive method, the texts discussed in the following chapters doubly intervene in the exclusionary discourses of contemporary media landscapes: they create spaces for sincere and pleasurable attachment to artistic objects and fellow audiences; while they critically detach themselves from normative narratives and images. Songs of love and redemption, after all, disturb more and *affect* differently if sung by bearded drag queens emerging from artificial flames or by bespectacled butches clasping hands with painted-on hearts.

NOTES

1. Most accounts of camp usage outside of mainstream media are found in (theater) performances, examples of which are discussed, among others, in Richard Niles' examination of Charles Busch's drag performances and José Esteban Muñoz's "*Choteo*/Camp Style Politics: Carmelita Tropicana's Performance of Self-Enactment," which adds considerations of intersectionality. Kate Davy's "Fe/male Impersonation: The Discourse of Camp" looks at lesbian theater performances at the WOW Cafe," while Sarah Warner examines the "acts of gaiety" that have permeated

lesbian performance and activism. For a more recent example, see Nishant Shahani's account of nostalgia, queer historiography, and camp in the oeuvre of the alternative "art-pop band" (1219) Antony and the Johnsons, founded by transgender singer Antony Hegarty.

2. Among the numerous authors to discuss camp's intimate relationship to mass culture are: Pamela Robertson, who calls the connection "parasitic" (122): Greg Taylor, who defines camp as "an active refashioning of mass culture" (51); and Matthew Tinkcom, who understands camp as a tactic employed by those omitted from representation "to appear [...] in those complicated moments of exchange under capital" (4).

WORKS CITED

30 Rock. Creat. Tina Fey. NBC, 2006–2013.

Babuscio, Jack. "Camp and Gay Sensibility." *Camp Grounds: Style and Homosexuality.* Ed. David Bergman. Amherst: University of Massachusetts Press, 1993. 19–37.

Buffy the Vampire Slayer. Created by Joss Whedon. The WB, 1997–2001, and UPN, 2001–03.

But I'm a Cheerleader. Dir. Jamie Babbit. Lionsgate, 2000.

Bergman, David. "Introduction." *Camp Grounds: Style and Homosexuality.* Ed. David Bergman. Amherst: University of Massachusetts Press, 1993. 1–16.

Burns, Lori, and Mélisse Lafrance. *Disruptive Divas: Feminism, Identity & Popular Music.* New York: Routledge, 2002.

Butler, Judith. "What is Critique? An Essay on Foucault's Virtue." *Transversal.* May 2001. Eipcp: European Institute for Progressive Cultural Policies. 1 Apr 2010 http://transform.eipcp.net/transversal/0806/butler/en#redir.

Cleto, Fabio. "Queering the Camp." *Camp: Queer Aesthetics and the Performing Subject – A Reader.* Ed. Fabio Cleto. Edinburgh: University Press, 2008. 1–42.

Creekmur, Corey K., and Alexander Doty. "Introduction." *Out in Culture: Gay, Lesbian, and Queer Essays on Popular Culture.* Eds. Corey K. Creekmur and Alexander Doty. London: Cassell, 1995. 1–11. Cassell Lesbian & Gay Studies.

Dambeck, Holger. "Eurovision Song Contest: So verzerrten die Jurys den Wählerwillen." *Spiegel.de.* 12 May 2014. SPIEGELnet. 17 July 2014 http://www.spiegel.de/wissenschaft/mensch/conchita-wurst-beim-esc-abstimmung-von-jury-und-zuschauern-a-968858.html.

Davy, Kate. "Fe/male Impersonation: The Discourse of Camp." *The Politics and Poetics of Camp.* Ed. Moe Meyer. London: Routledge, 1994. 111–127.

D.E.B.S. Dir. Angela Robinson. Screen Gems, 2004.

Dyer, Richard. "It's so camp as keeps us going." *The Culture of Queers.* Ed. Richard Dyer. London: Routledge, 2002. 49–63.

Foucault, Michel. "So is it Important to Think?" *The Essential Foucault: Selections from Essential Works of Foucault, 1954–1984.* Eds. Paul Rabinow and Nikolas S. Rose. New York: New Press, 2003. 170–73.

Gill, Rosalind. "Postfeminist Media Culture: Elements of a Sensibility." *European Journal of Cultural Studies,* 10.2 (2007): 147–171.

Hall, Stuart. "Notes on Deconstructing 'The Popular'." *People's History and Socialist Theory.* Ed. Raphael Samuel. London: Routledge & Kegan Paul Ltd, 1981. 227–239.

Hennessy, Rosemary. "Queer Visibility in Commodity Culture." *Cultural Critique* 29 (1994–95): 31–76.

Hoff, Hans. "Ein Triumph von Herz, Humor und Toleranz: Conchita Wurst beim ESC 2014." *Sueddeutsche.de.* 11 May 2014. Süddeutsche Zeitung Digitale Medien. 17 July 2014 http://www.sueddeutsche.de/medien/conchita-wurst-beim-esc-triumph-von-herz-humor-und-toleranz-1.1958322.

Hutcheon, Linda. *A Theory of Parody: The Teachings of Twentieth-Century Art Forms.* New York: Methuen, 1985.

Isherwood, Christopher. *The World in the Evening.* Minneapolis: University of Minnesota Press, 1999.

Jenkins, Henry, Tara McPherson, and Jane Shattuc. "The Culture That Sticks to Your Skin: A Manifesto for a New Cultural Studies." *Hop on Pop: The Politics and Pleasures of Popular Culture.* Eds. Henry Jenkins, Tara McPherson and Jane Shattuc. Durham: Duke University Press, 1995. 3–26.

Niles, Richard. "Wigs, Laughter, and Subversion: Charles Busch and Strategies of Drag Performance." *Journal of Homosexuality* 46 (2004): 35–53.

Muñoz, José Esteban. "*Choteo*/Camp Style Politics: Carmelita Tropicana's Performance of Self-Enactment." *Women and Performance: A Journal of Feminist Theory* 7: 2–8: 1 (1995): 38–51.

Osborne, Richard. "On Camp & Conchita: An Eurovision Victory For The LGBT Community." *The Quietus.* 12 May 2014. 13 June 2014 http://thequietus.com/articles/15224-eurovision-camp-conchita.

Pearson, Sarina. "Pacific Camp: Satire, Silliness (and Seriousness) on New Zealand Television." *Media, Culture and Society* 27 (2005): 551–75.

Peele, Thomas. "Introduction: Popular Culture, Queer Culture." *Queer Popular Culture: Literature, Media, Film, and Television.* Ed. Thomas Peele. New York: Palgrave Macmillan, 2007. 1–8.

Rich, B. Ruby. *New Queer Cinema: The Director's Cut.* Durham: Duke University Press, 2013.

Robertson, Pamela. *Guilty Pleasures: Feminist Camp from Mae West to Madonna.* London: Tauris, 1996.

Shahani, Nishant. "'Between Light and Nowhere': The Queer Politics of Nostalgia." *The Journal of Popular Culture* 46.6 (2013): 1217–1230.

Shugart, Helene A. and Catherine Egley Waggoner. "A Bit Much: Spectacle as Discursive Resistance." *Feminist Media Studies* 5.1 (2005): 65–81.

Sontag, Susan. "Notes on Camp." *Against Interpretation, and Other Essays*. New York: Picador, 2001. 275–292.

Taylor, Greg. *Artists in the Audience: Cults, Camp, and American Film Criticism.* 2nd ed. Princeton: University Press, 2001.

The Mary Tyler Moore Show. Creat. James L. Brooks and Allan Burns. CBS, 1970–1977.

The Monster Ball. Perf. Lady Gaga. Live Nation Entertainment, 2009–2011.

Thelma & Louise. Dir. Ridley Scott. Pathé et al, 1991.

Tinkcom, Matthew. *Working like a Homosexual: Camp, Capital, and Cinema.* Durham: Duke University Press, 2002.

Vänskä, Annamari. "Bespectacular and Over the Top: On the Genealogy of Lesbian Camp." *SQS Journal* 02 (2007): 66–81.

Warner, Sara. *Acts of Gaiety: LGBT Performance and the Politics of Pleasure.* Ann Arbor: University of Michigan Press, 2012.

Xena: Warrior Princess. Created by Robert Tapert. Renaissance Pictures, 1995–2001.

CHAPTER 2

The History and Theory of Camp

The World in the Evening's Charles Kennedy claims that camp is "terri- bly hard to define" (Isherwood 111), while Susan Sontag insists that to "talk about Camp is [...] to betray it" (275). Like many early scholarly texts on camp, these quotes emphasize how the concept is (supposedly) "notoriously evasive" (Medhurst 276) and defined by "its indefinability, its elusiveness, and its changeability" (Bergman 123). Some of the more recent texts, on the other hand, change the tenor to stress how camp "is so dead. Its ghost whispers can be heard beyond the creaking stairs leading to the attic" (Gaines and Segade). Similarly to Malik Gaines and Alex Segade, who preface this statement with the subheading "Further Notes on the Death of Camp," David and Harold Galef get their most important point across before their introduction by simply but provoca- tively using the title "What *was* Camp" (emphasis added) in their study of the phenomenon and its psychological effects in the early 1990s. Running counter to these extreme positions of certainty about camp's obsolescence, yet *un*certainty about its specific qualities, queer and femi- nist theory's re-evaluation of strategies like mimicry, appropriation, and parody has led to a proliferation of productive inquiry into the ongoing relevance of camp. This strand of scholarship constitutes the basis for my own understanding of camp's form and function as an excessively styl- ized parody and in-group humor, capable of intervening in naturalized and naturalizing discourses of gender and sexuality, while granting access to otherwise oppressive systems of meaning- and pleasure-making. This chapter therefore introduces the basic arguments of this re-evaluation of

© The Author(s) 2017   15
K. Horn, *Women, Camp, and Popular Culture*,
DOI 10.1007/978-3-319-64846-0_2

camp. Furthermore, to situate both my insistence on camp's continued relevance and the position of those who come to different conclusions concerning the legitimacy of contemporary uses of camp, a short history of the strategy and its contexts precedes these theoretical considerations. This sketched history illustrates how camp has evolved from a primarily private code of secret communication to a deconstructive method of cultural critique, and how these seemingly disparate aspects of its use are intimately related to this day.

1   STONEWALL, SONTAG, "SISSIES," SIRK

Part of camp's often (wrongly) diagnosed evasiveness can be explained by the fact that camp is firmly rooted in its historically specific origins in gay subculture at the same time as it is fully dependent on its variable contemporary context. Thus, in order to do justice to the complexity and specificity of camp, it is crucial to bear in mind its original status as "a means of communication and survival [for gay people]" (Bronski 42), particularly before the Stonewall riots and the advent of the gay rights movement in the late 1960s. David Bergman calls camp before Stonewall "an argot that provided an oppressed group some measure of coherence, solidarity, and humor" and a way "to talk to one another within the hearing range" of potentially hostile heterosexuals (13). Especially among drag queens, Andy Medhurst stressed, camp served to "undermine the heterosexual normativity through enacting outrageous inversions of aesthetic and gender codes" (279). Anthropologist Ester Newton offered a fascinating study of this in her 1979 publication *Mother Camp: Female Impersonators in America*. However, she cautioned that this version of camp was still a "pre- or proto-political phenomenon," as "the camp says, 'I am not like the oppressors' [, but] in doing so he agrees with the oppressors' definition of who he is" (100 n. 21), rather than negating their stigmatizing power.

The notion of stigma is a recurring theme in studies investigating camp's use in the rough timeframe of the 1940s to late 1960s, though later analyses retrospectively view camp in a more transgressive light than did Newton. Fabio Cleto, for example, called it an originally "survivalist strategy (working through a reinscription of stigma)" ("Queering" 8).[1] Sites at which camp is employed in this manner, according to studies from the 1980s onwards, include underground cinema and pulp fiction. In his study of directors like Andy Warhol, Jack Smith, and Kenneth

Anger, Juan Antonio Suárez views expressions of camp not as "adventures in taste as much as war cries, expressions of protest from communities actually claiming social and cultural spaces forcibly denied to them" (105). Gay male pulp is discussed, among others, by Fabio Cleto (in his foreword to Victor J. Banis' *That Man From C.A.M.P.*) and Michael Bronski (*Pulp Friction*) as an early site of resistance. Even more attention has been paid to lesbian pulp fiction by such authors as Ann Bannon and Vin Packer—due to its larger commercial success and hence more complicated relations to exploitation and voyeurism, and to identity-confirming aspects. Both strands of this low-brow fiction written at the height of paperback success after World War II, Patricia Julianna Smith describes as essential "iconoclasts" in what she calls "the queer sixties":

> these fictions rejected bourgeois morality and affirmed a gay lifestyle outside the bounds of heterosexual expectations. As such, they functioned as a considerable, if generally uncredited, aspect of the groundwork of Gay Liberation movements that would come to the fore in the 1970s and subsequent decades. (xxii)

While her definition of their camp value can still be considered "prepolitical," it is far less passive than Newton's. Similarly, most accounts of camp's usage in connection to Hollywood cinema from the 1930s to the 1960s already stress camp's combination of distancing qualities (in terms of heteronormative values) and communal aspects (in terms of shared queer values and responses), which inform my concept of detached attachment. In his analysis of MGM musicals, Steven Cohan for example, defines camp as a passing strategy which allows queer audiences to take pleasure in the same cultural products as the straight mainstream, yet to "reinvest them queerly" (*Incongruous* 18). With a rare focus solely on the production side and in connection to Marxist investigations of queer labor, Matthew Tinkcom provides a productive insight into camp's status as a tactic

> through which queer men of a particular historical epoch have made sense of their frequent omission from representation and sought to invent their own language to appear, in a particular fashion, in those complicated moments of exchange under capital. (4)

Moreover, Tinkcom is among the few scholars to reflect upon his omission of agents who are not white gay men (21). In general, however, most texts on the early history of camp follow Dyer's conviction that camp is "distinctively and unambiguously gay male" (49). This stance reflects gay and lesbian studies' origin in identity politics, and its resultant interest in uncovering biographies of historical figures and distinctly gay and lesbian forms of cultural production. Jack Babuscio argues in a similar direction with his definition of camp as "a relationship between activities, individuals, situations, *and* gayness" (20, emphasis in the original). He qualifies this statement by clarifying that not all gay men will necessarily respond to camp and that furthermore the person from which the camp product originates (e.g., director Josef von Sternberg), does not have to be gay him- or herself. Instead, he introduces the term "gay sensibility" to denote

> a creative energy reflecting a consciousness that is different from the mainstream; a heightened awareness of certain human complications of feeling that spring from the fact of social oppression. (19)

While he still thinks of this difference from the mainstream as created by gayness, he tentatively opens the discourse to include other forms of (gendered) oppression (28).

However, before camp is rediscovered from these proto-political gay origins as both political and queer in the 1980s, its usage takes a "detour" into the a-political and straight, of which the seminal "Notes on Camp" is the most well-known result.[2] The 1960s saw a shift in the perception of camp when gay activists and artists rejected camp and its effeminate gestures, allusions to Hollywood divas, and over-the-top performances of gendered identities, as a sign of internalized self-hatred, reactionary, and ultimately hurtful to the new political demands of the US gay rights movement. At the same time, camp found its way into popular culture and academic discussions about new aesthetics.[3] In accordance with the zeitgeist of the 1960s, Sontag described camp as a sensibility which, as Andy Medhurst summarizes, "advocated an arch skepticism towards established cultural canons" (279). She therefore contributed to "an avant-garde assimilation of camp" (Case 189). Problematically, however, in doing so Sontag claimed that camp is necessarily "disengaged, depoliticized—or at least apolitical" (277), a statement which is coherent with her own observations on camp, yet ignorant of camp's roots in minority culture.

The proliferation of this depoliticized and decontextualized notion of camp results in a theory of "mass camp sensibility," a term coined by Barbara Klinger to talk about the reception of Douglas Sirk's melodramas from the 1950s, which "entered mainstream culture ready to adore the mediocre, laugh at the overconventionalized, and critique archaic sex roles" (139). Similar observations can be found in Harry Benshoff's summary of 1960s movie culture in "Movies and Camp" or Andy Medhurst's reading of the original *Batman* series (1966–1968). Pop art also features prominently in this discussion for its inversion of artistic value and merit through elevating mass media products to pieces of art, and its subsequent disruption of cultural canons and aesthetic frameworks.[4] Its most prominent representative, Andy Warhol, literalized this connection in 1965 in one of his less often exhibited pieces, a film titled *Camp*, in which he does however stress camp's gay connotations.[5] In contrast to Sontag's claims and definitions like "mass camp," most of the supposedly mainstream and a-political cultural products from this era— like *Camp*—have since been reclaimed as representing a queer cultural canon and have subsequently become stable references in camp productions, such as Warhol and his influence on Lady Gaga's artistic vision or Douglas Sirk as the precursor to Rainer Werner Fassbinder. Nonetheless, camp's widespread discussion in mainstream media together with the supposed disappearance of its originating condition, the closet, has led several scholars to dismiss subsequent uses as camp lite (Galef and Galef) or pop camp (Robertson 129, Meyer 4), and "proper" camp as dead (e.g., Harris; Mistry).

Meanwhile a newly emerging political movement—no longer concerned with "acceptance" and/via "respectability"—and queer theory rediscovered camp as a politically useful strategy for criticizing oppression and uncovering the hypocrisy of American society in the 1980s. As David Bergmann summarizes: "[i]t took AIDS and poststructuralist theory to make camp intellectually and politically respectable again" (9).[6] This shift influenced camp's understanding in at least three meaningful ways: first, with queer activism's disregard for respectability and assimilation, camp's reliance on cultural waste, deviant gender representations, and connection to flamboyance ceased to be problematic; second, queer theory and its transferal of the theoretical basis from essentialism to performativity allowed for a much larger catalog of politically meaningful strategies; and finally, the de-essentializing and thus broadening of gay, to LG(BT), to queer meant that beyond the "in-group" of white gay men, many other individuals and groups who saw themselves outside of and in contrast to heteronormativity were acknowledged as able to participate in camp discourses. Moe Meyer bases his definition of camp as a queer strategy, for example, in the following reconceptualizing of queer[7]:

> As the rejection of a social identity based upon the differentiation of sexual practices, queer identity must be more correctly aligned with various gender, rather than sexual, identities because it is no longer based, and does not have to be, upon material sexual practice. (3)

Similarly, Annamarie Jagose argues for both the openness of the term itself and the inclusivity of queer critique:

> Institutionally, queer has been associated most prominently with lesbian and gay subjects, but its analytic framework also includes such topics as cross-dressing, hermaphroditism, gender ambiguity and gender-corrective surgery. Whether as transvestite performance or academic deconstruction, queer locates and exploits the incoherencies in those three terms [sex, gender, and desire] which stabilise heterosexuality.

Camp's thriving on incongruity thus is newly invested with political potential, as it aligns with queer theory's deconstructive framework. Accordingly, scholarly treatments of camp influenced by queer theory stress its "demystifying" (Cleto, "Gender" 203) and "denaturalizing" (Doty 83; Smelik 140; Devitt 32) qualities with regard to normative ideologies of gender and sexuality. In light of cultural and gender studies influenced by poststructuralist theory, camp can today be formulated as a subversive strategy in popular culture rather than just a taste for all things "good, because [they're] awful" (Sontag, "Notes" 292) or "the one thing that expresses and confirms being a gay man" (Dyer "So Camp" 59). Instead, Fabio Cleto summarizes that "under the aegis of queer theatricality camp has come to refer no longer to the limited field of gay 'effeminacy,' but to the whole apparatus of theatricalised performances of gender signs and gender roles" ("Gender" 203). Furthermore, camp has emerged as a method to enact "the refusal of the queer to be symbolically annihilated or to be subordinated to heteronorms" (Padva 222).

2   CAMP'S DOUBLE CODING: DETACHMENT/ATTACHMENT

As traced above and outlined in my introduction, this book argues on the premise that camp—indebted as it is to queer theory as much as it has developed from an argot for minority groups—is both disruptive and creative, and that these two uses are interrelated. It perceives camp as an aesthetic strategy, which relies on parody—often achieved through stylistic exaggeration, excessive theatricality, or other forms of overarticulation—irony, and humor to create incongruities and discrepancies within (popular) texts. Thus, it disrupts normative notions of gender and sexuality, oppressive ideologies more generally, as well as any given pretext's status as "original" or "natural." These effects define camp as detachment. To form camp's whole, however, the formation of alternative spaces of identification and belonging is equally crucial. Hence, any definition of camp needs to acknowledge its ability to advance "communal empowerment" (Denisoff 135) and thus the importance of understanding camp also as a form of intensified attachment.

From an aesthetic perspective, excess as "the engine of critical reflection" (Cleto, "Queering" 5) is fundamental to understanding camp's form and function, insofar as it "provides a freedom from constraint" (Sconce 551). Yet camp is simultaneously marked by excessive style *and* by "affect in excess of their apparent objective value" (Cohan, *Incongruous* 8).[8] Al LaValley connects the two aspects when he claims that "camp treasures excessive theatricality and outrageousness as an avenue of heightened emotion" (64). Whereas excessive stylization can be considered the strategy's most straightforward element, enhanced emotion is its most neglected aspect. This disregard for its affective dimension leads to—as, for example, the responses to the Eurovision Song Contest have shown—mislabelling any over-the-top object as camp as much as it results in the refusal to call camp by its name due to objects' and performers' supposed sincerity.

This study in contrast understands camp and its critical potential as inseparable from its affective dimension. With this I follow a point made most poignantly by Eve Kosofsky Sedgwick in her distinction between the oftentimes interchangeably used terms camp and kitsch:

> Unlike kitsch-attribution [...] camp-recognition doesn't ask, "What kind of debased creature could possibly be the right audience for this spectacle?" Instead, it says *what if*: What if the right audience for this were

exactly *me*? What if, for instance, the resistant, oblique, tangential investments of attention and attraction that I am able to bring to this spectacle are actually uncannily responsive to the resistant, oblique, tangential
investments of the person, or some of the people, who created it? And
what if, furthermore, others whom I don't know or recognize can see it
from the same "perverse" angle? (Sedgwick 156, emphases in the original)

This hope for and belief in others sharing "the same 'perverse' angle,"
which camp inspires, is the key to understanding its relationship to
community and affect: camp emerges as a way to relate oneself to the
"right audience" (join the in-group) through enjoying the camp texts'
celebration of a "perverse angle"; and it appeals to the "perverse angle"
through intertextual references to texts that are only canonical to the
"right audience." Camp is thus dependent on, as much as it is intent
on, drawing new demarcation lines between audiences—communities of
taste[9]—reflecting its history as a secret code of communication, even in
mass-mediated contexts.

2.1   Irony, Parody, and Discursive Communities

The idea of community—specifically as discursive community—also
informs camp's distancing qualities and hence its detachment aspect.
Linda Hutcheon has written extensively on postmodernism and attests
transformative power to all postmodern forms of parody despite opposing claims about the dominance of meaningless pastiche in contemporary
culture. Hutcheon describes parody as "repetition with a critical difference" (*Parody* 7). For her, the "critical difference" is produced through
a use of irony, which adds an evaluative edge and is therefore crucial to
differentiating between parody and pastiche as the kind of "blank parody" which Fredric Jameson describes in his discussion of the distinctly
unpleasurable conditions of late capitalism (15–16).

To establish irony's critical power and argue against its supposed
ambiguity, Hutcheon opens her consideration on the politics of irony
with the following guiding question:

Why should anyone want to use this strange mode of discourse where you
say something you don't actually mean and expect people to understand
not only what you actually mean but also your attitude toward it? (*Irony* 2)

it's a form of
coded language

The answer, for Hutcheon, lies in the interaction between what has objectively been "said" and the "unsaid," which is the utterance's implied meaning. Were the ironic meaning simply this "unsaid," irony would be but a mere play with words. But irony, Hutcheon contests, is more than that, as its "truth" lies in the mutual information of implied and uttered meaning in "a semantically complex process of relating, differentiating, and combining said and unsaid" (*Irony* 89). Here irony, and with it camp, develops its defining "evaluative edge" (ibid.). Yet, to make an ironic utterance legible as such, there need to be so-called markers that serve to alert the audience to the irony ahead. Successful ironic communication is consequently only possible if producer (or, in the mass communication context of popular culture, product) and audience agree on such markers as exaggeration and theatricality in the case of camp. If they do, they are part of the same "discursive community," which is "constituted by shared concepts of norms of communication" (*Irony* 99) and is fundamental to camp's repeated definition as a "relational" phenomenon, such as David Bergman's contention that the "camp effect requires a fit between performances and perception, between object and audience" (123). Steven Cohan echoes this sentiment and extends it to account for camp's effect as "the formation of a queer affect [...] because its irony affords a position of engagement, not alienation" (*Incongruous* 18).[10] The interpreter's engagement is equally important. Hutcheon makes clear in her argument that there "is no guarantee that the interpreter will 'get' the irony in the same way as it was intended. In fact, 'get' may be an inaccurate and even inappropriate verb: 'make' would be much more precise" (*Irony* 11). Yet she stresses that irony is not a reading against the grain. The community-specific meta-ironic markers either are or are not embedded in a text or utterance, and can only be read as intentional code for irony by the interpreter. In addition to illuminating how irony (and therefore camp) works, Hutcheon thus also clarifies how and when ironic communication is doomed to fail, namely, if the communication situation lacks a basic consensus on signs and values. Inside the specific discursive community, however, irony is never vaguely ambiguous, always evaluative, and, as such, crucial to an understanding of postmodern parody as "transformative in its relationship to other texts, [whereas] pastiche is imitative" (*Parody* 38).

Though Hutcheon is not talking about gender in her book on parody, and most accounts of gender parody are not directly referring to Hutcheon, they nonetheless follow a similar rationale, when they attest political power to parodic performances of gender. This conviction, which is also central to camp's queer formulation, may be best exemplified by Judith Butler, who describes gender parody as "subversive repetition" (*Gender* 146) in which "genders can [...] be rendered thoroughly and radically *incredible*" (141, emphasis in the original). Furthermore, where Hutcheon insists that irony gains its strength as "an effective strategy of oppositionality" from "intimacy" with dominant discourses (*Irony* 30), Butler equally evokes gender parody's necessary proximity to hegemonic discourses:

> to make gender trouble, not through the strategies that figure a utopian beyond, but through the mobilization, subversive confusion, and proliferation of precisely those constitutive categories that seek to keep gender in its place by posing as the foundational illusions of identity. (*Gender* 46)

Among the most influential scholars who have applied Butler's ideas to a camp analysis of popular media is Pamela Robertson, who coined the term "feminist camp" in her book *Guilty Pleasures: Feminist Camp from Mae West to Madonna*. Robertson advanced the argument that women can "reclaim camp as a political tool and rearticulate it within the theoretical framework of feminism," since "camp offers a model for critiques of gender and sex roles" (6). The basis for this rearticulation was her model of female masquerade, where the "credibility of images of the feminine can be undermined by a 'double-mimesis' or 'parodic mimicry'" (10).

Even though Robertson herself limited her discussion of this parodic mimicry to straight women and did not go into the possibility of lesbian camp at length, her work still constitutes an important reference point for thinking about female queer viewing practices. Robertson argued that camp functions not only as a distancing device for female spectators, but rather as a way of enhancing the pleasure they can derive from cultural products, which may—like many of Mae West's portrayals of women used as examples in *Guilty Pleasures*—at first glance, and outside a rather specific discursive community, not seem to be liberating and empowering at all. As with the "said" and "unsaid" of irony, camp allows for both the potentially misogynistic, homophobic, or merely normative mainstream entertainment on the one hand and the critical distance to what is depicted on screen/video/radio on the other, to coexist and interact with one another, and to be mutually transformed through its evaluative edge. It is precisely in this presence of that which is critiqued rather than the representation of a self-contained alternative, that camp's political potency emerges.

2.2   Politics

"Political" can have a wide variety of meanings. Delving into this discussion in his study of emotions, Jack Katz concludes that "[c]ollectively victimized peoples develop exquisite senses of humor and rich joking cultures as an alternative to mass depression" (146). This acknowledgment accounts for camp's inversion of insider and outsider by way of recoding "who is in on the joke." Camp is thus also a consciously exclusionary gesture. Katz's statement further explains camp's trademark inversion of what is treated as humorous and what as serious, as the in-group's values and experiences will unquestionably differ from mainstream notions of this distinction. One example, not directly related but nonetheless applicable to camp, is Butler's conviction that the "loss of the sense of 'the normal' [...] can be its own occasion for laughter" (138–39)—particularly to those who can only gain from irreverence towards the normative. Crucial to such laughter is that it thrives on the incongruities (but not ambiguities) between the playful and the sincere—"the refusal of *gravitas*; serious play with constructed superficiality" (Hemmings 164)—without giving up on either. Instead, emotional investment characterizes the relationship between audience and the text's politics or the unsaid—to use Hutcheon's terms—which here is constituted by camp's critical connotations. The affective component features twofold in these considerations: on the one hand, it denotes that camp connoisseurs are immersed in and *attached* to the cultural product in question and their fellow members of the "right audience" (Sedgwick 156); on the other hand, and intrinsically connected to this aspect, (queer) affect also extends to the underlying motives and themes of the given text, which are taken seriously no matter the exaggeration of their aesthetic representation. One, after all, "can't camp about something you don't take seriously" (Isherwood 110). Isherwood's dictum is explicated by Scott Long, whose comments on camp's relation to the absurd and the serious are worth quoting at length:

> camp plays with notions of seriousness and absurdity not to deny them but to redefine them [...] Its particular endeavor is to fix the nature of the

absurd: the society that laughs at the wrong things has gone wrong. To perceive the absurd is to realize that two conjoined ideas do not belong together. Behind camp is the expectation that, once the absurd is properly recognized, a sense of the serious will follow. (80)

In the combination of the sincerity of its motivation, the communal foundations of its humor and intertexts, and the demystifying qualities of its parodic irony ultimately lies camp's progressive potential, attested to by Michael Bronski (43), Richard Dyer (60), and Pamela Robertson (143), among others. With reference to Ann Pellegrini, progressive here is not understood as falling somewhere specific on the political spectrum, but rather as "a matter of ethical horizon: what might be" (184). Camp does not present a "utopian beyond" which disregards current issues, but instead presents a "subversive confusion [...] of precisely those constitutive categories"—to borrow from Butler's argument (46)—that structure our daily encounters with gender, sexuality, and the media. Overall, camp in popular culture "may not embody or produce political power, but its rhetorical push opens a space in which others might realize such power" (Harris 126).[11]

In the context of this book, these rhetorical pushes include a critique of the stereotyping of lesbian characters in Hollywood cinema and its heteronormativity in Chap. 3, questioning the basic assumptions and "rules" of postfeminist TV in Chap. 4, and finally in Chap. 5 the introduction of queer subjectivity into popular music as a critical alternative to the surveillance of female bodies and exploitation of gay images. The different readings offered in these chapters show how seemingly trivial media products like romantic comedies, sitcoms, and music videos can be employed to expose the absurdity of oppressive cultural frameworks and to empower members of the respective discursive communities to laugh *at* "what is wrong" (not the product itself, but the "absurd" which frames or hinders it) and *with* those "who are the right audience." Such a position of detached attachment is made possible by camp's overthrowing of hierarchies of form and content; the seemingly trivial form is privileged so that it produces an altogether new content and thereby a new level of potentially resistive and decisively queer consumption.

2.3   Queer Prospects

This brings me back to the term "queer" and how its employment as a defining characteristic of camp—the breaching, questioning, and redrawing of boundaries—might seem at odds with the structure of this book, whose chapters, after all, differentiate between lesbian, feminist, and queer camp. By way of explanation, I would like to differentiate between camp's queer politics and interests, and the media realities in which camp is found and against which it needs to position itself. Hence, while all the texts found here strive for "dethroning" a heteronormative framework that creates the aforementioned distinctions, they utter this critique from culturally specific vantage points. The different categories of camp hence are not meant to imply that the texts in question subscribe to essentialist notions of identity, or that feminist or lesbian camp and queer camp function fundamentally differently. Rather, the respective chapters and their different foci acknowledge how straight women, gay men, and lesbians have historically been constructed and treated differently in US (media) culture, and how their employment of camp as a strategy to defeat, or at least reject, essentialism (among other aims) must therefore come from separate cultural and social places.

The separate development of gay male and lesbian media consumption and cultural production, for example, has led to a heated debate about the possibility of lesbian camp, or rather the legitimacy of calling lesbian practices that resemble camp by that name, either due to exclusionary claims to the strategy by gay males, or for fear of making lesbian creations invisible or secondary to gay male culture. "Reserving" the term as well as the strategy of camp for gay males, however, does more to add to their hegemonic position and foregrounding within queer theory than the opening of the debate to include other communities and individuals. Additionally, gay camp's more public history should not deceive us into assuming that this unique status is based on its "actual" uniqueness—in fact, queer studies' impetus to address hegemonic statuses and to question their claim to "originality" and "normality," asks us to uncover precisely the potential of feminist, lesbian, and other neglected contexts for camp uses.

Chapter 3 expands on these matters in its tracing of lesbian camp through theory and popular culture. It first addresses the major protagonists in the debate, and then discusses the changes in lesbian identity in the years leading up to and during the era of New Queer Cinema, to show why gay and lesbian responses did not develop at the same time and take the same forms, and gives a cultural backdrop against which to read the analyzed examples of lesbian film production. Chapter 3 furthermore introduces a shared aspect of all three exemplary readings of camp texts after 2000. They are positioned in media discourses no longer defined by "the closet" or invisibility, but rather by "over-visibility" as the result of the commodification of gay and feminist images within a neoliberal market logic which assimilates differences into marketable "edginess." A "subculture's recognition of failed access to [...] the culture industry," which Pamela Robertson sees as the original impetus for camp (122), hence in contemporary contexts is not necessarily marked by repression, but rather distortion; commodified images of gayness emptied of queer subjectivity as much as of images of "strong women," which themselves function as new disciplinary regimes rather than alternatives to earlier repressive stereotypes. Assuming Sedgwick's "perverse" angle as the basis of shared cultural (and hence communal) values in this new cultural climate accounts for why camp does not need the closet and violent intolerance to sustain its merit. Rather, it can similarly thrive on rejecting the logic of repressive tolerance and, as such, present a way out of a cultural consensus and way in to an alternative web of affective connections.

NOTES

1. On camp's connection to stigma Gilad Padva comments: "Camp, as a queer creation and manifestation, objects to the stigmatization that marks the unnatural, extraordinary, perverse, sick, inefficient, dangerous, and freakish. [...] camp provides a different perspective that provokes heteronormative gender roles and codes of visibility and behaviour [...]" (216).
2. Naming Sontag in this context is not meant to infer anything about her sexuality, but merely refers to her statements within "Notes on Camp" as well the text's subsequent use. For a discussion of how Sontag's closeted life at the time of writing might have inflected on the text, see Ann Pellegrini's "After Sonntag: Future Notes on Camp," in which she considers diary entries (published in 2006) to better understand Sontag's "'peculiar' relation to homosexuality" (173). Terry Castle similarly reconsiders Sontag's remarks on homosexuality in light of these revelations in "Some Notes on 'Notes on Camp.'" For Sontag's own addendum to her statements, see "The *Salmagundi* Interview," in which she reconsiders camp's ability to create distance from gendered stereotypes (339).
3. For a summary of magazine articles and similarly "popular" treatments of the subject see Ken Feil's "'Talk About Bad Taste': Camp, Cult, and the Reception of *What's New Pussycat?*"

4. For more on camp in pop art, see: Feil ("Ambiguous 31"); Dick Hebdige, who describes Andy Warhol's art as involving "a committed, surgical examination of masculinity and femininity as masquerade" (112); Joe A. Thomas who claims that its "affinities with the camp sensibility have always provided Pop with a substantial gay audience" (265); and John Adkins Richardson who writes about the connection as a direct response to Susan Sontag's essay.

5. Gay allusions are mainly presented through camp codes, such as the stepping out of a closet, playing with a Batman-figure and several semi-theatrical performances, which blur the lines between genders as well as those between "acting out a role" and "being oneself."

6. For a discussion of camp's use in a narrower sense of the political, namely as part of activism, see Meyer's edited collection *The Politics and Poetics of Camp* and Deborah B. Gould's *Moving Politics*.

7. An interesting point in this reevaluation is raised by Doty, who connects camp's newly discovered progressive usage to queer activism's inclusion of lesbians: "Influenced by feminist and lesbian comedy over the past twenty years or so, many gays and bisexual men have adopted a more overt sociopolitical edge in their humor. This is perhaps most evident in uses of camp […] within progressive and radical queer politics (ACT-UP, Queer Nation) since the mid-1980s" (80).

8. Mark Booth suggested a similar definition—though with an emphasis on the person, rather than the object of camp appreciation—prior to Cohan in his study on camp originally published in 1983: "To be camp is to present oneself as being committed to the marginal with a commitment greater than the marginal merits" (69).

9. For a discussion of camp—though limited to gay male contexts—via Pierre Bourdieu "as an acquired disposition [used ….] to establish and mark differences by processes of distinction," see Farmer (111–12). Concerning the idea of taste in pop culture as "cultural capital," Roy Shuker claims that "the insider is able to join the game, provided he or she has the necessary background knowledge—cultural capital—to do so. All this is part of what has been termed the pleasures of the text" (15).

10. See also Feil ("Ambiguous" 38) and Babuscio (21).

11. The full quote, referring to the camp appeal of the TV series *Queer Eye for the Straight Guy* (Bravo, 2003–2007) also tackles its supposed capitalist limitations in fostering progress: "One can do queer work—and, I'd argue, effectively so—while working within a capitalist framework. Even progressive political action has to begin by addressing consumers, if only to rouse them, reshape their conceptions about the status quo" (Harris 126). For further discussion of *Queer Eye*'s camp (and its relation to postfeminism), see Cohan's "Queer Eye for the Straight Guise: Camp, Postfeminism, and the Fab Five's Makeovers of Masculinity."

WORKS CITED

Babuscio, Jack. "Camp and Gay Sensibility." *Camp Grounds: Style and Homosexuality.* Ed. David Bergman. Amherst: University of Massachusetts Press, 1993. 19–37.

Banis, Victor J., and Fabio Cleto, ed. *That Man from C.A.M.P: Rebel without a Pause.* New York: Harrington Park, 2004.

Benshoff, Harry M. "Movies and Camp." *American Cinema of the 1960s: Themes and Variations.* Ed. Barry Keith Grant. New Brunswick: Rutgers UP, 2008. 150–171.

Bergman, David. "Introduction." *Camp Grounds: Style and Homosexuality.* Ed. David Bergman. Amherst: University of Massachusetts Press, 1993. 1–16.

Booth, Mark. "CAMPE-TOI! On the Origins and Definitions of Camp." *Camp: Queer Aesthetics and the Performing Subject – A Reader.* Ed. Fabio Cleto. Edinburgh: UP, 2008. 66-79.

Bronski, Michael. *Culture Clash: The Making of Gay Sensibility.* Boston: South End, 1984.

Butler, Judith. *Gender Trouble: Feminism and the Subversion of Identity.* New York: Routledge, 2008.

Camp. Dir. Andy Warhol. 1965. Museum of Modern Art, New York City.

Case, Sue-Ellen. "Toward a Butch-Femme Aesthetic." *Camp: Queer Aesthetics and the Performing Subject – A Reader.* Ed. Fabio Cleto. Edinburgh: UP, 2008. 185–99.

Castle, Terry. "Some Notes on 'Notes on Camp'." *The Scandal of Susan Sontag.* Eds. Barbara Ching and Jennifer A. Wagner-Lawlor. New York: Columbia UP, 2009. 21–31.

Cleto, Fabio. "Gender, and Other Spectacles." *Camp: Queer Aesthetics and the Performing Subject – A Reader.* Ed. Fabio Cleto. Edinburgh: UP, 2008. 202–06.

———. "Queering the Camp." *Camp: Queer Aesthetics and the Performing Subject – A Reader.* Ed. Fabio Cleto. Edinburgh: UP, 2008. 1–42.

Cohan, Steven. *Incongruous Entertainment: Camp, Cultural Value, and the MGM Musical.* Durham: Duke UP, 2005.

———. "Queer Eye for the Straight Guise: Camp, Postfeminism, and the Fab Five's Makeovers of Masculinity." *Interrogating Postfeminism: Gender and the Politics of Popular Culture.* Eds. Yvonne Tasker and Diane Negra. Durham: Duke UP, 2007. 176–200.

Denisoff, Dennis. *Aestheticism and Sexual Parody: 1840–1940.* Cambridge: CUP, 2001.

Devitt, Rachel E. "Girl on Girl: Fat Femmes, Bio-Queens, and Redefining Drag." *Queering the Popular Pitch.* Eds. Sheila Whiteley and Jennifer Rycenga. New York: Routledge, 2006. 27–39.

Doty, Alexander. *Flaming Classics: Queering the Film Canon*. New York: Routledge, 2000.

Dyer, Richard. "It's So Camp as Keeps us Going." *The Culture of Queers*. Ed. Richard Dyer. London: Routledge, 2002. 49–63.

Farmer, Brett. *Spectacular Passions: Cinema, Fantasy, Gay Male Spectatorships*. Durham: Duke UP, 2000.

Feil, Ken. "Ambiguous Sirk-Camp-Stances: Gay Camp and the 1950's Melodramas of Douglas Sirk." *Spectator* 15.1 (1994): 30–49.

———. "'Talk About Bad Taste': Camp, Cult, and the Reception of *What's New Pussycat?*" *Convergence, Media, History*. Eds. Janet Staiger and Sabine Hake. New York: Routledge, 2009. 139–51.

Gaines, Malik, and Alex Segade. "Séance in the Dark Theater: Further Notes on the Death of Camp." *The Journal of Aesthetics Protest*. 2006. 17 Feb 2010, http://www.journalofaestheticsandprotest.org/new3/segadegaines.html.

Galef, Harold, and David Galef. "What was Camp." *Studies in Popular Culture* 13.2 (1991): 11–25.

Gill, Rosalind. "Postfeminism." *The International Encyclopedia of Communication*. 2008. Blackwell. 13 Apr 2012, http://www.blackwellreference.com/subscriber/tocnode?id=g9781405131991_chunk_g978140531995255-1.

Gould, Deborah B. *Moving Politics: Emotion and Act Up's Fight against AIDS*. Chicago: University of Chicago Press, 2009.

Harris, W. C. *Queer Externalities: Hazardous Encounters in American Culture*. Albany: SUNY P, 2009.

Hebdige, Dick. "Fabulous Confusion: Pop Before Pop?" *Visual Culture*. Repr. Ed. Chris Jenks. London: Routledge, 2002. 96–123.

Hemmings, Clara. "Rescuing Lesbian Camp." *Journal of Lesbian Studies* 11.1 (2007): 159–166.

Hutcheon, Linda. *A Theory of Parody: The Teachings of Twentieth-Century Art Forms*. New York: Methuen, 1985.

———. *Irony's Edge: The Theory and Politics of Irony*. London: Routledge, 1994.

Isherwood, Christopher. *The World in the Evening*. Minneapolis: University of Minnesota Press, 1999.

Jagose, Annamarie. "Queer Theory." *Australian Humanities Review*. 1996. 20 Jul 2011, http://www.australianhumanitiesreview.org/archive/Issue-Dec-1996/jagose.html.

Jameson, Fredric. "Postmodernism and Consumer Society." *Postmodernism and its Discontents*. Ed. E. Ann Kaplan. London: Verso, 1988. 13–29.

Katz, Jack. *How Emotions Work*. Chicago: University of Chicago Press, 1999.

Klinger, Barbara. *Melodrama and Meaning: History, Culture, and the Films of Douglas Sirk*. Bloomington: Indiana UP, 1994.

LaValley, Al. "The Great Escape." *Out in Culture: Gay, Lesbian, and Queer Essays on Popular Culture.* Eds. Corey K. Creekmur and Alexander Doty. London: Cassell, 1995. 60–70.

Long, Scott. "The Loneliness of Camp." *Camp Grounds: Style and Homosexuality.* Ed. David Bergman. Amherst: University of Massachusetts Press, 1993. 78–91.

Medhurst, Andy. "Batman, Deviance and Camp." *The Many Lives of the Batman: Critical Approaches to a Superhero and his Media.* Ed. Roberta E. Pearson. New York: Routledge, 1991. 149–163.

Meyer, Moe. "Introduction: Reclaiming the Discourse of Camp." *The Politics and Poetics of Camp.* Ed. Moe Meyer. London: Routledge, 1994. 1–20.

Mistry, Reena. "Madonna and *Gender Trouble.*" *theory.org.uk,* Jan 2000. Communications and Media Research Institute (CAMRI), University of Westminster. Ed. David Gauntlett. 8 Oct 2010, http://www.theory.org.uk/madonna.htm.

Newton, Esther. *Mother Camp: Female Impersonators in America.* 2nd ed. Chicago: University of Chicago Press. 1979.

Padva, Gilad. "*Priscilla* Fights Back: The Politicization of Camp Subculture." *Journal of Communication Inquiry* 24.2 (2000): 216–43.

Pellegrini, Ann. "After Sonntag: Future Notes on Camp." *Companion to Lesbian, Gay, Bisexual, Transgender, and Queer Studies.* Eds. George E. Haggerty and Molly McGarry. Malden: Blackwell, 2007. 168–193.

Richardson, John Adkins. "Dada, Camp, and the Mode called Pop." *Pop Art: A Critical History.* Ed. Steven Henry Madoff. Berkeley: University of California Press, 1997. 154–161.

Robertson, Pamela. *Guilty Pleasures: Feminist Camp from Mae West to Madonna.* London: Tauris, 1996.

Sconce, Jeffrey. "'Trashing the Academy': Taste, Excess, and an Emerging Politics of Cinematic Style." *Film Theory and Criticism: Introductory Readings.* 6th ed. Eds. Leo Braudy and Marshall Cohen. New York: OUP, 2006. 534–53.

Sedgwick, Eve Kosofsky. *Epistemology of the Closet.* Updated with a new preface. Berkeley: University of California Press, 2008.

Shuker, Roy. *Understanding Popular Music.* 2nd ed. New York: Routledge, 2001.

Smelik, Anneke. "Gay and Lesbian Criticism." *The Oxford Guide to Film Studies.* Eds. John Hill and Pamela Church Gibson. Oxford: OUP, 1998.

Smith, Patricia Juliana. "Icons and Iconoclasts: Figments of Sixties Queer Culture." *The Queer Sixties.* Ed. Patricia Juliana Smith. New York: Routledge, 1999. xii–xxvi.

Sontag, Susan. "Notes on Camp." *Against Interpretation, and Other Essays.* New York: Picador, 2001. 275–292.

————. with Robert Boyars and Maxine Bernstein. "The *Salmagundi* Interview." *A Susan Sontag Reader.* Ed. Susan Sontag. New York: Vintage, 1983. 339–346.

Suárez, Juan Antonio. *Bike Boys, Drag Queens & Superstars: Avant-garde, Mass Culture, and Gay Identities in the 1960s Underground Cinema.* Bloomington: Indiana UP, 1996.

Thomas, Joe A. "Pop Art." *The Queer Encyclopedia of the Visual Arts.* Ed. Claude J. Summers. San Francisco: Cleis, 2004. 264–265.

Tinkcom, Matthew. *Working like a Homosexual: Camp, Capital, and Cinema.* Durham: Duke UP, 2002.

CHAPTER 3

The Great Dyke Rewrite: Lesbian Camp on the Big Screen

About halfway through director Jamie Babbit's feature film debut, *But I'm a Cheerleader* (1999), Hilary (Melanie Lynskey), a teenage girl at a Gay-to-Straight Conversion Camp, is asked to name her "root," that is the origin of her homosexuality. Her reasoning is simple: She went to an all-girl boarding school—an explanation seemingly so self-explanatory that neither the other self-help group participants nor the camp leader question it. While sociology, medicine, and psychology might be unsure about what exactly "causes gayness"—nature vs. nurture, gay genes vs. homosexual hormones—the film has an easy answer; the only circumstance more damning for an innocent and confused girl's sexuality than women's prisons and the vicinity of female vampires is the reclusiveness of all-girl boarding schools.

As a cinematic trope the boarding school setting dates back to at least 1931, when a nearly all-female crew produced *Mädchen in Uniform* (Dir. Leontine Sagan, Carl Froelich), based on Crista Winsloe's drama *Gestern und Heute* (1930). The German film, which was widely distributed in the US despite problems with censorship, critiqued patriarchal power structures and innovated early sound film production, yet today it is best remembered for how the film itself and "the story associated with it have [...] become symbolic, as it were, of Lesbianism, as far as motion pictures are concerned" (unofficial memo from the Hays office qtd. in White, *Uninvited* 18). History proved the Hays office right, as the associated story—emotional turmoil at all-girl boarding schools resulting in female bonding, homoerotic moments, and declarations of love between

© The Author(s) 2017
K. Horn, *Women, Camp, and Popular Culture*,
DOI 10.1007/978-3-319-64846-0_3

women—and its symbolism have been carried from Hollywood's classical era—the tragic, star-studded (and suicidal) *The Children's Hour* (1961, Dir. William Wyler)—to contemporary LGBT film productions—such as the equally tragic *Lost and Delirious* (2001, Dir. Léa Pool) and the *Mädchen in Uniform* adaptation *Loving Annabelle* (2006, Dir. Katherine Brooks). Rather than simply continuing this trend *But I'm a Cheerleader* intervenes in the perpetuation of the boarding school trope through its stylistic and narrative devices and its open acknowledgment of this cinematic legacy. While Hilary's revelation about her educational past in *But I'm a Cheerleader* is only a fleeting moment in a scene full of other revelations about the supposed origin of these teens' sexual orientation that are either more relevant (to the plot) or more emotional (for the characters), her statement is still key to understanding the film's engagement with Hollywood's representation of lesbian characters and lesbian clichés more generally. In this short moment *But I'm a Cheerleader* points to the heavily censored history of female–female desire on screen, mocks the absurd and dark one-dimensionality of the boarding school trope, and connects itself to this troubled past by choosing an (at least temporarily) all-girl educational environment created to smother exactly those desires it has come to symbolize in the cultural imagination.

Such moments of meta-awareness are presented in the context of a John Hughes inspired narrative and a John Waters inspired visual style. The film thus combines several genre traditions, each of which creates a different set of expectations and meaning making cues. The same playful, yet contradictory, combination of over-the-top aesthetics with genre parody, dark themes with happy endings, and traditional narratives with the depiction of lesbian desire also characterizes the spy movie spoof *D.E.B.S.* (2004, Dir. Angela Robinson), which even more overtly than *But I'm a Cheerleader* uses intertextual references as both foil and support for its own narrative. Both films employ strategies that mark a larger cultural trend emerging after the lesbian chic of the 1990s, a camp take on lesbian representation. Other strands of this development, including the re-publication of pulp novels, the rise in burlesque- and musical-inspired performances, country music, and, most notably, iconic TV series such as *Buffy the Vampire Slayer* (1997–2003) and *Xena: Warrior Princess* (1995–2001) have received extensive academic coverage.[1] Cinema, however, has been curiously absent from this discussion. Part of the reluctance to engage with lesbian camp practices in cinema can be traced to academic discourses in which gay male camp and

Hollywood cinema have become all but synonymous with each other. Additionally, economic hurdles are higher in cinema than other media, which has historically led to a dearth of alternative voices such as women's, both gay and straight.

Two convergent cultural developments of the 1990s have created an environment in which camp could finally materialize as a prominent strategy in films for lesbian audiences: the proliferation of "lesbian chic" in mainstream media, which influenced lesbian media consumption and representation, and consequently a willingness to engage in more playful ways with questions of gender and sexuality; and the success of New Queer Cinema which paved the way for queer themes in feature films and a re-evaluation of intertextuality and camp aesthetics. Together they provide both the access to and visibility in popular culture which have hitherto been claimed as lacking for lesbian subjects and thus precluded them from participating in camp discourses widely regarded as a male prerogative. I therefore outline the most relevant premises of these two simultaneous and yet vastly different phenomena, and how their contrariness—born from the mainstream, created to resist it; made to please, meant to disrupt—are reflected in *But I'm a Cheerleader* and *D.E.B.S.*, as two examples of lesbian camp on the big screen. By reframing them in this manner these films emerge as major components of B. Ruby Rich's hope for "the Great Dyke Rewrite" of popular culture ("New Queer" 19). This rewrite is made possible by the films' use of common Hollywood themes to tell their stories, whereby they modify mainstream genres to include non-straight romances. Additionally, by consciously engaging with the cinematic history of lesbian representation, they reinscribe (pleasurable) lesbian presences into themes and tropes that had hitherto besubtextualen connected to doomed and/or lesbian desire. Thus, these films and other examples of contemporary lesbian camp offer a critical engagement with and intervention into the history of lesbian representation. Furthermore, they represent new forms of cinematic pleasure, as they infuse stereotypes which have historically as well as more recently been used mainly to disavow lesbian identity and sexuality with a sincerity of affect that recodes them as objects of identification and desire.

1   New Queer Cinema

In 1992 B. Ruby Rich recognized a new trend in queer film production while attending several LGBT festivals, which were notably on the rise in the early 1990s. She aptly titled this newfound trend New Queer Cinema. The term acknowledges both the movement's indebtedness to New American Cinema—as exemplified in its return to auteur approaches, its stark differentiation from "the mainstream," and its favoring of demonstratively artistic forms—and the films' connection to Queer Theory, which changed how identity was constructed and politics understood. As in academia, where gay and lesbian studies were starting to give way to queer studies, the turn from gay and lesbian cinema to (New) Queer Cinema denotes, among other things, the willingness "to investigate the darker aspects of queer representation and experience and to attend to the social, psychic, and corporeal effects of homophobia" (Love 2). Combined with the films' often frank depiction of sexuality and its disregard for respectability concerning both artistic and queer identities, this attention to hitherto repressed stories and individuals earned the movement the moniker radical. As this is a status notoriously difficult to keep up, it was rather fitting when the same author who had named the movement was also among the first to disavow it. In "Queer and Present Danger," published in 2000 and thus almost simultaneously with the release of *But I'm a Cheerleader* and four years prior to *D.E.B.S.*, Rich states that the movement had changed "from radical impulse to niche market" (24) and had thus lost its original appeal and artistic integrity.[2] To state the lack of longevity of this "new kind of film- and video-making that was fresh, edgy, low budget, inventive, unapologetic, sexy and stylistically daring" (24), however, is different from denying its long-lasting influence, particularly on LGBT film productions.

Indeed, New Queer Cinema left its mark on queer representation and the film industry: it launched the career of several, by now canonic, directors such as Todd Haynes and Gus van Sant; the movement aided the growing demand and market for independently produced films; and it revived the US festival scene. Furthermore, New Queer Cinema was sexually explicit, stylistically experimental, and often communal in its production and distribution. Maybe most importantly, however, it introduced festival and movie audiences to gay and lesbian images, and to a lesser extent to queer and trans ones, on a scope never before witnessed in the US. It did so in a manner that turned away from many gay-themed movies produced in the 1980s, which either tried to use film to plead for acceptance of homosexuals or painted them merely as support-ing cast providing comic relief or "cutting edge." Quite the contrary, many of New Queer Cinema's movies put their gay characters front and center and were unapologetic about their flaws and sexuality. For this introduction of a wide range of hitherto unimaginable protagonists, many directors looked for inspiration to earlier moments in film history to put their (anti-)heroes into contexts their audiences would under-stand. Whether drawing on avant-garde filmmakers like Kenneth Anger and Andy Warhol, or Hollywood auteurs such as Douglas Sirk and James Whale, New Queer Cinema established itself as radical and oppositional to mainstream conventions of representation by referring to and con-sciously diverging from those norms, particularly through its style. These aspects shaped not only the films of New Queer Cinema "proper," but have also profoundly influenced many queer productions that either hap-pened on the "sidelines" of the movement or followed it.

Concerning the defining aesthetics of New Queer Cinema, Rich admits that there hardly an overarching theme as—unlike cinematic movements such as dogma—it lacked any manifesto or preordained core group. Nonetheless she detects a "common style" in the works by the early defining directors such as Gregg Araki, Todd Haynes, and Gus van Sant, which she playfully refers to as "Homo Pomo":

> There are traces in all of them of appropriation and pastiche, irony, as well as a reworking of history with social constructionism very much in mind. Definitively breaking with older humanist approaches and the films and tapes that accompanied identity politics, these works are irreverent, ener-getic, alternately minimalist and excessive. Above all, they're full of pleas-ure. ("New Queer" 16)

Considering the impact of AIDS/HIV on the LGBT community at large, even from a non-artistic point of view it is hardly surprising that many New Queer Cinema films would rely less on a colorful and celebra-tory style, and more on a dark and minimalist one. Furthermore, given the background of the stereotypical "flaming sissies" in Technicolor musicals as the most visible male queers in cinematic history—besides perverted criminals that is—a turn away from such imagery seems only logical. Excess and minimalism, however, are not necessarily opposites.

In fact, many films from the era managed to be stylistically minimalistic and excessive at the same time. The subdued atmosphere in Todd Haynes' *Safe* (1995), for example, is minimalistic in many ways despite its lush 1980s mise en scène, costumes, and decor. The equally threatening yet simple soundtrack emphasizes the claustrophobic monotony of the almost monochrome imagery. In combination with the slow storytelling and reduced dialogue even these restrained stylistic devices become not only expressive, but excessive through the emphasis put on them—particularly as they are contrasted with repeatedly used, seemingly uncontextualized symbols, such as the milk drinking of Julianne Moore's characters. Similarly, while many New Queer Cinema films are shot in black and white in rural environments or indoors—which can be considered minimalistic compared to the explosion-heavy action movies, dramatic wide frame landscape shots, and colorful outdoor scenes in romantic comedies dominating cineplexes at the time—the lack of color is contrasted with non-linear editing and obtrusive soundtracks, creating an overall atmosphere in which style is very much at the forefront of the audience's perception. This focus on aesthetics, however minimal they might be, goes against the narration-focused style established in Hollywood cinema and thus draws attention to the relationship between style and meaning in New Queer Cinema. This relationship is crucial to the films' politics, depends heavily on intertextuality, and is therefore directly linked to the reworking of the history of cinematic sexuality to which Rich alludes in the quote above.

Two of the earliest examples of "appropriation and pastiche" employed to engender the deconstruction and revisioning of film history are *Meeting of Two Queens* (1991, Dir. Cecilia Barriga) and *Dry Kisses Only* (1990, Dir. Jane Cottis and Kaucyila Brooke), which Rich herself cites as examples for New Queer Cinema in general as well as "the Great Dyke Rewrite" more particularly. Both films are heavily invested in the rewriting of the cinematic past of (rumored to be) lesbian characters and stars. In 1934 renowned fashion photographer Edward Steichen created a photomontage for the magazine *Vanity Fair* in which Greta Garbo, The Swedish Goddess, and Marlene Dietrich, The Blonde Venus, appear as if they were about to kiss. As European actresses who had reached the peak of their fame through a combination of androgyny and seduction, Garbo's and Dietrich's sexuality, and in particular their potential homosexuality, was an intriguing publicity item as well as a calculated risk (should the public decide that tinseltown was once again descending into sin) for their respective studios. The photomontage thus can be read both as wish fulfillment for audiences intrigued by their queer allure—there is the obvious implication of mutual desire—and as a deferral and even denial of such rumors. It was, after all, an obvious fake combination of their faces outside of any meaningful context. Cecilia Berriga's short film *The Meeting of Two Queens* might be understood as a video version of Steichen's photomontage, but with the crucial difference that Berriga's film arranges short scenes of flirtation and seduction from several films starring Greta Garbo and Marlene Dietrich so that they tell the story of their tragic love affair with each other. She thus writes the story of the attraction between two of Hollywood's biggest stars *into* the narratives of the movies that made them famous, which makes their desire for each other not only central to their star image, but also pushes the heteronormative context of the scenes' origins to the sidelines. Similarly, *Dry Kisses Only* manipulates clips from Hollywood's classical era to make obvious what was once hidden beneath censorship requirements and genre conventions yet still "there"—the desire between the films' female protagonists. These two films thus confirm Rich's claim that neither New Queer Cinema's style nor queerness are incidental. Rather, gay cinematic history and contemporary queer desire form the films' central concern (there is no story outside of their queer focus) and style is consciously used not only to enhance the films' queer appeal, but also to comment on and intervene in the repressive, self-censoring framework of Classical Hollywood Cinema.

As found footage films that offer more than the retelling of a singular story, namely investigations into a medium, an industry, and reception processes, they also illuminate how and why Harry Benshoff and Sean Griffin refer to New Queer Cinema as "metacinema." The authors claim that—despite the often radical choice of content—the movement's main appeal lies in its invitation to audiences to actively think about the relation between medium and message, and between story and storytelling respectively. Like Rich, Benshoff and Griffin emphasize the connection to queer theory and activism, the stylistic diversity of New Queer cinema, which they see manifested in genre parodies, as well as the transgression between fictional and documentary filmmaking, and also in performance styles and visual excess. "In other words," they claim, "New Queer Cinema is a metacinema that simultaneously represents queer characters and concerns but also comments upon the form of those representations" (221–22). Similarly, Michelle Aaron insists that New

Queer Cinema has done more for queer representation than to "open up a space for avowing, for affirming, homosexuality" (187). Rather than focusing on the metarepresentational aspects of films, however, she shifts focus to the "New Queer Spectator," who "becomes an important coordinate in our continuing understanding of the machinations of cinema" (187), as New Queer Cinema also provided a contemplation on the role of spectatorship in the creation of (alternative) meaning.

1.1   Camp and New Queer Cinema

From New Queer Cinema's willingness to embrace the decoding power of its audience, alongside its insistence on defamiliarizing and queering conventional stories and aesthetics, emerge the intersections with camp discourses. The establishment of a new relationship to codes, audiences, and movie history, and its stereotypical and oppressive representation of queer characters through camp, are among New Queer Cinema's most relevant and long-lasting influences on LGBT movies. As Rich remarks on this intersection in her inaugural study, the "queer present negotiates with the past, knowing full well that the future is at stake" ("New Queer" 22). Her explanation of the relevance of the negotiation of a queer (filmic) past is worth quoting at length, as it sheds light on one of the most significant ways in which New Queer Cinema has influenced the proliferation not only of camp in general, but also of lesbian camp as I trace it through post-New Queer Cinema film.

> There are two ways to dismiss gay film: one is to say. "Oh, it's just a gay film"; the other, to proclaim, "Oh, it's a great film, it just happens to be gay." Neither applied to the films in Park City [the festival where Rich first became aware of a shift in gay film production], since they were great precisely because of the ways in which they were gay. Their queerness no more arbitrary than their aesthetics, no more than their individual preoccupations with interrogating history. (22)

As both the filmic movement and queer theorists and activists distanced themselves from concerns about positive representation, while at the same time the interest in intertextuality and appropriation rose, the "signature gay style" camp lost its stigma of internalized homophobia, and became instead a valid form of artistic expression. More than just "one way to be gay" on an aesthetic level, camp obtains its relevance to

New Queer Cinema through its status as an historically queer style as well as its intertextual quality, which makes it is doubly bound to LGBT film histories. It thus offers a unique possibility to express New Queer Cinema's investment in the past and its metacinematic qualities. In fact, Glyn Davis calls camp "a key aspect of many a New Queer Cinema film," a conviction echoed in almost all major publications on New Queer Cinema (see: Banks; Morrison). Freed from the concern for respectability and focused on the meaning-altering potential of style, New Queer Cinema perceived of camp as not only suitable to convey queer theory's deconstructionist ideas, but also as a way for directors to set their films visually apart from mainstream productions. Camp provided an alternative way to tell stories, which not only distorted the narratives and images perceived as oppressive, but also connected a movement built on historiographical interests and interventions to avant-garde queer art of past decades as well as queer appropriations of Hollywood texts.[3] As such, most texts and anthologies on New Queer Cinema offer not only camp readings of films by auteurs like Todd Haynes, Gregg Araki, or Derek Jarman, but also point to the significant role camp has played in the films and auteurs by which New Queer cinema has been inspired— reinforcing camp's status as a way to negotiate cinema's queer past.

In fact, there is probably no aspect of popular culture more closely connected to camp than the movies, a relationship which has been analyzed in diverse contexts ranging from Hollywood musicals to queer independent cinema.[4] In his study entitled *Working like a Homosexual: Camp, Capital, and Cinema*, for example, Matthew Tinkcom discusses diverse queer filmmakers working between the 1940s and 1960s, such as MGM director Vincente Minelli or underground auteurs Kenneth Anger and Andy Warhol.[5] The author invites us to understand camp as

> the tactics through which queer men of a particular historical epoch have made sense of their frequent omission from representation and sought to invent their own language to appear, in a particular fashion, in those complicated moments of exchange under capital. (4)

Without the recourse to Marxist critique on which Tinkcom bases his theories, but with an interest in a similar period Steven Cohan approaches the MGM musical and its queer potential in *Incongruous Entertainment: Camp, Cultural Value, and the MGM Musical*. Jack Babuscio's reading of the camp aesthetics in cinema goes even further back in time to examine style in the films of director and creator of Marlene Dietrich, Josef von Sternberg. Another "women's director." Douglas Sirk, has been reestablished in a similar vein as a critical voice inside the Hollywood industry, most prominently by Barbara Klinger, who described Sirk's lasting appeal as "mass camp," but also in a more overtly queer context by scholars like Ken Feil or Ryan Powell, who use "gay camp" and "performative camp" respectively as analytical tools.[6] Even this comparatively small sample of articles on gay male camp practices in cinema reveals the relative agreement on the ubiquity as well as the relevance of camp to queer cinematic discourses.[7] It also reveals how the intertwining discourses on camp and New Queer Cinema are, in fact, so aligned that they share the same blind spot: women.

1.2   Women in (New) Queer Cinema

Female directors and producers played a crucial role in the movement, primarily in films with a gay male focus, such as Christine Vachon as the producer of Todd Haynes' *Poison* (1991) and numerous other important films of the movement, or Jenni Livingston as the director of *Paris is Burning* (1990), a documentary about the Black and Latino voguing scene in New York. Stories with a female focus, however, were as far and few between in New Queer Cinema as texts on lesbian camp were among a sea of publications on gay camp. Benshoff and Griffin describe the issue as

> a structural bias in the funding and distribution of New Queer Cinema [... due to which] New Queer works by women and people of color were much more likely to be shorter than feature length or shot on video and therefore less likely to earn theatrical releases.[8] (237)

Rich even claims that over the years "the imbalance has only worsened, [e]ven including the low-budget productions where more lesbians have tended to work" (*New Queer* 202). Without denying the underlying sexism apparent in the lack of funding for stories by and about queer women, other scholars view lesbians' investment in low-budget productions quite differently as not only a passively received injustice, but also an active artistic choice. Patricia White, for example, refers to them as "minor lesbian cinema,"[9] whose format is defined, among others, by length (short), material (video or 16 mm rather than 32 mm film) and "de-aestheticization" achieved through hand-held cameras and black and white images ("Lesbian" 419). Filmmakers are motivated to concentrate their artistic expression on this sub-genre, White explains, by their desire to resist "commodification or authorization" by (male dominated) New Queer Cinema as well as (straight originated) lesbian chic ("Lesbian" 41). Like White's definition of "minor lesbian cinema," Rhona Berenstein describes the artistic deviations in films by pioneering lesbian filmmakers as politically motivated. Rather than looking at the style of these films, however, Berenstein focuses on the way they construct narratives. She observes an attraction to the disruption of conventional storylines and narrative techniques, which she relates to the association between (Hollywood) narratives and "patriarchal oppression" (133). The refusal of conventional narration leads to a focus on avant-garde and documentary films, which often goes together with White's aesthetic markers of minor lesbian cinema. As mainstream cinema's main intent is the generation of "visual pleasure," achieved if not mainly than at least consistently through the objectification of women, lesbian cinema's relation to "pleasure" itself is a troubled one: Berenstein calls it an "attraction to unpleasure" (133).[10]

The politically motivated refusal to partake in narrative conventions that aim at the audience's absorption into the narrative is also one of the most significant stylistic markers of one of the most notable lesbian contributions to New Queer Cinema, the 1994 debut feature Go Fish, written and directed by Roche Troche and starring Guinevere Turner (who also co-wrote). Go Fish tells the conventional story of the dating adventures and eventual relationship between Max (Guinevere Turner) and Ely (V.S. Brodie) who meet through mutual friends. The main narrative is punctuated by several dream and "talking head" sequences, which either comment on the ongoing story ("will they/won't they?") or on questions of sexuality and gender identity that are often only indirectly addressed in the story itself. Many of the sequences break the fourth wall and therefore also the illusion of a closed fictional world upheld in conventional Hollywood cinema. Despite the low-budget, black and white aesthetics and the stress on disruptive storytelling techniques, the effect of "unpleasure" is mitigated by the introduction of humor on the diegetic level of the "love story" as well as into the metanarrative elements—indicating a larger shift within lesbian filmmaking in the late 1980s and early 1990s when "unpleasure" had become a cliché itself. In combination with the self-conscious exploration (and send-up) of stereotypes within queer communities, the film becomes an odd blend of "minor lesbian cinema" (low-budget aesthetics), New Queer Cinema (metanarrative elements) and romantic comedy (plot). Due to this mixture of the serious and the frivolous, B. Ruby Rich claims, she is tempted to use the term "lesbian camp" to describe the film, but eventually decides not to, since such a definition might be considered a historical inaccuracy due to camp's close association with gay male discourses outlined above, while her "species is, after all, better known for camping" ("New Queer Cinema" 19).[11] In a later article (reflecting a broader reassessment of camp's identity politics) Rich reviews the movie as "the living proof that lesbian camp does exist and even has a lineage," with the qualification "except that Troche and Turner have never seen it" ("Goings" 94).[12] While the former statement as a self-deprecating joke about stereotypes through a double entendre might itself be considered camp, the second statement, perhaps unwittingly, points to the essential problem, not only of New Queer Cinema and/or camp, but also of cinema more generally, of seeing lesbians.

While Rich's re-evaluation of her assessment on the state of lesbian camp is testament to a larger, yet very recent cultural shift, both her initial hesitancy to use the term at all and her later reservations about the filmmakers' familiarity with traditions of lesbian camp result from lesbian women's overall fraught relationship to visual media and mainstream representation. Terry Castle, a literary scholar, argues in her monograph *The Apparitional Lesbian* that the issue of lesbian invisibility in culture predates film. Yet in an acknowledgment of the moving image's power to influence minorities' representation, she opens her book in a self-described "polemical" manner by describing one of the major (invisible as such) lesbian movie icons:

When it comes to lesbians [...] many people have trouble seeing what's in front of them. The lesbian remains a kind of "ghost effect" in the cinema world of modern life: elusive, vaporous, difficult to spot—even when she is there, in plain view, mortal and magnificent, at the center of the screen. Some may even deny that she exists at all. [...] What we never expect is precisely this: to find her in the midst of things, as familiar and crucial as an old friend, as solid and sexy as the proverbial right-hand man, as intelligent and human and funny and real as Garbo. (2–3)

In her study of lesbian representability in classical Hollywood cinema Patricia White similarly described representations of lesbian lives and desires as "elusive" (*UnInvited* xii). She contended that therefore lesbian audiences in particular, were (and are) dependent on "reading the codes." More recently, Suzanna Danuta Walters supported these claims about queer women's particularly fraught relationship to mainstream representation in her assessment of the "explosion of gay visibility" in the 1990s and early 2000s in US media. Walters pointed out that the "problems of representing gays are compounded when homophobia meets sexism" (161). While single men and even groups of single men do not threaten the established order of patriarchal Hollywood cinema (after all, entire genres depend on the coming together of groups of men), the same cannot be said for women. Walters thus cautioned that "if *heterosexual* women without men (single mothers, 'career women,' outlaws) have been punished for their errant ways, then we can imagine the cinematic treatment of *homosexual* women without men" (161). Indeed, the history of lesbians in Hollywood cinema is equally as plagued by "unpleasure" as its independent counterpart, though in very different ways. While gay men were, sometimes at least, afforded the role of comic relief, lesbian appearances in major productions were usually accompanied by death and madness, or what Walters names "the Freudian realms of pathology and deviance" (161). Among the main tropes of representation is the "threatening, dark" lesbian (though never named as such) in a position of power—usually dead by the end of the movie—prying over a younger (blonder) innocent woman who seeks solace in the arms of a man. Variations of this trope range from prison warden (*Caged*, 1950, Dir. John Cromwell) and housekeeper (*Rebecca*, 1940, Dir. Alfred Hitchcock), to nun (*Black Narcissus*, 1947, Dir. Michael Powell and Emeric Pressburger) and vampire (*Dracula's Daughter*, 1936, Dir. Lambert Hillyer).[13]

Patricia White refers to these characters as an "uncanny appearance" (*UnInvited* xxiv). The term denotes not their proximity to the horror genre, but rather their status as "coded figures" who appear repeatedly in cinematic history despite censors' best efforts to contain their threat (and allure). White contends that though her readings depend on codes and subtextual meanings, these figures of lesbian desire are nonetheless "uninvited not because they are forbidden entry but because they are already at home" (*UnInvited* xxiv). One could thus think of films like *Dry Kisses Only*, *Meeting of Two Queens*, and by extension also of *D.E.B.S.*

and *But I'm a Cheerleader*, as attempts to canonize the uncanny by making the subtext maintext and by literalizing the coded depiction. The latter two also aim at removing the second connotation of the "uncanny." They are not only concerned with outing the "coded figures" of the not-yet-fully-straight girl at boarding schools and the ambiguously sexed, yet scary villain, but also with removing the stamp of "unpleasure" from the depiction of lesbian sexuality and identity. At the same time, given the circumstances of their release, there is yet another "stamp" associated with lesbian sexuality in the media these post-New Queer Cinema films must engage with. While from a historic perspective, death and madness are the main tropes of female–female sexual desire, the 1990s introduced quite a different image of lesbianism, which proved problematic for lesbian audiences not for its lack of visibility, but for its (exploitative) affluence of it.

2   LESBIAN CHIC

The 1990s earned their monikers "decade of the dyke" (Rich, "Goings" 97) or "a decade in love with lesbianism" (Ciasullo 605) for more than one reason. One of the most important consequences of New Queer Cinema on both cultural and economic levels has been the realization that films by queers for queers with queer content could be a financial (and critical) success. And even as women as part of the movement were largely absent, Karen Hollinger still noted that the 1990s might have been the first decade in which "lesbian-identified directors producing lesbian content with lesbian audiences in mind were not the singular exception anymore" (81). Rhona Berenstein refers to the phenomenon as "the New Wave of lesbian features" (134). Many of these films were not met with critical acclaim, yet they clearly denoted a new direction in lesbian film production, as they were not aimed at museum or festival screenings, but meant for wide release.[14]

Largely independent from lesbian producers, however, another cultural shift developed: lesbian chic. Despite the lack of political motivation behind this "fad," lesbian chic fundamentally changed gay women's relationship to and representation in mainstream media, as "[h]omoerotic images of women in film, television, and other media [became] hip, hot, and increasingly prevalent" (Reichert et al. 123). A growing number of out celebrities like k.d. lang, Martina Navratilova or Melissa Etheridge, the spread of "sweeps week lesbianism" and the landmark outing of Ellen Degeneres' character on her sitcom *Ellen* (1994–1998) in 1997 further added to its widespread influence.[15] As a secondary phenomenon camp is always under pressure to change in accordance with shifting paradigms of identity, sex, and gender, as well as taste and conflicting ideas about what culture is and who wields power over it. The growth in the visibility of lesbian images in pop culture thus provides the crucial foil against which lesbian camp products can position themselves. The increased lesbian visibility is precisely what *D.E.B.S.*, *But I'm a Cheerleader*, and other contemporary films must engage with, and why they were slightly "delayed" in relation to similarly prominent and reflexive gay male stories. That lesbian camp gained currency after the "lesbian chic" craze is notable also in examples from other media, such as: the rerelease of lesbian pulp novels by Cleiss in 2000, the success of *Xena: Warrior Princess*[16]; performances at the WOW Café in New York and other queer venues[17]; and web series such as *Girltrash!* by *D.E.B.S.* director Angela Robinson.

Equally relevant as noting the increase in visibility is the close analysis of the specific form this visibility took, since as simply a positive step to more cultural presentation and acceptance, lesbian chic was not. One aspect of lesbian chic does not denote the aforementioned proliferation of not overtly homophobic images of lesbian in mainstream culture, but rather a stylistic and political change within the community:

> It could be argued that lifestyle lesbianism promotes assimilation over separation, style over substance, and is a sign of our growing conservatism. Yet many lesbians today don't see it that way. Instead, they experience this new attention to lifestyle as a freedom, a testament to the fact that their identity is now a matter of personal choice rather than political compulsion. (Stein 481)

Starting in the 1980s, lesbian fashion and lifestyle underwent a drastic change away from the flannel and denim anti-style, which had long been a way for lesbians of "resisting dominant cultural definitions of female beauty and fashion as a way of separating themselves from heterosexual culture politically and as a way of signaling their lesbianism to other women in their subcultural group" (Clark 82). Instead, gay women adopted more stylish, consumerist attitudes and took "a great deal of pleasure in playing with the possibilities of fashion and beauty" (82). Stein witnessed the emergence of the lipstick lesbian and a growing openness to understanding "roles" (such as butch-femme) as an erotic play and experiment with different styles, rather than as a fixed identity reflecting one's social and sexual position. She spoke of a development from "political lesbianism" to "lifestyle lesbianism" (482). Stein acknowledged the potential danger of drifting further into invisibility by giving up known codes of lesbian identity in favor of more "stylish" appearances, yet still reasoned that this shift did not necessarily imply the loss of political investment:

> the new lesbianism deconstructs the old, perhaps overly politicized or prescriptive notion of lesbianism by refusing ghettoization, acknowledging internal group differences, and affirming the value of individual choice when it comes to style and political and sexual expression [...] some might argue that if we define politics broadly as a series of contests between competing cultural images—of what it means to be a woman or a lesbian, for example—then the new lesbian style can be seen as a political act, a public assertion of lesbian identity. (482)

In her article "Commodity Lesbianism," Danae Clark not only traced the same development and reached a similar conclusion, but even highlighted that "some credit for the changing perspectives on fashion might also be given to the recent emphasis on masquerade and fabrication in feminist criticism and to the more prominent role of camp in lesbian criticism" (82–4). Both scholars refer to personal styles in clothing and appearance. Their arguments can, however, easily be transferred to artistic expression by and for lesbians, including a turn away from "minor lesbian cinema" to movies that are more accessible to straight audiences, yet still distinctively queer.

The "lesbian style wars" were a minor part of lesbian chic, yet related to a bigger aspect, which resulted mainly from a corporate interest in finding a new "edgy" topic to spice up products without alienating audiences and consumers. Repeating a trend surfacing in the 1920s and 1930s, the original "lesbian chic" so to say, lesbian chic once again entered mainstream media in the 1990s at the same time as panic arose that lesbians might not be detected by their physical difference but actually live invisible among "us" (Hankin xviii). As mentioned before, despite the focus on gay women, their aesthetics and erotics, and notwithstanding the increase in out performers of significant status within the neoliberal entertainment industry, the terms of lesbian chic were largely defined by others. Thus, Rich and several other scholars (see Ciasullo; Ladenson 417; Hamer and Budge 11) rightfully cautioned against any premature enthusiasm about the quantitative change in visibility and representation: "Lesbian visibility was attained at long last, freed from the stale stereotype of asexual spoilsport, but the terms of visibility were set by the media and would eventually prove problematic" (*New Queer* 104).

Among the earliest indicators of this new visibility was a 1993 *Vanity Fair* cover not all too different from Steichen's photomontage which depicted bisexual Marlene Dietrich and (presumably) lesbian Greta Garbo as almost kissing for the same magazine. This time around, the celebrities and motive in question were the 1990s only visible butch celebrity, singer k.d. lang, getting a shave from the decade's most desirable (presumably) bisexual model Cindy Crawford. The obviously gendered action is further emphasized through the two women's clothing, hair, and make-up. k.d. lang is wearing a men's suit and tie with her short dark hair slicked back, whereas blonde, long-haired Cindy Crawford is wearing a bathing suit which reveals a plunging neck line and her famously long legs. Even more provocative than the gender-bending cover, the image accompanying the article shows Cindy Crawford, her mouth slightly open and looking at the lips of the woman beneath her, leaning over a seated k.d. lang, who has her eyes closed and hands on the model's thighs as they appear—like Garbo and Dietrich—about to kiss. The magazine spread is not only remarkable for being among the first to depict an out lesbian celebrity as desirable, but also—and maybe even more so—for embracing lang's butch identity and enjoying the "erotic play," as Stein puts it, associated with it. As such *Vanity Fair*'s profile on lang was not only among the first of its kind, but also among the last. "Visibility means not only that one is present but that one is being watched," Ann Ciasullo explains and adds: "It also means that certain images get singled out as watchable" (584). In the case of lesbian chic, the butch was not and thus, after this short and sexy moment in the spotlight, her figure soon vanished from mainstream representation.[18] Even as k.d. lang still graced the cover of *New York Magazine* for the second "inaugural" article of lesbian chic, "The Bold, Brave New World of Gay Women," the text itself was concerned with widely different figures. The magazine's seven-page spread mentioned k.d. lang and Lea DeLaria, alongside decidedly more feminine performers such as Madonna and Sandra Bernhard, to introduce its readers to the idea of lesbian chic, before it underscored that lesbians were now sexy and hip enough to be featured in Banana Republic adds. Author Jeanne Russel Kasindorf marveled at these "brave, bold new gay women" who go shopping for wedding rings and seem to come out by the dozen, share gossip about the Madonna–Sarah Bernhard–unnamed model love triangle, and watch *Seinfeld*'s (1989–1998) and *Friend*'s (1994–2004) lesbian characters on primetime TV (in both cases as the male protagonist's ex-girlfriend). Importantly, according to the article, the new gay women do not just shatter the lesbian stereotype of being miserable, but also of looking unattractive: "Now 'lipstick lesbian' and 'designer dykes' share the bar with the 'butch/femme' group" (34). Kasindorf left little room to wonder which of the two groups consti- tuted the new and desirable, and media representation supported her. From the aforementioned ex-girlfriends of sitcom lead characters to *Basic Instinct* (1992, Dir. Paul Verhoeven) to clothing ads, mainstream incarnations of the new lesbian are characterized by "the sanitizing [...] through her feminizing" (Ciasullo 584–85); they are made unthreat- ening, even appealing to mass audiences, by looks and lifestyles which make them indistinguishable from straight women. Another characteris- tic of "the new lesbian" is that, at least in fictional representations like TV and film, she is more often than not experimenting. The girl-on-girl make-out session quickly became a staple of teen movies from *Cruel Intentions* (1999, Dir. Roger Krumble) to the *American Pie* (1999, Dir. Paul Weitz, Chris Weitz) franchise, while the sweeps week kiss on TV transcended channels and genres. Even if a show or film allowed its gay character to admit to their homosexuality, the focus on the realization of the women's sexuality, their initial awkwardness, and their coming out stressed the supposedly transitional nature of women's homosexuality. "Therein lies the rub," as Ann Ciasullo noted, "in mainstream cultural representations of lesbianism, there is [...] always the possibility—or is it the promise?—that she who is lesbian [...] can 'unbecome' lesbian" (592). By focusing only on visually non-threatening femme women who have at one point in their life considered themselves straight and might do so again soon (without ever considering labeling these women as bisexual), the lesbian in US media in the 1990s was seen less as a politi- cal or sexual identity, and more as a *sexualized* identity meant to attract (straight, often male) audiences (see also Ladenson's "Lovely Lesbians"). Her sexualization as an object to be watched went hand in hand with the delegitimization of her actual sexuality,[19] as sex between women was

not shown and relationships were often cut short. The rhetoric introduced in the early publications on lesbian chic about how gay women
are "just like" straight women, insofar as they enjoy gossip and fashion,
comes full circle when the formerly countercultural identity of the lesbian is as much defined in relation to men as her heterosexual counterpart. Gay women's inclusion in and visibility within mainstream culture
thus came not only at the expense of "a politicized version of lesbian
identity" (Hamer and Budge 11), but even at the risk of the credibility of her identity beyond that of stock character and eye candy. While
mainstream representation had presumably moved beyond the point at
which a movie was counted as offering its lesbian character a happy ending if she at least survived the credits, now the benchmark seemed to
be, whether the woman was still (or had ever been) considered gay or
whether she had grown out of this "phase" by the end of the movie.[20]

3   GIRLS GONE CAMPING: *BUT I'M A CHEERLEADER* AND *D.E.B.S.*

Against a backdrop of tragedy, which often dominated the themes of
New Queer Cinema (Rich, "Queer and Present" 24), and a history
of "unpleasure" associated with lesbian cinema and lesbians in cinema more broadly, and a de-association of lesbian imagery with lesbian
lives and love in the 1990s, emerged the "new wave of lesbian feature
films" (Berenstein). *But I'm a Cheerleader* and *D.E.B.S.* are late examples of this corpus and, while they differ from most of their predecessors
through their use of style, irony, and reflexivity—in short, camp—the use
of comedy is a trademark shared not only between the two films in question. With the high-profile exceptions of such dramas as *High Art* and
When Night is Falling, most lesbian movies produced during and particularly after the heyday of New Queer Cinema fall under the category
of romantic comedy. On the one hand, the prevalence of *comedy* in lesbian feature films from the mid-1990s onwards "suggests that love relationships among women do not, as was once the case, insure cinematic
suicide" (Berenstein 129). On the other hand, the *romances* provided in
these films produced stories of enduring love, or at least enduring sexual identity, against the invalidation of lesbian sexuality by contemporary
mainstream media. Hence, to simply dismiss the films of this "new wave"
for their formulaic structures and conservative aesthetics is to miss how

they participated in rewriting the terms of lesbian (in)visibility. Through their reliance on camp *But I'm a Cheerleader* and *D.E.B.S.* combine the new wave's interest in pleasure and affirmative representation with New Queer Cinema's legacy of intervention in cinematic discourses and normative representation. As romantic comedies with a camp twist, so to say, they embrace the emotional core of their respective stories and invest with sincerity what lesbian chic has made a superficial fashion, even as their excessive style allows for distancing laughter towards the norms of representation that have long repressed or distorted lesbian visibility.

3.1   Lesbian Film After New Queer Cinema

In presenting stories of love between women, lesbian romantic comedies are caught between two very different traditions of "romantic" movies, the straight romantic comedy and the "lesbian disaster movie," as Jackie Stacey puts it in her discussion of how *Desert Hearts* (1985, Dir. Donna Deitch) and its happy ending (one of the first of its kind) both furthered and broke with the latter tradition.[21] Thus positioned at the crossroads of different filmic traditions and cultural ideologies, the new wave of lesbian features was, in fact, "new" in many regards, but hardly perceived as inventive by either critics or scholars. This "lack" became even more apparent through the films' temporal proximity to those associated with New Queer Cinema. The latter had paved the way for queer representation in film, but it also set the standard against which later movies were judged—often unfavorably. Berenstein herself suggests that these new lesbian feature films did not exhibit the same characteristics as their gay male counterparts, namely Rich's "holy trinity" of New Queer cinema: pastiche, irony, and the reworking of history informed by deconstructive theories. Their "redeeming quality," according to Berenstein, however, is to be found in their even more drastic difference from lesbian features produced before the 1990s:

> they are exploring new venues of pleasure for lesbians. They're transforming the dark and sinister identity of previous lesbian portrayals into a fun and desirable identity, they're offering images of lesbian sex and desire, and they're making spectators laugh. (134)

While I agree with Berenstein's assessment that for lesbian features to be funny is a radical move in its own right, I would be hesitant to dismiss the whole "new wave" of said features as lacking any connection to and influence from New Queer Cinema. Instead, pastiche, irony, and an interest in history and social constructionism can be found already in early examples of lesbian feature films, namely the often quoted *Go Fish* and the even more overtly political (and hybrid) *The Watermelon Woman* (1996, Dir. Cheryl Dunye). The combination of New Queer Cinema's defining features, in an admittedly light and romance-focused context, continues to be important in later lesbian feature films.

Moreover, several filmmakers emerging from or inspired by New Queer Cinema contradicted the general conflation of a turn to genre with a turn away from the principles of New Queer Cinema. Filmmakers like Todd Haynes and John Cameron Mitchell used the classical Hollywood genres par excellence of melodrama and musical respectively, to continue the cinematic story started in New Queer Cinema. Both are genres with a long history of gay signification and appropriation, as both are connected with the kind of excess associated with camp, stylistically, emotionally, and on the level of its gender representations. Haynes, who seems almost "classical" in his continued dedication to "the women's film," newly interprets the 1950s melodrama with his 2002 movie *Far From Heaven*, in which he presents an update of Sirk's style and ethos with the added awareness of intersectionality.[22] *Hedwig and the Angry Inch* (2001, Dir. John Cameron Mitchell), on the other hand, the story of a young East German gay boy who comes to the US as the wife of a US soldier after a "botched" (in the words of Hedwig her/himself) sex-change operation, takes the musical genre to its logical extreme in its obsession with the bridging of differences, personal growth, the per formativity of identity, and search for harmony.

The romantic comedy on the other hand is a genre which is more easily associated with the upholding of Hollywood standards of heter-onormativity. By definition, films of this genre are concerned not only with straight courting, but also inevitably end with its success and (the promise of) the creation of a nuclear family. At the same time, however, "as a genre, comedy is fundamentally queer since it encourages rule-breaking, risk-taking, inversions, and perversions in the face of straight patriarchal norms" (Doty 81). This contradictory description of the romantic comedy is echoed in the first comprehensive study on lesbian romantic comedies, *Girl Meets Girl*, in which Kelly Ann McWilliam argues for a nuanced reading of this corpus of films, which is "conserva-tive *and* progressive, conventional *and* subversive" (6).[23] She agrees with

Berenstein's assessment that the romantic comedy has, indeed, become the major genre for lesbian features films—particularly for those produced with a crossover appeal (=cinematic release) in mind—yet differs from Berenstein by looking at romantic comedies as providing more than laughter and "positive" representations of lesbian desire. Beyond the "liberal prestige films" with a penchant for drama[24]—among lesbian-themed movies most famously, and successfully if awards are any indication, *Boys Don't Cry* (1999, Dir. Kimberly Peirce)[25] and *The Kids Are All Right* (2010, Dir. Lisa Cholodenko)—romantic comedies such as *Imagine Me and You* (2005, Dir. Ol Parker) and *Kissing Jessica Stein* (2001, Dir. Charles Herman-Wurmfeld) have without a doubt proven to be the easiest way to box-office success. While their success surely has many reasons, one factor is probably that New Queer Cinema's establishment of metacinematic techniques seems to have had little impact on these films and they challenge viewing habits the least. As genre films their style and story is as predictable as it is inoffensive. There are, however, exceptions to this rule, which prove that even the genre of romantic comedy can be used to challenge both its own generic conventions and heteronormativity.

Even before *But I'm a Cheerleader* tackled gay re-education camps, two other romantic comedies infused the genre's stereotypical narrative with biting criticism of homophobia and anti-gay politics. Interestingly, both films are also noteworthy for their embrace of camp—be it in on the level of characterization or style. The movies in question are *It's in the Water* (1997, Dir. Kelly Hard) and *Better Than Chocolate* (1999, Dir. Anne Wheeler).[26] *It's in the Water* tells the story of a small town which is divided by the building of a hospice for people dying of AIDS-related complications. The town's inhabitants are further divided on a filmic level using camp, as the homophobic, upper-class women who lead the protest are painted as caricatures in dress as well as behavior. McWilliam therefore argues that camp is used as an "othering" strategy to compare the towns' moral leaders negatively with the lesbian and gay central characters who constitute the "new normal," and that employed in this manner camp renders homophobia "the ridiculous and excessive butt of the film's joke" (100–01). The title, *It's in the Water*, illustrates the comic excess of the town's homophobia, which stems from a rumor spread early in the film that gayness is caused by consuming the local tap water. The irrational fear of "catching the gay" is presented alongside the equally irrational fear that the hospice will become a health issue for the whole town. The hospice as a place is relevant not only to the overtly political aspect of the movie, but becomes an equally significant (if highly unusual) space for the dual romance plot. In the gay male romance plot the newspaper owner's son, hitherto closeted and engaged to a woman, finds the strength to take a stand against his father and come out to him, as fighting erupts over how to report on the protests against the hospice. Moreover, a discussion about anti-gay activism during the ex-gay self-help session he attends spurs his interest in his future lover, who is the only one attending (having mistaken the group for an AA meeting as is later revealed) to openly oppose any action against the hospice. A lesbian romance is similarly intertwined with this gay-coded place. It occurs between married Alex (Keri Jo Chapman), a volunteer at the hospice, and her former best friend Grace (Teresa Garrett), a nurse, who has just returned to her hometown after divorcing her husband. The film does not shy away from extending its elaboration on the workings of homophobia into the love plot, when it shows the consequences of Alex's decision to leave her husband to be with Grace: the rejection of neighbors; the closing of her (shared) bank account; and a rift between her and her mother. While the film closes with the seemingly typical image of the two happy couples embracing, celebrating their victory over the hardships their love had to endure, its ending is anything but typical. Sharing the scene with the two couples is Alex's best friend, and the only character to be out from the beginning of the film, Spencer (John Hallum), who had just given the eulogy at his lover's funeral. By clashing the images of happy gay couples with the background of a church, in which the town had attended the funeral of someone they all knew but still failed to visit when he was dying of AIDS, the film refuses—despite its lighthearted tone—to paint a picture of happily ever after, which ignores the politics of complacent silence and outspoken homophobia that continue to threaten gay happy endings.

The Canadian movie *Better than Chocolate* is a more straightforward romantic comedy, as it focuses primarily on the falling in love and early stages of a relationship of only one couple. Kim (Christina Cox) and Maggie (Karyn Dwyer) meet early in the movie, fall in love at first sight, encounter some difficulties mainly related to family and outing, and are reunited in the end. Beside this basic plot, however, the movie also sheds light on transphobia within the LGBT community via the treatment of Judy (Peter Outerbridge), a friend of Maggie's boss at an LGBT bookshop. The bookshop itself becomes the site of an additional subplot, which is more issue-focused than the genre generally calls for, namely enacting and protesting censorship laws pertaining to the different interpretations of "obscenity" in the arts. In all three storylines, the movie does not shy away from showing or at least alluding to anti-gay and anti-trans violence despite its generally lighthearted, and at times, camp tone. Beside its painting of some protagonists as caricatures rather than realistic depictions of well-developed characters, the film's camp appeal mainly comes from its oversaturated colors and the incorporation of scenes from a nightclub the characters frequent, where elaborate drag performances contrast starkly with the movie's issue-driven scenes. As with *It's in the Water*, camp becomes a way to reconcile the depiction of horrific events with the movie's genre-typical portrayal of love and romantic fulfillment; the stylistically exaggerated portrayal of both films' respective antagonists allows protagonists as much as audiences to laugh at them and thus provides a form of in-group humor which serves as "a means of transcending the pain inflicted by prejudiced people" (Wolfe 381). On the other hand, camp—particularly in *Better Than Chocolate*—is also used to celebrate the queerness of its protagonists, which had often been downplayed in other romantic comedies, and thus aids the "triumph" of the films' queer protagonists in dual ways.

3.2   Romancing the Queer: Rewriting the Script of Romance

Arguably, neither *But I'm a Cheerleader* nor *D.E.B.S.* overtly tackle topics quite as political as *It's in the Water* or *Better Than Chocolate*. Yet, even as they turn away from matters of HIV and censorship, they are still invested in the foundations and effects of homophobia, insofar as *D.E.B.S.* has been read as a (however comic) parable on the then ongoing policy of "Don't Ask, Don't Tell" in the US military (Vesey 2011), and "conversion camps" like the one lampooned in *But I'm a Cheerleader* continue to exploit the internalized homophobia of gay Americans under the guise of religious beliefs and pseudoscientific claims to this day. Furthermore, both films embrace New Queer Cinema's legacy by taking on metacinematic issues, such as the analysis of historic representation, the burden of stereotypes, and the question of how style influences stories and, ultimately, who gets to tell whose story. Where *Go Fish* and *Watermelon Woman*, a quite literal exegesis of the lack of black female stars and filmmakers in Hollywood, address issues of (mis- and under)representation via collage aesthetics and interview-style commentary, *But I'm a Cheerleader* and *D.E.B.S.* reflect the zeitgeist of the early 2000s by engaging in less literal, but no less effective ways with the "celluloid closet" through the embrace of genre and pop culture. Rather than carving out a niche at the margins of mainstream culture, they position themselves right at the center, as they write their narratives at the heart of Hollywood's most cherished story, that of boy gets girl. The effect of this rewriting of an, or rather *the,* heteronormative genre as "girl gets girl" is, however, not confined to a gender swap within the cast of lead characters.[27] *But I'm a Cheerleader* and *D.E.B.S.* use camp on several layers, from dialogue to soundtrack, and from costume to setting, to differentiate themselves from and comment on stereotypes and formulas. They thus provide a critique of the genre and of traditional representations of gay women on screen, as well as the pleasurable movie experiences constituting the "Great Dyke Rewrite."[28]

Like any genre, romantic comedy is embedded in, partially created by, and expressive of ideological beliefs, in this case most centrally "the universality of heterosexuality" (Allen 72), which is also representative of Hollywood cinema's general "heterosexist bias" (Benshoff 61). Allen explicates that the genre suggests that "romantic love [...] is a heterosexual phenomenon" (72), and thus also "reinforces a number of our cultural beliefs, not only about love, but also about sexuality, gender and gender relations" (73). Thus, the genre lends itself perfectly to stories which try to challenge the "natural" correlations between these three notions. Furthermore, and at least equally importantly, the genre not only believes in, but depends on "true love." More than any other genre, romantic comedies imply that the central couple is meant for each other, that their love is "real"—no matter the unlikelihood of their encounters or the concerns of family and friends (or, in the case of gay protagonists, of society). For audiences starved for the representation of (meaningful) relationships between two women, rather than singular incidental characters giving products a touch of lesbian chic, the romantic comedy thus provides an ideal shortcut, insofar as "genre provides the viewer with a set of expectations, [...] it offers variation on a fantasmatic script" (White, *UnInvited* xxi).

This romance script has allowed for a wide range of variations of representations of masculinity, femininity, and heterosexual relationships since its inception in Clark Gable's and Claudette Colbert's tumultuous courtship in *It Happened One Night* (1934, Dir. Frank Capra)—from the 1930s Screwball Comedy to the 1950s "sex comedy"[29]; the "nervous romances of the late 1970s and early 1980s" (Krutnik, "Conforming" 138); to the "new" (139) or "neo-traditional" (McDonald 85) romances personified by Meg Ryan in the 1990s—the romantic comedy has evolved at the intersection of its generic rules and "a shifting environment of sexual-cultural codifications" (Krutnik, "Faint Aroma" 57–8). These changes include feminism, the sexualization of culture, conservative backlashes, and the loosening of mores concerning sex before (and outside) of marriage, attitudes towards divorce, and so forth. Steve Neale even defines the emergence of the new romance in light of developments like the AIDS crisis and sociopolitical changes, in particular relating to the interaction between the sexes and ideas of family and partnership (287). Neale thus touches upon many of the concerns which also govern New Queer Cinema.

In other regards, however, the genre has allowed for very little deviation from known patterns. The central couple's race, age, and sexual orientation have remained stable over 60-plus years. As Neale noted in 1992, "there exist no romantic comedies in which the members of the couple are lesbian or gay or Asian or black, and only one—*Minnie and Maskowitz* (1971)—in which the couple are markedly 'old'" (288).[30] Similarly set in stone is the narrative progression of romantic comedies, namely the three-act structure of the "meet-lose-get formula involving two protagonists" (Mernit 13). It is within the confines of this formula that queer romantic comedies are read and understood as such, and it is these three basic narrative moments finally, to which *But I'm a Cheerleader*, *D.E.B.S.*, and others can add meaningful differences from their heterosexist genre predecessors.

The first of the three narrative turning points, "meet," is also the one discussed most in literature on romantic comedies. Neale argues it is the one moment in which the different cycles most differ from one another, because "ideology is always at stake [...] in the mode and context of the meeting" (288). "The meet cute"[31] is the scene in which two people who had been strangers hitherto meet and fall in love, usually at first sight though they might only realize that later. Neale asserts that the characteristics of this "meet cute" depend very much on the cycle of romantic comedies. Whereas nervous comedies of the 1960s and 1970s, such as Woody Allen's films, focus on "ordinary" moments like spilling someone's coffee, the screwball as well as the new comedy prefer the extraordinary (287–88), as when Meg Ryan falls in love with Tom Hanks via listening to his "radio grief therapy" in *Sleepless in*

Seattle (1989, Dir. Nora Ephron), or Katherine Hepburn infuriates Cary Grant by wrecking his car in the beginning of *Bringing Up Baby* (1938, Dir. Howard Hawks). Equally "fated" occasions of strangers meeting also set the action in motion in lesbian romantic comedies. In *Kissing Jessica Stein*, for example, the eponymous (hitherto straight-identifying) Jessica Stein recognizes her soul mate in an answer to her rather obscure "lonely hearts ad," and hence decides to not let gender get in the way of her happiness just as Meg Ryan's character Annie Reed will not be discouraged by the geographical distance between her life in New York and the Seattle-based voice she fell in love with over the radio. Closer to the "sex comedy" tradition of false or mistaken identities, *Out at the Wedding* (2007, Dir. Lee Friedlander) introduces the lesbian love interest Risa (Cathy DeBuono) when she literally falls from the ceiling of a coffee shop (she was rewiring a lamp) just as Alex Houston (Andrea Marcellus) contemplates how to find a suitable gay woman to pose as her fiancée in front of her family—though Risa later ends up with Alex's sister. McWilliam argues that the introduction of lesbian "characters and content" inevitably destabilizes the genre "in significant ways" (24). Taking into account Neale's and Krutnik's observations on the romantic comedy's reluctance to embrace any couple other than its standard, McWilliam is certainly right to insist on the transformative potential of the insertion of non-straight lovers into a genre based on the "selling" of heteronormativity. I would, however, differentiate between "lesbian characters" and "lesbian content" rather than assume that the two necessarily entail each other. The above-mentioned films and several others, such as *Imagine Me & You* and *Gray Matters* (2006, Dir. Sue Cramer), offer generic meet cutes that either are inspired by straight romantic comedies—dogs feature prominently in the meet cute in *Gray Matters* just as they do in either the meet cute or overall plot of romantic comedies *The Truth About Cats & Dogs* (1996, Dir. Michael Lehmann), *As Good as It Gets* (1997, Dir. James L. Brooks), and *You've Got Mail* (1998, Dir. Nora Ephron)—or easily transferable into them, as when in *Imagine Me & You* the bride meets the future love of her life at her own wedding. In contrast, the meet cute scenes in *But I'm a Cheerleader* and *D.E.B.S.* are queer not only because of the gender of the characters involved. Rather, the scenes in which the two protagonists meet and/or interact for the first time negotiate the generic tropes of the romantic comedy with the historic tropes of lesbian representation. The scenes thus destabilize the genre to a much greater extent than romantic comedies which minimize their lesbian content despite the homosexuality of their protagonists. Rather than simply add another set of lovers into a pre-existing formula as if sexuality was inconsequential, *But I'm a Cheerleader* and *D.E.B.S.* make queerness and tropes of queer representation central to the crucial moments of their respective courtship plots. They take seriously the difference (and difficulty) of same-sex romance and adapt the heteronormative formula to fit their protagonists rather than strip the protagonists of their specificity and history to make *them* fit *it*.

But I'm a Cheerleader's Megan and Graham meet for the first time when Megan is given a tour through the premises of True Directions—a rehabilitation camp for homosexual teenagers, at which her parents have just dropped her off to undergo a 12-step program which will put her back on the path of heterosexuality. The setting itself precludes the interchangeability of this scenario for a straight romance, yet the scene includes even more signifiers of difference. As the audience learns while Megan takes the tour under the tutelage of camp member Hilary (Melanie Lynskey), Megan is the only one of the "rehabbers" who has not yet completed step one of the program, namely admitting to her homosexuality. In fact, the film's exposition has introduced Megan as the ultimate "all-American girl"—as she herself puts it in her introduction during the first group therapy session: "I shouldn't even be here [...] I'm a Christian [...] I get good grades [...] I go to church, I'm a cheerleader!" Yet her parents and friends have become suspicious of her behavior, and thus decide to send her to rehabilitation camp despite Megan's refusal and (self-)denial. Megan's "good girl" persona is so ingrained that when Hilary informs Megan that "inappropriate behavior" will not be tolerated in the room where all the girls sleep, Megan needs clarification. This lays the groundwork for the following meet cute, as the camera turns to Graham (Clea DuVall), another camp member. Graham is lying on one of the bright, pink beds, smoking, when she corrects Megan's assumption that "inappropriate" meant swearing with a deadpan "inappropriate as in fucking." The scene thus follows the generic logic of the romantic comedy by setting up the central couple as both antagonists—divided by their obstinate and conflictive characters—and as stereotypes of movie lesbians. While Megan is introduced as hinging on asexual in her refusal to either acknowledge her homosexuality or act on her assumed heterosexual desires, Graham is almost reduced to (perverse) sexuality. Unable to read her own desires due to internalized homophobia and misogyny (thinking of an independent female sexuality seems to have been impossible for Megan) until forced into introspection by intruding outside forces, Megan is every bit the reincarnation of Martha Dobie, Shirley MacLaine's tragic character in *The Children's Hour*. Martha can only understand her feelings for her colleague and friend Karen Wright (Audrey Hepburn) as lesbian desire, when rumors started by a student at the school they jointly manage make her aware of the possibility of such deviant longing. Her suicide right after this confession saves the narrative from the need to investigate whether her feelings might have been reciprocated by Karen, whose face in close-up ends the movie on a rather ambiguous note as she leaves behind not only sites of her homosexual accusation—the school and Martha's funeral—but also her male fiancé.

Megan is, however, more than Martha's heir—though the school setting and the movies' focus on the power of rumor do put them near to each other. More generally, Megan represents a type of movie lesbian, as Richard Dyer explicates in his influential essay "Stereotyping," who is defined not by her looks or character but by her position within a movie's narrative structure. Dyer uses the term "sexually malleable" to describe women who are "not just passive, they are nothing, an absence [...] things happen to her, people struggle to make her what they want her to be" (279–80). Such a character is also often marked by her relative youth—think Birdie in *The Killing of Sister George* (1968, Dir. Robert Aldrich)—positioned opposite the "'committed' lesbian" who is often presented as older, more (sexually) experienced, and trying to emulate men's position in society and within their relationship to the "malleable" girl (280). Indeed, the movie's opening positions Megan precisely in the role of the innocent young girl who will follow any lead, as the audience has already witnessed her "playing along" with her boyfriend's sexual advances, even though she is clearly not interested in, let alone aroused by their making out. She shows herself cooperative at camp (such as writing a song for one of the assignments) although she had been distressed about her parents' intervention, and even admits to her homosexuality rather quickly during the first therapy session despite her initial insistence that she was "normal." While later developments in the movie expand her character beyond the type, for the meet cute and early interactions with her future love interest, Megan's characterization fully embraces the stereotype.

Similarly, Graham is shown as the cliché "committed lesbian." Not much older, yet wise beyond her years, she is ahead of Megan in sexual as well as personal development. Everyone is made to wear bright pink (the boys bright blue), yet Graham's haircut, choice of jewelry, lack of make-up, and body language mark her as androgynous—like Dyer's older women in perfectly cut pant suits, this is expressed more in a rejection of femininity than an embrace of masculinity (despite the symbolic cigarette). Her gender-neutral name furthermore puts her in a long tradition of lesbian characters, such as *The Killing of Sister George*'s titular character and *Desert Hearts*' Cay.[32] She is unapologetic about her sexuality and rejects convention. Yet Graham's introduction does not stop at these historic markers. Instead she is also equipped with the indicators of lesbian chic, namely the sexualization of her lesbian identity. The first images of Graham are framed to show her whole body as she is lying on the bed (as opposed to a medium close-up of her upper body in the following shot), thus drawing attention to her bare legs exposed by the short uniform skirt. Added to this sexualized depiction are Graham's first lines, "inappropriate as in fucking," whose explicitness clashes with the infantilizing quality of her costume and surroundings. She thus not only looks the part of lesbian chic—draped on a bed, with attitude to spare, yet no history (as of now) or community—but also performs lesbian chic; she figuratively becomes the "edge" added to an otherwise bland context. As Megan turns to leave, a point of view shot by Graham lingers on her back, where the hospital gown Megan was made to wear until completion of step one exposes bare skin and underwear, thus further aligning Graham with sexuality.

Their "formal" introduction during group therapy in the next scene picks up this theme, as Graham simply states "we met," winking at a slightly uncomfortable, yet increasingly intrigued Megan not yet able to read the codes of flirtation between two women. This relatively unmarked phrase is presented as Graham's authentic reaction, as it is uttered spontaneously and accompanied by Graham's trademark shrug. Admonished for her lax attitude by camp leader Mary Brown (Cathy Moriarty), Graham gets up and adds with a mischievous grin: "I'm Graham and I like girls ... a lot." As opposed to her initial "we met," for this phrase Graham clearly takes on a role. Both her voice and body language change as she stands for her "outing" as the impersonation of lesbian chic; a combination of hyper-sexuality and coolness, which nonetheless shies away from labels and makes lesbianism a lifestyle rather than an identity. The focus is on something Graham *does*, and might not even do exclusively—liking girls—rather than something she *is*—a lesbian. Yet Mary still voices her objection, as Graham has presented the wrong type for the current setting. Hence, she finally follows the group therapy protocol as she adds with a mock-depressed tone "and, uhm, I'm a homosexual," thereby relying on medical terms, which pathologize "her condition," rather than using terms which have been adopted as self-describing options, such as gay, lesbian, or queer. Both her mocking tone and her obvious adoption of several roles available to her from a hegemonic script of lesbian identity, send up not only the current absurd situation. By extension—as she, Megan, but also the other participants are clearly presented as (stereo)types—her going through the motions of adopting identities ridicules the supposed shame associated with admitting one's homosexuality in historical contexts (Martha, after all, was drawn to suicide within minutes of her realization in *The Children's Hour*) as well as the idea of edginess in contemporary ones. At the same time, it draws attention to the constructedness of such time-bound notions by exhibiting them all at once. By combining this endeavor with the extended meet cute scene of the romantic comedy, *But I'm a Cheerleader* also draws attention to the "unmarked" status of heteronormative sexuality. After all, straight couples almost never need to declare their heterosexuality publicly before the love story can get underway.

D.E.B.S. takes a similar route, insofar as it once again introduces the "committed lesbian" during the meet cute through the gaze of the hitherto straight-identifying girl, and infuses the scene with "lesbian content" beyond the gender of super villain Lucy Diamond (Jordana Brewster) and super spy in training Amy (Sara Foster). The future couple first meets at a restaurant, where Amy is part of a surveillance operation trying to gain intelligence on Lucy Diamond, the head of a large crime conglomerate. What is meant to be an investigation into Lucy Diamond's alleged hiring of Russian assassin Ninotchka (Jessica Cauffiel),[33] is actually a blind date between two women who have recently broken up with their respective girlfriends. None of the attending spies, however, reads the scene for what it is, despite the obvious clues: two people meeting at a fancy restaurant; dressed to impress; one ordering for the other. The reason for this misinterpretation is revealed later, when—confronted with the truth about the meeting between Lucy and Ninotchka—Amy is caught off guard and admits that despite years of spying on this world-famous criminal nobody knew she "was a –." Though the word lesbian is not uttered, it is quite clear that Amy's "blank" insinuates just that. Given the bland disregard for the clues they had all just witnessed, this surveillance mishap points to the invisibility of lesbian sexuality, at the same time as it presents the private moment between Amy and Ninotchka as a public spectacle. Besides Amy and her three fellow D.E.B.S., who are suspended from the ceiling, the audience is also made aware of the presence of several men from different agencies ogling the couple. Amy's point of view, however, is privileged by the camera. The first close-up of Lucy's face is presented through her binoculars. As in *But I'm a Cheerleader* the shot emphasizes the other woman's desirability. Yet *D.E.B.S.* is even more overt in defining Amy as the origin of the desiring gaze, as the dialogue over the close-up has her struggling for words to define Lucy. When she says "Wow, Lucy Diamond is …," the next shot once again returns to the close-up, very much implying that the sentence would end in "hot." She saves face for the moment by inserting "real." Nonetheless, her lingering gaze has laid the groundwork of sexual tension for their first face-to-face interaction. In both cases, the blatant avoidance of specific terms, even as camera angles, editing, and so forth clearly convey the protagonists' queerness (which will later be made overt), mocks the homophonic dismissal of subtext or "reading between the lines," which have structured much of lesbian engagement with film as wishful thinking.

The blossoming love story is temporarily stalled, when *D.E.B.S.* emphasizes its status as a genre hybrid and the stakeout goes awry.[34] Amy's ex-boyfriend Bobby (Geoff Stults), who is working for another surveillance agency, shows up to demand back a bracelet from her, which during the struggle between the two drops right into Lucy Diamond's soup. Realizing she is surrounded by agents and spies, Lucy draws her gun, which prompts a lengthy action sequence including slow-motion sequences of exaggerated stunt movements. After the chase sequence, the film returns to the conventions of the romantic comedy, and in particular the meet cute, when Lucy and Amy, both looking in the other direction, bump into each other in an empty warehouse. As this is still set within the framework of a spy movie, however, the script of the meet cute is recreated with guns drawn—and additional incentive to Amy to lie about her sexual attraction to Lucy. When Amy is "rescued" by the other D.E.B.S. and Lucy has vanished without a trace but the floor is covered in diamonds, Amy is forced to conceal the true nature of the interaction. Their flirting subsequently becomes distorted as a moment of mortal danger when scrutinized by her peers and parental figures at their spy academy.

In both films the meet cute scenes fulfill the generic conventions of the romantic comedy by introducing two strangers not only to each other, but also to the audience. The scenes furthermore set the protagonists as antagonists in the tradition of the screwball comedy, while indicating their mutual attraction. At the same time the scenes emphasize the meeting's association with moments of illicit interaction and illegal actions, with shame, secret, and even pathology, thus merging the codes of romantic comedy with the stigma of lesbian historic representation. Presented in the "light entertainment" context and celebratory tone of the romantic comedy, however, the stereotypes are not rejected, but rather negotiated in such a way as to refuse the power of interpretation by, as Dyer puts it, "heterosexual society [which defines] us for ourselves, in terms that inevitably fall short of the 'ideal' of heterosexuality" to "bolster heterosexual hegemony" (278). Furthermore, by making the lesbian content instrumental to the narrative, the films avoid the problem of making their lesbian leads merely incidental, and thereby avoid creating a new version of "the same old story" with only lesbian chic added to the equation. Instead they rewrite both the "old story" of stereotypes by embracing rather than rejecting them, and the "old story" of straight meet cutes by stressing the social privileges associated with scenes of public heterosexual courtship in which only individual traits stand in the way of a couple's happiness.

The same approach of infusing the romantic comedy tropes with specifically queer contents and concerns is also used for the "lose" and "get" aspects of the plot. As Neale argues, part of the "lose" formula is often a "would-be-suitor or a possible but unsuitable partner for one or other of the members of the couple" (288). This would-be-suitor is often representative (particularly in the screwball comedy) of the path too conventional for the members of the couple, or it stands for the characteristics of one of the partners that stand in the way of the couple's happiness. In *But I'm a Cheerleader*, as well as in *D.E.B.S.*, this character is present in the form of the (ex-)boyfriend who is both "too conventional" and indicative of deeper problems in one of the protagonists: for Amy, Bobby represents the sense of duty which keeps her at the D.E.B.S. academy, even though she dreams of attending art school in Europe; while for Megan her picture-perfect quarterback boyfriend serves as a stand-in for her initial trait of unreflectively fulfilling roles in life she assumes to be the norm. Both boyfriends are quickly discarded by the plot, which underlines their status as symptoms rather than independent characters. Their easy rejection also emphasizes that for the queer couple, issues leading to their break-up are not internal, as favored by screwball and sex comedies whose romances seem to be foredoomed due to the protagonists' incompatible characters. Rather, *D.E.B.S.* and *But I'm a Cheerleader* equally stress the role external forces play in the failure of queer romance. In both cases, the couple must keep their relationship a secret—Megan and Graham violate the camp rules by engaging in "inappropriate behavior," and Lucy is "engaging with the enemy." Interestingly, both intrusions into their privacy, which lead to the discovery of their hitherto secret relationship, happen either right after (*But I'm a Cheerleader*) or during (*D.E.B.S.*) the first time the couple has sex, thus also alluding to the policing of young women's sexuality more generally.

Moreover, and in stark difference to most heterosexual romantic comedies which feature similar occasions—interrupted sexual encounters are, after all, not too rare in Hollywood cinema—*D.E.B.S.* and *But I'm a Cheerleader* stress how the intrusion not only "kills the mood," but ends the whole relationship and leads to brutal forms of punishment (though those are softened in their representations due to the genre constraints). Upon discovery Megan is expelled from the camp, yet forbidden to return to her parents and thus virtually made homeless, while Amy is kept at the academy for publicity reasons, yet ordered back into the closet by being forced to deny her relationship with Lucy and instead made to attend prom accompanied by Bobby. The films thus do not portray their central romances as the very personal development seen in most conventional romantic comedies. Rather, both films stress the power that "outer forces" and authorities wield over the couple, as their judgment of and intervention into the relationship not only interfere with happy endings, but also turn the private expression of emotion into a public—and publicly regulated—spectacle.

Hence, it is only logically consistent that both films also make the final act, the "get," a public event. The happy endings accomplished in this public manner not only present a triumph of true love in general, but the affirmation of the existence and legitimacy of queer love more specifically. Megan and Graham are reunited at Graham's camp graduation ceremony, when Megan declares her love in front of the "congregation" (the scene is eerily reminiscent of a wedding) with a cheerleading chant. Amy, on the other hand, uses her graduation speech to come clean about the real nature of her hostage taking.[35] In a revealing turn of events—and structural reversal of the genre—both "malleable girls," the ones seduced by the "committed lesbian," therefore are the ones to actively pursue their love. They do so by using a role they had thought in conflict with their homosexuality: cheerleader and honor student respectively. The films thus reject the one-dimensional stereotype of "the lesbian" who adds little else to the narrative besides her sexuality. Additionally, both very public outings at the end are met with rejection by at least a minority of the spectators. Despite the happy ending, the films do not depict a utopian outcome, as the underlying threat of homophobia is not entirely written off. In summary, all three decisive narrative components of the romantic comedy are rewritten in a way which stresses—rather than glosses over—the differences in obstacles faced by queer and straight couples. The films thus use romantic comedy to accentuate how love might be a universal *feeling*, but loving someone in a norm-based society is not a universal *experience*. Thereby, they actively counter the logic of lesbian chic and neoliberal media that "promote a 'universalising' portrayal of lesbian desire, which makes it a desire 'like any other' [and hence] see lesbian desire as incidental, private, and thus politically inconsequential" (Pick 109).

The critical differences from the genre norm do not end at the structural or narrative level. Rather, both films highlight their distanced attitude towards conventional representations of romantic love even before the credit sequence shows the films' title, namely via their title song. One of the stylistic characteristics of the romantic comedy is the use of (love) songs, which not only differentiates the genre from other genres, but also cycles within the genre. In this context, Ian Garwood underscores the importance of the title sequence to determine the way a film employs music as well as the mood of a movie. The use of Jimmy Durante's version of "As Time Goes By" at the beginning of *Sleepless in Seattle* (1993, Dir. Nora Ephron), for example, serves "as a guide to the spirit in which the film should be viewed, rather than locating its affect within a specific moment" (284). Adding that "other romantic comedies often also feature title sequences which seem to offer general guidance and advice to the viewer through song" (285), Garwood, however, cautions that title sequences can also establish an ironic, rather than "sincere" (as he calls *Sleepless in Seattle*) approach to love and romance, exemplified among others by Ani DiFranco's sugary performance of "Wishin' and

Hopin'" in the title sequence of *My Best Friend's Wedding* (1997, Dir.
P. J. Hogan). Here the song signals the movie's unorthodox happy end-
ing, when one of the reigning queens of the 1990s romantic comedy
(Julia Roberts) does not get together with her love interest (Dermot
Mulroney), but shares the last dance with her gay best friend (Rupert
Everett). Following from and supporting their distancing from genre
norms, *But I'm a Cheerleader* and *D.E.B.S.* begin with songs even less
romantic (and more ironic) than "Wishin' and Hopin'."

3.3   Riot Grrrls at the Disco: Compilation Soundtrack and Meaning

Over the slow-motion montage of the limbs of cheerleaders suspended
mid-air, *But I'm a Cheerleader* opens to the first notes of April March's
"Chick Habit," a cover of Serge Gainsbourg's "Laisse tomber les filles."
As in the original, April March's English lyrics warn a man about his
"chick habit"—his use and abuse of women—which will likely get him
in trouble, even threatening a violent outburst by the women he has
wronged. The dark and sinister topic of the song, while obvious from
the lyrics such as "you're gonna need a heap of glue/when they all catch
up with you/and they cut you up in two," is disguised by the song's
upbeat melody, the singer's nasal, yet high voice, and an instrumental
arrangement reminiscent of 1960s girl groups. The incongruity of content and form foreshadows *But I'm a Cheerleader*'s use of excessive style
and light cinematic format (the romantic comedy) to convey its critique
of institutionalized homophobia. Jamie Babbit repeats this technique in
her 2007 feature *Itty Bitty Titty Committee*, whose opening credits con-
sist of black and white, overexposed footage of women dancing at a punk
concert accompanied by the sounds of a riot grrrl song, which anticipates
the movie's interest in alternative, feminist culture and "Do it your-
self" styles. Her approach is thus similar to the Canadian comedy *Better
Than Chocolate*, whose focus on queer-specific locations and issues is also
reflected in its soundtrack. It consists of equal parts disco songs with
sexually explicit lyrics and lesbian "classics" by singer-songwriters such as
Ferron and feminist music icon Ani DiFranco, plus the song "I'm not a
f*** drag queen," originally written by transgender activist Star Maris
and sung by Peter Outerbridge in his role as the transsexual lesbian Judy.
The film opens with a drag/lip-synch show at the local queer bar, Cat's
Ass, to West End Girls' "Sexy." In less than a minute, however, the scene
is intercut with two skinheads attacking the protagonist, still in costume,

calling her "little baby angel dyke" in a back alley. The hate crime is only averted because the second protagonist intervenes in another instance of the meet cute, updated to a queer context. *D.E.B.S.* on the other hand opens its film with an exposition via montage and voice-over, which seemingly explains the spy background for the movie's storyline, yet in fact offers a thinly veiled summary of filmic stereotypes associated with lesbian movie characters.

> Voice-over: There is a secret test, hidden within the SAT. This test does not measure a student's aptitude at reading, writing, and arithmetic. It measures the student's innate ability to [here the screen shows a multiple-choice answer sheet gradually revealing the terms mentioned by the voice-over to accentuate their importance in contrast to the generic half total of a classroom setting shown before] lie, cheat, fight, and kill. Those who score well are recruited into a secret paramilitary academy. Some call them [close-up of the revealing multiple-choice answers again] seductresses. Some call them spies. Fools call them innocent. They call themselves D.E.B.S.

In her review of the movie, Alex Vesey notes that

> characterizing these traits as desirable for female cadets to embody may be somewhat misogynistic. Yet I think *D.E.B.S.* is effective enough as satire to suggest [...] the tactical maneuvers white, queer, and women and girls of color have to enact in order to combat patriarchal strategizing. ("Bechdel")

The correlation between the two identities—lesbian and spy—is further transported in the title song which sets in immediately after the voice-over, Disposal Unit's "Parade." The film skips the song's intro, starting it with the lines "It doesn't matter who you are/If you can believe there's something worth fighting for." Soundwise, "Parade" is an energetic mix between girl pop and alternative rock. On both levels, the song works well for the action genre aspect of this hybrid film, yet—like "Sexy" and "Chick Habit"—it seems highly unusual for a romantic comedy, at least until the movie exposes just how much energy and fight is necessary to be able to "be who you are." The soundtrack's significance is thus twofold. On the one hand, it marks a distinct deviation from the genre norm, thereby adding to a reworking of the genre and its accommodation to the queer content rather than the other way around. Moreover, the affect, or more broadly, the mood created by the soundtrack is essential to how the images are perceived. On the other hand, the soundtrack—due to its specific connection to affect—more than probably any other part of the movie that is not character or dialogue, becomes one way to create a (or at least address) a specific community. Soundtracks, particularly compilation soundtracks, thus create a meaningful way to "queer" a work on several levels, making it more accessible to LGBT audiences, and more fitting for LGBT narratives. Beginning with the idea of "fitting" narratives, I want to outline the ways in which a soundtrack engages with genre conventions.

Particularly in recent, "new" romantic comedies their nostalgic mode is reflected in their soundtrack. The films' notions of old-fashioned romance are, as Neale claimed, chiefly expressed through "standard songs," which help establish "true—and by implication, lasting—love" (296). He referred among others to the jazz-centric soundtrack of *When Harry Met Sally* (1989, Dir. Rob Rainer) and the combination of opera and pop standards such as "That's Amore" in *Moonstruck* (1987, Dir. Norman Jewison). An even more overt mode of expressing romantic compatibility through music is the film musical, elements of which are unsurprisingly also appropriated in the romantic comedy. Garwood cited a choreographed dance sequence in the 1998 romantic comedy *The Object of My Affection* (in which a straight woman falls for her gay best friend) as evidence of "the willingness of the romantic comedy to hark back to the forms of the Hollywood musical" (292). A montage set to Gene Kelly's "You Were Meant for Me" presents the "couple" at dance class until they are not only in sync with the song, but also each other. Such "old-fashioned" dance routines and soundtracks also played an important role in several lesbian-themed productions of the early 2000s which used the genre conventions of the romantic comedy in far less negotiated ways than my previous mentioned examples. In *Gray Matters*, for example, dancing complex routines from classical Hollywood musicals is the reason siblings Gray (Heather Graham) and Sam (Tom Cavanagh) are constantly mistaken for a couple, and later also an important step in the story of how Gray falls in love with her brother's fiancée. In *Out at The Wedding* a waltz at a ballroom dance competition is the final phase of courtship between the protagonist's supposedly straight sister and the woman she hired to pose as her girlfriend for the duration of the sister's stay in NY (covering the fact that she has a black boyfriend). *Kissing Jessica Stein* opens to an old-fashioned tune, while

Imagine Me & You derives its title from a 1960s love song which plays over the lover's reunion.

Soundtracks thus differentiate *But I'm a Cheerleader* and *D.E.B.S.* not only from straight romantic comedies, but also from most contemporary lesbian movies, and they do so in meaningful ways. Just like the old-fashioned love song emphasizes traditional ideas of love and courtship and their nostalgic tendencies, the music in *But I'm a Cheerleader* and *D.E.B.S.* reinforce their parodic mode. Many of the songs from *But I'm a Cheerleader*, for example, have a nostalgic retro-sound—harking back like "Chick Habit" to musical traditions of the 1960s, for example—which might seem to support a neo-traditional approach to love and romance in the same way that the use of "standard love songs" does for the new romance. Yet the effect is broken either by incongruous lyrics and themes, or electronic musical effects which reject musical pastiche in favor of critical appropriation, as it draws the audience's attention to these discrepancies rather than allow them to be lulled into the soundscape of a supposedly "easier" past. The soundtrack thus reflects *But I'm a Cheerleader*'s visual framework, which falsely suggests nostalgia, instead offering a biting critique of the reactionary glorification of an oppressive past. In *D.E.B.S.* the soundtrack reflects the hybrid quality of the movie—its combination of action and romance which enables the film's joyful spin on the homophobic story of the threatening queer villain—while also flaunting its obvious queerness in contrast to the narrative of secrecy and hiding.

Both soundtracks are compilations consisting mainly of pop songs rather than original songs or instrumental scores. While compilation scores fulfill the same role as "classical scores," that is the creation of atmosphere and conveying of emotion, the distinction is crucial. As Ronald Rodman argued pop scores "may be viewed as 'postmodern', in that they decenter the role of the unique musical work, and draw upon discourses around the musical work such as style and celebrity" (121). Anahid Kassabian similarly argued that such scores "bring the immediate threat of history [...] it means that perceivers bring external associations with the songs into their engagements with the film" (2). Kassabian discussed, among others, the lesbian classic *Desert Hearts* as a noteworthy example of using a compiled score, in this case consisting primarily of Western and Rock'n'Roll songs, to create a multiplicity of meanings:

These songs are important in the score not because country and western has a precise, guaranteed meaning, but rather because they do not belong to the tight meaning system of classical Hollywood scoring practice. Instead, each of us brings meanings from the individual and collective uses of songs in our everyday lives. [...]

The choice of popular music thus helps make *Desert Hearts* something other than an archetypal Hollywood romance. It avoids the trap of trying to represent lesbian sexualities in terms of Hollywood heterosexist feminine sexuality. By bringing memories, with their associated emotions, from audience members' unconsciousness into consciousness, it both particularizes Cay and Vivian's relationship and provides particularizable paths of entry for identification. And, since Patsy Cline—two of whose songs are used in the film—has a wide following in gay and lesbian communities, it manages to address two distinct audiences—heterosexual and lesbian—along different lines at the same time. (73)

Yvonne Tasker offers a similar reading of the film's score, when she claims its references as camp appropriations of pop culture by lesbian audiences, before concluding that to "suggest that a film which opens with Patsy Cline singing 'Leavin' on Your Mind' isn't located in lesbian culture seems rather bizarre" (182).

Comparable strategies are at work in *Better Than Chocolate*, whose soundtrack, however, lacks any pretense of trying to address a dual audience and instead underscores its queer intent. Ani DiFranco's and Ferron's star texts align them not only with lesbian audiences, but also with particularly queer love songs, whose combination of the private and the political, of entertainment and activism mirrors the movie's larger themes. *But I'm a Cheerleader* and *D.E.B.S.* similarly use music genres and artists that resonate with queer audiences. *But I'm a Cheerleader* uses songs by groups associated with the riot girl movement and independent girl groups like Go Sailor and Dressy Bessy. *D.E.B.S.* incorporates bands with large queer fan bases, such as Goldfrapp, and musical styles with queer subtexts like 1980s glam rock whose appeal lies in narratives of young, discontented boys maturing into "indeterminately gendered subjects" (Peraino 229–30). Among others, the two films thus not only reject the assimilationist tendencies of romantic comedies like *Gray Matters*, but also achieve what Simon Frith has identified as musical authenticity—an idea most often used for films dealing with foreign locations or different eras, yet equally applicable to subcultures (84–5). Frith further explicates how soundtracks are "important in representing *com-munity* [...] in both film and audience" (86). This authenticity and sense of community, is one of the crucial contributions to the films' overall perspective of creating a mood, in which the use of stereotypes becomes readable as camp reappropriation rather than exploitation.

The use of unconventional (love) songs also helps the central charac-ters, as Kassabian has shown for *Desert Hearts*, escape some of the clichés of cinematic representation of romance, sexuality, and femininity. This effect is best exemplified by the songs used in pivotal moments of both films' romance story lines. For Amy and Lucy, the first of these scenes is their initial conversation at a bar, after Lucy has "abducted" a consent-ing Amy, since otherwise a meeting between the two would be impos-sible. The background sound to Amy's admission that she is "really glad she met Lucy" and their subsequent almost-kiss—interrupted by fellow D.E.B.S. Janet (Jill Ritchie) who accompanied Amy—is Goldfrapp's "Strict Machine." The dance track reminds viewers of the couple's pres-ence at an underground (potentially queer) bar even as the medium close-up focuses on their faces and emotions rather than their surround-ings. Later, their first kiss starts without any additional sounds and is then accompanied by an instrumental whose volume is gradually raised, yet remains faint in comparison to that of some of the pop songs used throughout the rest of the movie. In connection with the secluded set-ting and the low-key backlighting, which make Amy and Lucy appear almost glowing, the reserved use of music emphasizes the intimacy of the moment, and thus counteracts the fanfare associated with the sweeps week kiss, which more often than not is characterized by the presence of an audience. The lengthy conversation about their pasts and future hopes, about committing without question to the D.E.B.S. versus "liv-ing a life of crime" is accompanied by the mellow song which might have been expected during the make-out scene, Jessy Moss "Telling You Now." This musical choice alerts audiences to the relevance of this scene, and thus the emotional bond between the two lovers, which extends beyond sexual attraction. Their interrupted first time of having sex is then again accompanied only by a slow instrumental, which once more underlines the intimacy of the moment and its centrality to the plot rather than its shock value or voyeuristic appeal.

In contrast, the montage sequences that summarize the early stages of their relationship prior to this scene, and Lucy's subsequent attempts to win Amy back, exude playfulness and fun, which counter the usually

tragic or sad mode of equivalent scenes in the "lesbian disaster movies." The latter montage is accompanied fittingly by the upbeat "A Little
Respect" by Erasure, whose out singer Andy Bell sings the lines about
unrequited love full of yearning. Their courtship plays out to the British
new wave band New Order's song "Temptation." While this 1980s hit
includes lines such as "No, I've never met anyone quite like you before,"
which subscribe to the same romantic ideals as the romantic comedies'
"standard song," it is both musically and lyrically far removed from the
clichéd love songs to be expected in this context. *D.E.B.S.'* end credits and Lucy's and Amy's final escape from convention and authorities
(as they literally drive into the sunset together) is set to The Weekend's
"Into the Morning." The energetic indie pop song and its lyrics, "It
was young love at its best and it's you that I'll remember," underscore
McWilliam's finding that the happy ending in lesbian romantic comedies "valorizes 'happy right now' over 'happily ever after,' by focusing
on and privileging the present" (136–7). McWilliam ties this focus on
the present to Stacey's arguments about the "lesbian disaster movie,"
concluding that with this kind of cinematic legacy "it is arguably less
important whether the central couple stay together forever, than that
they simply reach the end of the film without being maimed, rejected,
killed, depressed, or in jail" (136). But *I'm a Cheerleader* ends on a similar note, as the credits roll to "Together Forever in Love." Megan's and
Graham's reunion, however, which takes up the last scene before the
credits, is treated in a more traditional manner and accompanied by a
reprise of "their" song, "Glass Vase Cello Case" by Tattle Tale, which
had played in the background of their first sex scene earlier in the movie.
The mostly instrumental and minimalistic song (the complete lyrics are
"breathe into my hands/I'll cup them like a glass to drink from/are
you still ... still breathin?") captures the combination of hesitancy and
urgency expressed in their love-making. Gender-neutral, without any
narrative drive, and free of overused metaphors of sex and love or the
pomp associated with the string orchestras of conventional music scores
(the song's "bare" acoustic sound is achieved mainly with a single guitar and violin), "Glass Vase Cello Case" fulfills the common intent of
pop songs in love scenes, as it "delineates the emotion to identify with"
(Kalinak 20). It does so, however, without putting the queer romance
in secondary position to straight romances by "copying" their musical
language.

Overall, the song choices in *D.E.B.S.* contrast not only with the use of standard pop songs for they "possess a sense of confidence in their own romantic sentiments" (Garwood 284), but also with new romances' less nostalgic contemporary, the chick flick. While chick flicks rely on pop compilation albums as much as *D.E.B.S.* and *But I'm a Cheerleader*, the intended effect is quite different. According to Lisa Rüll, "a fairy-tale sensibility often pervades such movie narratives and several of the selected pop songs reflect this old-fashioned sentimentality" (83). Rüll further argues that chick flicks do not use pop songs in incongruous ways to "avoid postmodernist juxtapositions" (83), which *D.E.B.S.* and *But I'm a Cheerleader* consciously embrace. Furthermore, "upbeat tracks suitable for dancing" are usually reserved for use in credit sequences (83). On all these accounts, *D.E.B.S.* and *But I'm a Cheerleader* resist convention in favor of anti-nostalgia and queer authenticity, which not only accompanies, but rather accentuates the stylistic excess that is characteristic of both movies and is formative of their camp appeal.

3.4 Rainbow Colored and Typecast: Stylistic Excess and Stereotypes

Style—colors, costumes, mise en scène, sound effects, and characterization—enhances the films' abilities to parody intertexts, and enables their camp critiques of narratives and ideologies perceived as equally normative and oppressive, which they achieve, among other ways, by reversing the role of "freak" and protagonist. Their demonstratively artificial and (artificially) bright style, however, is not only used to refer to and set themselves apart from mainstream movies, but also to distinguish them from other queer movies, particularly New Queer Cinema. "Indeed," as Rich notes, "tragedy seems paradoxically to have been the favored tone of much of the New Queer Cinema" ("Queer and Present" 24). The movement's dark themes more often than not also translated to "dark" aesthetics, to which the prominence of black and white features such as *Poison* and *Swoon* (1992, Dir. Tom Kalin) attests. Yet even movies shot in color, such as *Safe*, often relied on muted colors and minimalist soundtracks and/or sounds more generally. On the other hand, the artistic ambitions (and financial restrictions) of many New Queer Cinema films meant that even some comedies, among them *Go Fish*, relied on a black and white aesthetic, which made them easily readable as "avant-garde" without so much as watching even one complete scene of the film. As such, *D.E.B.S.*'s and *But I'm a Cheerleader*'s exuberant styles serve to turn away from realist mainstream traditions and artistic queer influences. Like the structural deviations from genre conventions and the non-traditional use of the soundtrack, the visual style of the movies becomes a way to create a critical difference from norms at the same time as it creates new references and affective connections. Furthermore, the movies also posit themselves through their style outside of (and revolting against) the niche New Queer Cinema had allotted to movies by and about queer women.

3.4.1 Spatial Clichés

A huge part of the films' stylistic excesses stems from the mise en scène, which includes not only the way the locations are presented on screen, but also the kind of location chosen as the film's setting. Spatial aspects are, in fact, crucial to understanding how *But I'm a Cheerleader* and *D.E.B.S.* displace stereotypes through excess and thus ultimately how camp plays into their creation of cinematic pleasure. The presence of queer bar spaces in both movies interlocks with the aforementioned inclusion of "tracks suitable for dancing," from which conventional feature films shy away. As an essential component of lesbian representability from a short scene in *Wings* (1927, Dir. William A. Wellman), and Marlene Dietrich's entrance into the American consciousness in *Morocco* (1930, Dir. Josef von Sternberg), to the lavish sequences in *The Killing of Sister George*, and finally the numerous gay bars frequented in films and TV shows during the era of lesbian chic, the bar has surfaced as one of the two "chronotopes" of lesbian representation, as Lee Wallace defines them. She borrows the term chronotope from Vivian Sobchack's analysis of the setting's role in defining the elusive genre of Film Noir. Similarly, Wallace argues that places alone can define, or invoke, sexuality, particularly in the case of lesbians, whose burdened relation to visibility in Hollywood cinema relies heavily on coded representation. She therefore claims that there are two spaces which have "catalyzed lesbian possibility for the duration of the twentieth century" and emerged as "privileged locations of the lesbian-life world," namely the bar and the schoolroom (5). Both are present in *But I'm a Cheerleader* and *D.E.B.S.* and strikingly absent from most other contemporary romantic comedies.[36]

The conscious omission of places marked as queer in films such as *Imagine Me & You* and *Kissing Jessica Stein* further supports their "universalizing" impetus—to borrow a term from Maria

Pramaggiore[37]—already reflected in their choice of conventional soundtracks and adherence to genre conventions more generally. Pramaggiore used the distinction between "minoritizing" and "universalizing" interests to discuss the different approaches to genre in lesbian romantic comedies in the early 1990s, mainly *Go Fish* and *The Incredibly True Adventure of Two Girls in Love*. The former, Pramaggiore argued, accentuates its characters' and narrative's queerness rather stressing "universal" aspects such as first love and teenage revolt, like *Two Girls in Love* does. Even more so than this film from 1995, however, many romantic comedies after 2000 put much effort into aligning their protagonists' lesbian love stories with family and tradition, specifically traditional (read: universal) romance as symbolized by marriage and weddings. Hence, they rely on a markedly different "chronotope" than the bars and schools which align *But I'm a Cheerleader* and D.E.B.S. with their queer predecessors. Instead, (straight) wedding banquets dominate films from *Saving Face* (2004, Dir. Alice Wu), where the central lesbian couple is last seen dancing at a wedding among their conservative families, to *Kissing Jessica Stein*, in which attending a straight wedding becomes the defining moment of the couple's developing relationship. In *Out at the Wedding* a whole wedding party assuming the protagonist is gay is considered worrisome, but at least preferable to unveiling her interracial straight relationship, while *I Can't Think Straight* (2008, Dir. Shamim Sarif) opens to the lavish preparations of a soon-to-be-aborted straight wedding. Finally, in *Imagine Me & You* the future lesbian couple meet at one of the women's wedding with a man. In none of these films, except for a gay ballroom dance contest attended with their parents in *Out at the Wedding*, do these couples enter a queer bar or any other space which might hint at a community outside of (biological) family. The choice of space thus supports an overall approach to genre in which queer characters are added, yet queer content and connotations are kept at a minimum. Moreover, courtship in these more "universalizing" romantic comedies takes place almost exclusively in either private spaces or empty public spaces (such as the "date" in *Imagine Me & You*, where the couple dances at a video arcade rather than a club). Thus, the films follow the dictum that queer individuals "are expected to confine the expression of their sexuality to the private sphere so as not to contaminate the public" (Lister 123). *D.E.B.S.*'s and *But I'm A Cheerleader*'s use of locations runs counter to such universalizing notions and instead embraces queer spatial (and other) stereotypes.

The queer bar features prominently in *D.E.B.S.*, since it constitutes the background for the couple's first date, when Lucy "abducts" Amy after their first meeting is cut short. In *But I'm a Cheerleader*, Megan follows Graham and the other rehabbers as they escape from the confines of True Directions to spend a night dancing at a local gay bar, the Cocksucker, where the girls first kiss. Both bars are reintroduced at later moments in the movies and thus represent stable elements of their now queer life, when Amy and Lucy are spotted on a date by Ninotchka, and Megan goes to the Cocksucker alone only to run into the woman (Julie Delpy) who set in motion the actions which led her to be kicked out of rehab. *But I'm a Cheerleader*'s bar scenes are stylistically set apart from the excessive style used throughout most of the film to—borrowing from Al LaValley's definition of camp's purpose—"make the ordinary surreal" (65). Conversely, these restrained scenes help to make the "extraordinary" real. Just as the soundtrack at several moments takes a break from the dance and pop tracks that make up the majority of songs featured in the films to make room for either instrumental or near-instrumental scores to emphasize the emotional relevance of a scene, also visual restraint works to take some scenes out of the themes of satire and parody in favor of intimacy between and attachment to its protagonists. In *But I'm a Cheerleader* such a visual break occurs not only for Megan's first time of having sex with a woman—which marks, as mentioned before, a turning point in the movie insofar as it leads to her public punishment—but also for Megan's first time of entering a queer bar. Rather than presenting the audience (and Megan) with the kind of huge, stylish, and extravagant club filled with highly attractive, visibly queer extroverts, and lavish interior usually presented in mainstream films (e.g. *First Wives Club*, 1996, Dir. Hugh Wilson), or series (*Sex and the City*, 2x06 "The Cheating Curve"), *But I'm a Cheerleader* portrays the Cocksucker as a seedy small-town gay bar. It is thus presented as an island of realism in a sea of surrealism. Even as the place is more run-down than in vogue, cinematography and editing ensure the depiction of this semi-public queer space in a more positive light than usual, insofar as the repeated representation of arrival scenes at lesbian bars— from *The Killing of Sister George*'s Mercy Croft (Coral Browne) literally descending into the depravity of the bar, to Michael Douglas lost in a sea of women in *Basic Instinct*—"produces and upholds heterosexuality's spatial hegemony by continually emphasizing the accessibility of lesbian bars to heterosexuals" (Hankin 25). This "accessibility," Hankin claims, is particularly used within the context of lesbian chic for heterosexuals to "confirm and reinvigorate their heterosexuality through the space of the lesbian bar" (32–3). She furthermore points to examples from *Foxy Brown* (1974, Dir. Jack Hill) to *Bound* (1996, Dir. The Wachowskis) and *Basic Instinct* to show how the lesbian bar space is often associated with "narratives revolving around criminality" (26). While this is to a certain extent the case in *D.E.B.S.*, as Amy is after all abducted, the scene nevertheless plays out in a way which emphasizes the bar's potential for social mingling and initiating romance over its connection to organized crime. In fact, neither scene—contrary to contemporary mainstream representations—presents the bar as a shortcut to indicating the liberal character of straight protagonists and their willingness to branch out and break the patterns of their lives as they flirt with non-normative sexuality only to ultimately dismiss it as mere fun. Rather, the bar becomes the place where Megan and Amy—the initial "fish out of water"—finally confirm their feelings for another woman, turning the story of harmless flirtation into one of successful seduction. The scenes thus help to validate a queer space devalued by lesbian chic and vilified by Hollywood film.

In addition to this positive rewriting of the script of lesbian interactions at bars, the films' combination of the bar with the other chronotope of lesbian representability, the school, is noteworthy for its potential to intervene in the cinematic meaning of both places. According to Wallace, the two places are "connected historically in relation to the trope of the sexual closet," insofar as the "highly gendered butch-femme culture of the midcentury lesbian bar" presents the other extreme to "the passing culture of female friendship associated with the women's college" (9). As such, the bar scenes serve to counteract not only the repressive, subtext-laden environment associated with the schools as portrayed in both films, but also the (boarding) school trope more generally. By putting the same protagonists within the contrasting environments of the hyper-visibility of lesbian desire within bar spaces on the one hand, and the invisibility of sexual relationships between women within schools on the other, the films stress the contingency of such codes of representation. The supposed depravity of one place clashes with the assumed innocence of the other and undermines both associations.

Furthermore, by combining school and bar within films about young people's coming of age, the latter space is introduced into yet another genre (as in the romantic comedy) from which it is usually absent, the teen film. In their discussion of teen films of the 1980s and 1990s, Steve

Bailey and James Hay defined three locations as "critical sites [...] in which social identities of youth find articulation:" home, school, and mall (218). The last is described as a place of "courtship and romance," and thus a "counterspace to the school and the home" (226). They fail to mention, however, the extent to which the opportunity to spend time in a mall and experience romance in such a relatively public space (semi-public as they call it, but still open to authority figures like parents and teachers) hinges upon white, straight privilege. The feeling of autonomy and the possibility of courting other teenagers in such an environment is barred to queer couples. In accordance with the minoritizing interest of the two films in question, the chronotope of the bar thus occupies the narrative space vacated by the mall. Whereas the mall represents an ambiguous site of both "an increasing personal autonomy and of a simultaneous conformity to social norms" (218), the bar unambiguously confirms the former and rejects the latter. Considering that the denial of lesbian identity in recent teen movies is a substantial aspect of the two films' use of the representational stereotypes that will be discussed below, this spatial replacement also aids rewriting the trope, particularly apparent in teen movies, of the "lesbian until graduation." By allowing the school and the bar—substituting for the teen movie's mall as the first step into "the real world"—to overlap temporarily, *D.E.B.S.* and *But I'm a Cheerleader* intervene in the teen movie's spatiotemporal heteronormativity. They undermine the genre's construction of lesbian sexuality as a terminable experience and draw attention to the privilege associated with traditional teen movie sites of romance.

3.4.2 Cheerleaders and Color Blocking

Beside the choice of location their stylistic composition adds crucially to the films' politics. *But I'm a Cheerleader*'s visual style is primarily one of visual exuberance and its comedy one of frustrated expectations about the connection between appearances and matter. Most of the movie's scenes are full of bright colors repeated on several surfaces to create the impression of conformity despite glaringly artificial costumes and sets. An early scene, for example, leading up to the intervention staged by Megan's parents and friends, shows the family dinner routine. In the sequence brown and yellow colors dominate the screen, yet a slightly different shade of color sets Megan visually apart from her home and parents, even before the unveiling of her vegetarianism—which is picked up later during the intervention as a sign of her homosexuality—through a shot that shows the different contents of each family member's plate and indicates her difference from the nostalgic suburban idyll. The next morning, the end of her and her family's daily routine is heralded by the jarring arrival of the True Directions instructor Mike (RuPaul) in a pink van and dressed in tight bright blue clothes, bearing the slogan "Straight is Great."[38] As soon as Megan leaves the suburb for camp, these two colors dominate the entire rest of the movie, as the rehabbers are made to wear uniforms according to their biological sex: boys in blue, girls in pink. The use of these colors constitutes one of the movie's many hints to the contingency of symbols, as pink is used inside the camp to denote girly femininity, whereas in the context of the ex-ex-gays later introduced pink—as part of the pink triangle– becomes a sign of queer radicalism. In the same vein, many of the exercises in "true womanhood"/"true manhood" include movements and directions—such as a vacuum cleaning instruction which consists of pushing a phallic-shaped object towards the thighs of a fellow female camper—whose ambivalence makes them highly homoerotic despite the intent to convey traditionally gendered behavior.

Throughout the movie homoerotic images thinly veiled as straight imagery make up a large part of its humor. Overtly, this clash between straight and gay readings mainly functions as a basis for the situational comedy created by the incongruous images. The homoerotic iconography can, however, also be understood as a comment on "the kind of dismissive attitude that sees queer understandings of popular culture as being the result of 'wishful thinking' about a text" (Doty 4). As with *D.E.B.S.*'s emphasis on the silencing of Amy's queer voice in the beginning of the film, which allows her friends to continue to read her as straight, even as the subtext of lesbian attraction becomes almost blatantly obvious, *But I'm a Cheerleader* uses its visual double entendres to debunk the insistence on straight readings as itself a form of "wishful thinking." Conversely, a figure like Mary's son Rock (Eddie Cibrian), whose name evokes closeted romantic comedy star Rock Hudson and whose looks resemble the Castro Clone, becomes a symbol of straight society's inability to read queer characters, even as all the boys—including instructor Mike—ogle him and his phallic tools while he takes on the "manly" jobs around the camp. Yet Mary still uses him as the model of straight masculinity in a later part of the rehab, where the teens are made to re-enact "simulated sexual lifestyle" under her direction to re-engage with heterosexuality. Other situations backfire in less obvious, yet equally meaningful ways, as when Megan, for example, is instructed to "put [her] feelings down in song" to address and overcome her latent homosexuality. While she eventually comes up with a song that rejects homosexuality and celebrates the joys of conversion, the exercise's success rings hollow as performing acoustic songs about your innermost feelings on a guitar was already a tradition of lesbian singer-songwriters clichéd enough to be spoofed in *Ellen*'s coming out episode, aired in 1997 on national television to a mainstream audience.

Overall, the conversion camp's continued attempts to instill something supposedly natural, like sexuality and gender identity, in its rehabbers only serves to emphasize how both are constructs whose "correct" performance takes effort. Here, the setting and camp exaggeration of gender stereotypes interacts with the genre, as the romantic comedy's romance plot often necessitates moments of play. These lend themselves perfectly to the film's re-education plot, in which rehabbers take on traditionally male and female roles in the household, since—as Neale elaborated concerning romantic comedies—"it is relatively common for some or all of the fun to stem from playing—or from having to play—at being a married couple" (292). As Megan and Graham are accidentally grouped together for the rehab exercises, it gives the audience ample evidence of their compatibility and them plenty of opportunity to "play house"—and explore the queer and particularly queerly sexual possibilities which arise from that situation. Neale adds that such scenes of play further help the protagonists get to know the other's true identity as well as learn about themselves (289), which only increases the irony of the role the True Directions program has in the creation of the queer couple, and in teaching Megan about the futility of fulfilling normative roles of gender identity.

The film's critique of such norms is not limited to heteronormativity, but equally sends up homonormativity, among other ways through the inclusion of a couple of militant ex-ex-gays. While they preach that there is "no right way to be gay," their home is a museum of queer paraphernalia, LGBT slogans, and rainbow symbols, which create an atmosphere no less surreal than Mary's color-coordinated recreation of a 1950s lifestyle. Clichés of gayness are not only embodied, but also problematized in the movie, when the rehabbers themselves are exposed as prejudiced. The group's most overtly masculine female participants, a softball player named Jan (Katrina Phillips), who sports facial hair and a mohawk, comes out as straight in one of the therapy sessions—condemning how people constantly disregard her identity when they (wrongly) deduce her sexuality from her gender representation. Despite Jan's outburst her fellow rehabbers continue to assume that she is simply in denial about her homosexuality rather than confronting their own prejudice and correcting their assumptions. Furthermore, Jan's desperate "I can't help it"—as if she would prefer to be gay simply to better fit—reverses "dominant homosexuality-is-a-choice rhetoric" and thus "allows for a profound critique" (Mulkey 61). While this scene exposes the complexity of letting go of the assumed connection between gender presentation and sexuality (the paradox of the straight softball player), the film overall offers a happy ending in that regard by allowing Megan to conciliate being gay with being a cheerleader.

In her 1973 short film *Home Movie*, filmmaker Jan Oxenberg uses documentary footage from her own youth to illustrate the coming out process and contemporary issues of lesbian identity. One of the scenes shows her younger self as a cheerleader, while her adult voice-over comments "The thing I liked most about cheerleading was being with the other cheerleaders" (qtd. in Weiss 45). Later scenes show her instead engaged in sports herself, on which Andrea Weiss commented how the movie thus ends with an "image of strength" and in a liberating tone, as the former cheerleader finds her place on the field in the company of other dykes, rejecting socially sanctioned ideals of femininity, which the cheerleader embodies "because she uses her body (voice, hands, legs, hips) to support the team and to encourage the community or the body of fans to do the same" (Miles 224). Yet such a reading perpetuates the consideration of cheerleaders not as athletes, but as "a sideshow spectacle" (225). *But I'm a Cheerleader* thus also offers an update on *Home Movie*'s ending. Rather than rejecting her former role, Megan overcomes its connotative burden. And, rather than overcoming a "preconceived notion that cheerleaders represent wholesomeness," which Natalie Adams attested to in her study on cheerleading "American Icon"(3), Megan rejects the idea that this wholesome image and gayness are mutually exclusive, when she wins back her girlfriend with a cheer. In *But I'm a Cheerleader* it is therefore not the young lesbian (cheerleader) who has to change, but her surroundings. Megan can reconcile her attraction to Graham with her cheerleader identity and can stay the same, while her parents need to re-socialize at a PFLAG event they are shown attending during the end credits.

3.4.3 Villainous Lesbians and Innocent School Girls

Where *But I'm a Cheerleader* incorporates stereotypes from different aspects of life and very much focuses its camp send-up on normative notions of gender identity, *D.E.B.S.*' style and content is defined by its celebration of cinematic trash—the girls' guns are shiny and giant to the point of impracticality, and clash with the innocence implied by the D.E.B.S. school girl uniform while taking on the status of fashion accessories. Similarly out of proportion—and outdated in their design—are Lucy Diamond's weapons with which she threatens the extinction of Australia. Props like Lucy's supposedly high-tech gadgets flaunt their makeshift quality in the same way the D.E.B.S.' technological innovations, such as hologram conversations and laser-based warning systems, display their cheap CGI generation. Adding to the movie's anti-realist aesthetics, its sound design exaggerates the intentionally bad CGI effects by evoking early science-fiction sounds or adding consciously artificial noises to gadgets, such as the sucking sound which accompanies Lucy's ascent to Amy's bedroom window. Even more "retro" is *D.E.B.S.*'s combination of scene transitions with audio-effects. Like its lengthy fight sequences and slow-motion montages of the D.E.B.S.' "heroic" actions, they further position the film as an homage to science fiction and action B-movies. The success of this strategy becomes apparent from the way critics have tried to define and describe the film mainly through comparisons to other iconic and contemporary films, varying from "feminist alternative to *Charlie's Angels*" (Stuller 10) to B. Ruby Rich's assertion that " 'lesbian *Spy Kids*' is what one pundit already dubbed *D.E.B.S.*, but I prefer 'a *Kill Bill* for dykes'" ("Out at Sundance" 22). Included in her 2013 retrospective on New Queer Cinema only as an afterthought to lament the turn to commercialism that Angela Robinson's career supposedly took after *D.E.B.S.*, Rich redefined the film as a "lesbian version of James Bond [with] posses of female spies, one hot villainess in hot pursuit, and a love story for the ages" (*New Queer Cinema* 266). Adam Vary dubbed *D.E.B.S.* "the gay spy movie" in his article "The New New Queer Cinema" in which he discussed a new cycle of gay—mainly gay male—genre films, which dominated the mid-2000s festival scene, such as *Eating Out* (2004, Dir. Q. Allan Brocka). *D.E.B.S.*, he claimed, was "one of several movies this year that could essentially be called 'gay and ____'" (44). The choice of action and spy movies as the main source of allusions was neither coincidental (as his article and the blank after "gay and" implies), nor merely a tribute to genre's potential for visual excess.

Rather, the inclusion of action elements reflects how "equivocal play with gay and lesbian desire and identity has become a defining feature of the genre" (Tasker 72) and, in particular, "the lesbian potentialities of the active body" (84). Jeffrey A. Brown similarly related the action heroine's appeal to her "polysemic sexuality" (200) and her status as a "symbol of polymorphous sexuality" (17).

Beyond the action heroine's general appeal as a queer figure, the TV series *Charlie's Angels* (1976–1981) takes on special importance in contextualizing *D.E.B.S.*[39] The D.E.B.S. are markedly represented as stand-ins for Charlie's Angels, including slow-motion takes of their hair flowing in the air, their communication with their superior via intercom, and their assembly as a group of young women, different in looks and character, as a secret crime-fighting force. This intertext is noteworthy particularly for the double-codedness of the original *Charlie's Angels*, which is picked up and enhanced in *D.E.B.S.* While Fabio Cleto named *Charlie's Angels* (together with *Batman* and *The Avengers*) as an early example of pop camp (122), other scholars stressed its relevance to the history of lesbian appropriation of mainstream media (Mizejewski 70; Brown 201–2). Whereas the 2003 remake *Charlie's Angels: Full Throttle* (Dir. Joseph McGinty Nichol) follows the logics of lesbian chic and pays titillating tribute to the queer subtext of the original series by showing ex-angel turned villain Madison Lee (Demi Moore) on two different occasions almost kissing current angel Natalie Cook (Cameron Diaz), the series actively worked "to undercut potential lesbian implications" (Schwichtenberg). Particularly the episode "Angels in Chains," which plays in a women's prison, has reached cult status as one of the occasions at which "the lesbian possibilities [...] surfaced as part of the general soft-porn scenario" (Mizejewski 70). Such connotations were, however, swiftly disavowed as "female adversaries emerge as lesbian stereotypes— butch or high-heeled killers—in ways that reassured us of the Angels' absolute difference from such nasty women" (70). Hence, Lucy's successful seduction of Amy, the "top angel," marks the belated triumph of lesbian (sub-)text over repressive self-censorship, while the comparatively restrained representation of their intimate moments rejects the original's exploitative toying with such themes.

Lucy is, moreover, coded as more than simply a random "female adversary" in the *Charlie's Angels* universe and thus broadens the film's intertextual density; she is one of the defining elements which also makes *D.E.B.S.* a *James Bond* spoof. As cinema's most virile, sexy lady-killer, who also fights criminal super-villains, James Bond has encountered several "evil" lesbians over the course of both his literary and cinematic career. Elisabeth Ladenson describes the two most famous lesbians from the James Bond canon—Rosa Klebb in *From Russia with Love* (1963, Dir. Terence Young) and Pussy Galore from *Goldfinger* (1964, Dir. Guy Hamilton)—as embodying "the repellent butch-versus-comely fem scenario" (419).[40] Lucy Diamond resembles Pussy Galore in "the sheer extravagance of both name and character that lures James Bond, and also lures the public" (422). Yet with her gadgets and ability to convert the women meant to fight her through seduction, Lucy equally represents James Bond himself. As Lucy in this scenario takes on the role of the queer enemy of state, at the same time as she personifies the characteristics of the traditionally straight male Lothario, she contradicts Hollywood's historic insistence of the lesbian's "lack." Through the inversion of seducer and seduced, *D.E.B.S.* ultimately puts overly masculine James Bond in close proximity to the overly feminine girl heroines of *Charlie's Angels*, thus collapsing the heteronormative logic of both primary texts. Moreover, through its trash aesthetics, which refuses to take its criminal content serious, *D.E.B.S.* spoofs the trope of the "evil lesbian" more generally. This moniker denotes not only criminal intent, but also sexual prowess in Hollywood cinema, as well as lesbian independent cinema. In both, women usually "need to be coaxed into their lesbianism, usually by dykes who are more experienced and often darker in skin tone and hair color" (Berenstein 125)—blonde, Caucasian Amy and brunette, Latina Lucy are cases in point.

The contrast between dark and light—whether in skin or hair color or both—runs through cinematic presentations of lesbianism from 1970s lesploitation films to contemporary TV series.[41] While it does not always signify to the same extent a difference in character and power position within the relationship, the coupling of a blonde and a brunette woman has still become as much of a cliché as the cinematic correlation between visual and emotional darkness, and therefore between lesbianism and danger (see Kessler 18). Painting Lucy Diamond as the pursuer of "innocent" Amy and as a national threat references the over-determination of queer characters as metaphorically dark in Hollywood history, which is continued in the "lethal lesbian" fad Rich observes alongside lesbian chic (*New Queer* 108). Yet the film rejects the consequences of such logic by giving Lucy a happy ending. At the same time, it dismantles these negative connotations by ridiculing Lucy's criminal ambitions—she threatens to annihilate Australia with a homemade looking atomic bomb because her heart has been broken—and presents her pursuit of Amy—by becoming a "better person"—in the style of makeover montages. The latter sequence is noteworthy for the way it plays with the importance of perception in narrative film, insofar as it qualifies Lucy's status as a super villain and her attempt at redemption by aligning it with the teen movie's and romantic comedy's trope of "new identity" through "new looks." The ultimate send-up of the vilification of queer characters is presented at the end, when graduation and the lovers' reunion clash with the show-down typical of action and spy movies. As Amy comes to accept her feelings for Lucy and comes out during her graduation speech and Lucy sneaks into the ceremony in her final attempt to win her back, Amy's ex-boyfriend and Homeland Security agent Bobby jumps at the chance to finally catch the evil mastermind. His quest to end Lucy's career is, however, quite obviously inspired more by the threat Lucy poses—like her cinematic predecessors—to "the social order" (Kessler 18), namely his heteronormative relationship with Amy, than to national security. As he tries to hunt her down with the support of a group of men behaving like frat boys, and the D.E.B.S. superintendent who forced Amy to give up on Lucy in the first place, their cause is clearly a homophobic one. The gay panic embodied in the attempted annihilation of the lesbian is taken to its extremes, when the whole crowd starts to run amok after Lucy is spotted by a random guest who then warns "everybody run for your lives" while a close-up captures his face distorted by fear. The subsequent shots capture hundreds of guests in slow motion as they run in different directions, bump into each other, and stumble over furniture in an exaggerated flight from an imaginary evil they have not seen and which poses no threat to them. This highly energetic sequence of panicked, anonymous masses, intercut with Bobby on his mission to kill Lucy is contrasted with the mellow, lyric-less song "Girls." This takes the audience back to Lucy's and Amy's first encounter, which also resulted from a chase sequence. The incongruity between the thoughtless masses' fearful, over-the-top reaction, and the sweet reunion between the central couple, whose love is furthermore finally condoned by their friends, ensures audiences' identification with the queer outsiders, and paints Bobby and his cohorts as freaks. Just like Amy's final words in her speech, "I have a date with the devil," as she looks up to a smitten—not at all devilish—Lucy, the final chase sequence, and the film overall present a toying with (negative) stereotypes, and thus one

of the key issues of queer media representation.[42] For queers in particular—as an "invisible" minority—stereotypes are also one way to see and
be seen on screen, even when their role is not big enough to warrant a
time-consuming coming-out scene or being "out" is neither an option
for the character nor the film at large. Hence there is always a "tension
within stereotyping between offensive imagining and productive visibility" (Halberstam 180). *D.E.B.S.* is rescued from the risk of "offensive
imagining" through its presentation of Lucy within a distinctly queer
context, whose camp aesthetics translate to the inversion of value judgments—among others by painting homophobes as freaks and normativity as highly artificial—and whose genre appropriation emphasizes queer
experience through intertextual references to subcultural canons and a
disruption of Hollywood's heteronormative genre frameworks. *D.E.B.S.*
thus presents a handling of cinematic stereotypes akin to Richard Dyer's
claims established in "Stereotyping." In this article, Dyer insisted that
the simple rejection of stereotypes would "bolster heterosexual hegemony" (278), as it entails the acceptance of heteronormative definitions of
what is and is not acceptable. Rather, Dyer argued, what "we should be
attacking in stereotypes is the attempt of heterosexual society to define
us for ourselves" and that subsequently "the task is to develop our own
alternative and challenging definitions of ourselves" (278). By relying on
stereotypes, yet presenting them in contexts which encourage their positive appraisal and giving them different storylines, *D.E.B.S.* ensures that,
for example, the stereotype of "the evil lesbian" exceeds the limits of the
trope's hegemonic function of dismissing both the character and her sexual identity. Lucy's portrayal instead shows how the trope can be recu-
perated as a tool of productive visibility and as a countermeasure against
the oppressive power of homophobic definitions.

   While Lucy's embodiment of the villainous queer is *D.E.B.S.'* most
obvious engagement with a trope, it is not the only one. Amy herself represents a different cliché and—similar to the naming of Lucy's
blind date as Ninotchka—a nod to those audience members aware of
Hollywood's production code era representation of gay women; her plan
to run off and be a painter in Barcelona calls to mind one of the only
semi-canonical representations of a lesbian woman before *The Children's
Hour*. In *Young Man with a Horn* (1950, Dir. Michael Curtiz), Lauren
Bacall plays the wife of Kirk Douglas' character Rick, whom she leaves in
the end for "a vacation" with a fellow female painter. Moreover, Lucy's
character relates the story of the stereotype of lesbianism as "immature

sexuality" (Dyer 280), and even more specifically contemporary clichés of the "lesbian until graduation." This trope is found both in retrospective aspects of lesbian chic narratives—older women talking about their sexual experimentation in college, like Jennifer Aniston's character in *Friends*—as well as in teen movies, which in the late 1990s regularly included scenes of "girl on girl" action—and bear little consequence for the character development of the girls involved. A prime example is *Wild Things* (1998, Dir. John McNaughton), which features a steamy make-out session between two young women that illustrates the combination of the sexualization of their bodies and actions with the de-homosexualization of their emotions and identities. In her analysis of *Wild Things*, *American Pie*, *Cruel Intentions*, and other teen movies that had been released either shortly before or simultaneously with *D.E.B.S.* and *But I'm a Cheerleader*, Tricia Jenkins noted their majority featuring images of lesbian sexuality, but rarely depicting the women involved as "traditionally lesbian" (492). She therefore spoke of "The Heterosexualization of Lesbianism in the Recent Teen Film" in the subtitle of her article. Interestingly, among the actresses involved in this trend is Clea DuVall, who portrays Graham in *But I'm a Cheerleader*. She had previously starred in the alien-invasion horror/high-school movie *The Faculty* (1998, Dir. Robert Rodriguez) as a girl who only fakes being gay as part of her rebellious phase, but ends up happily with one of the male protagonists.[43] The movies' focus on young adults thus bears a relevance beyond McWilliam's explanation of how the relatively young age of protagonists of lesbian romantic comedies is tied to the films' politics of painting their happy ending as temporary (rejecting the monogamous impetus of both classical romantic comedy and new romantic comedies, which envision true love as eternal). Rather, the films also provide poignant counter-narratives to the delegitimization of queer teens and young adults, who supposedly will grow out of their gay phase.

As such, *But I'm a Cheerleader* provides a radical intervention in hegemonic discourses as it represents not only a "taboo" sexuality, namely homosexuality, but additionally the sexuality of a "taboo" group, young women, who despite their constant sexualization are seldom allowed sexual agency. For this effort *But I'm a Cheerleader* received an R rating from the MPAA who, according to director Jamie Babbit, mainly took issue with a scene about half an hour into the narrative, when Megan sneaks out of the bedroom to masturbate.[44] The scene unfolds after Megan has got to know Graham better through some of the therapy sessions, and Megan learns that Graham was sent to True Direction after she had been caught with another girl. The slow-motion sequence of Graham as she gets ready for bed in the shared bathroom, framed as Megan's point of view shot, alerts the audiences to Megan's growing attraction, which is finally confirmed as she dreams about kissing Graham. She is awoken from the dream by the sounds of moaning and small electroshocks from the bed next to her, where she spots a fellow female rehabber—Sinead, who introduced herself by stating "I like pain"—masturbating with the "aversion therapy shocker" while watching Graham. The next scene is comparatively brief, not at all explicit as the frame never shows Megan below the waist, and of narrative importance mainly because Megan discovers two of the other rehabbers kissing, which gets them kicked out and foreshadows Megan's own fate. Still, the scene is rich with references and illustrates the film's use of intertextuality and stereotypes. Megan pleasures herself while holding the shocker meant to induce pain whenever she has "inappropriate" thoughts about another woman, yet uses the electroshocks to aid her arousal rather than to thwart it. The scene references the painful (pun intended) history of LGBT individuals in the US, as it evokes cinematic associations of deviant sexualities of all kinds with S/M and the historical treatment of homosexual "patients" with electro shocks. It does so, however, while showing Megan's sexual awakening as a crucial and pleasurable moment in her life. It thus rejects the negative connotations of earlier images and rewrites them via queer sexuality, at the same time as it lays the groundwork for Megan "graduating" into homosexuality rather than maturing out of it.

4   SUBTEXT TO SINCERITY

The movies' "campy" aesthetic is the one element most often commented on by critics and scholars, though on its meaning there is little agreement. Evaluated against New Queer Cinema, the films are judged to be too tame, and with reference to John Waters, *But I'm a Cheerleader* especially is assumed to lack bite. Especially in combination with the romance plot, the style seems to puzzle film and queer scholars alike, even as Susan Driver described it as "by far the most popular film" among the subjects of her study on queer teen media consumption (118). Critic Cynthia Fuchs, for example, lamented the film's reliance on caricatures because it supposedly makes "Megan's and Graham's

emotional development look trivial because it's so couched in camp."
A review of *D.E.B.S.* struggled with similar issues as it summarized that
"*D.E.B.S.* is a patently ridiculous teen-spies scenario that's played mostly
for laughs but oddly enough only works when it's being downright sincere" (Barsanti). Yet, it is not "odd" at all that at the films' core there is
sincere sentiment—love and heartbreak—as this is precisely what makes
them camp rather than merely "campy." Their visual and sound effects,
as well as their use of genre conventions, create the difference and distance from the dominant which is necessary for camp to work as a parodying strategy that denaturalizes and critiques, yet camp also "involves an
'extreme' identification with and affection for dominant texts" (Feil 38),
which allows for the emotional investment at the heart of camp pleasure.
But I'm a Cheerleader *and* D.E.B.S. rely on the audience's knowledge
of the conventions they break with as much as on the audience's interest in the inter- and subtexts they use—they are metatexts on the history
of lesbian (non–)representation at the same time as they take a "detour
into the commercial world of happy-ending popcorn movies" (Rich,
New Queer xxiii). In doing so, they refuse the either/or logic of mainstream and minor cinema, New Queer Cinema, and queer prestige movies in favor of rewriting the script of movie lesbians, which strives for the
creation of a pleasurable present without losing sight of its troubled past.
They queer the romantic comedy when they adapt the formulas beyond
a mere adding of lesbian protagonists, reinterpret homophobic stereotypes though a joyful rejection of the stigma, and reclaim a sexual identity coopted by mainstream media through lesbian chic—young femmes,
who in *But I'm a Cheerleader* and *D.E.B.S.* are portrayed with affection
and as individuals developed far beyond a role as eye candy and added
edginess to which that media "fad" confines them. Unquestionably these
films are commercial to a degree most "proper" New Queer Cinema
productions were not. They are neither "artsy" nor provocative in the
overt manner of their predecessors. Instead, they oppose the way lesbian
sexuality has been exploited for almost as long as visual media has existed
by infusing those very images with depth, sincerity, and pleasure through
the very queer strategy of camp, so that they can finally be enjoyed by
queer audiences without necessitating coded readings. The final camp
send-up of the censored history and demonization of queer characters
is achieved through both films' packaging as teen movies. Yet, unlike
the contemporary teen-focused movie actually called *Camp* (2003,
Dir. Todd Graff), in which "emasculated sissy boys literally beg for

acceptance and produce a mainstream audience that congratulates itself
for generously granting its tolerance to these poor queer souls" while a
straight romance takes center stage (Castellanos 114), *D.E.B.S.* and *But
I'm a Cheerleader* redefine the genre's stereotypes of bad boy and good
girl queerly, put those romances front and center, and do not backpedal
towards the end, when the couple rely on grand (public) gestures à la
John Hughes, to express their feelings. Rather, the genre's trademark
iconography comes back with a vengeance shortly before the credits,
when both films' couples reunite and drive away from policed sexualities in extravagant, slightly old-school cars—teen movies ultimate symbol of the rebellious teenager in their escape from conformity (Bailey and
Hay 229). As the films create an atmosphere of sincerity with respect to
the central lesbian love stories, and authenticity in its embrace of queer
audiences, the framing of these final moments of revolt in an "infanti-
lized" genre like the teen movie, however, does not minimize the critique embedded in the films. Rather, the contrast throws into sharp relief
exactly what kind of relationship Hollywood has deemed dangerous and
threatening.

Both directors have continued to rely on satire, caricature, and camp
in their works. Jamie Babbit, for example, received praise from B. Ruby
Rich for her later feature *The Itty Bitty Titty Committee,* which chroni-
cles the actions of a queer feminist action group. Rich praised the film
as an homage to the lesbian classic *Born in Flames* (1983, Dir. Lizzie
Borden), claiming that Babbit had found a "route out of lifestyle narratives" and making a strong case for the power of the carnivalesque,
producing something "slyly empowering" through the movie's "meta-
filmic incorporation of popular culture and lesbian history" (*New Queer*
205). In her capacity as writer and director for *The L Word,* Angela
Robinson introduced hints of camp when she sent up the dyke drama
cliché—which is, after all, perpetuated by *The L Word*'s own often soap-
opera-like structures and stories—in the opening of episode "Luck Be
a Lady" (4x06). Breaking with the visual style of the series by using a
split-screen sequence in which the change of frames is accompanied by
sound effects much like those used in *D.E.B.S.,* Robinson increased the
absurdity of an already over-the-top sequence not only through the trash
aesthetics, but also the narrative condensation which emphasizes the
convolutions of the plot. It does so, however, by stressing the diversity
of the "types of lesbians" shown on screen—tech-savvy and urban, professionals and parents, mothers and models—while also accentuating the

interconnectedness of their lives, and thus the importance of community. Her latest feature *Girltrash: All Night Long* (2014, Dir. Alexandra
Kondracke), a prequel to her successful web series *Girltrash!*, promised
to continue Robinson's exploration of mainstream genres for queer purposes as the movie combines noir aesthetics with a musical setup—while
featuring actresses from some of the most commercially successful TV
representations of lesbian relationships, namely *South of Nowhere* (2008–
2008) and *The L Word* (ensuing artistic differences between PowerUp
and Angela Robinson unfortunately led to the writer's distancing from
the project upon release). In lieu of a *Warrior Princess* movie adaptation
the creators of *Xena*, meanwhile, used their iconic stars Lucy Lawless
and Renée O'Connor in a cameo as not-quite-straight-nuns in their
modern spin on the lesploitation genre, *Bitch Slap!* (2009, Dir. Rich
Jakobson). Like its predecessors, the movie (with CGI as outrageously
bad as *D.E.B.S.*') offers scantily clad women engaged in gross violence
spouting one-liners—yet this time, at least, the lesbian characters are not
the butt of the joke. Another genre of the 1950s is used in Madeleine
Olnek's *Codependent Lesbian Space Alien Seeks Same* (2011), "a throw-
back to old-school sci-fi cheesiness [employing] a George Kuchar-like
aesthetic for a retrofitted lesbian fairy tale that thrillingly reinvents lesbian camp" according to Rich (*New Queer* 279). "The Great Dyke
Rewrite" of pop culture, it seems, has not yet exhausted itself.

NOTES

1. See, for example, Joanne Morreale on *"Xena: Warrior Princess as
   Feminist Camp,"* Elizabeth Whitney on performance art in *"Pop Culture
   Princess,"* and Martha Mockus' *"Queer Thoughts on Country Music and
   k.d. lang."*
2. While the exact moment of the "end of New Queer Cinema" is up for
   debate, the influence of market value on the development, or rather
   decline, of New Queer Cinema is supported by several scholars (e.g.
   DeAngelis; Bronski).
3. See, for example, Benshoff who describes the works of Kenneth Anger,
   Andy Warhol, Jack Smith and others as "deliberate camp glosses on
   Hollywood formula, style, and industrial practice" (119).
4. For a historical overview over gay film consumption and camp's role in it
   see Al LaValley's "The Great Escape."
5. For more on Anger, camp style, and old Hollywood, see Vincent
   Brook, "Puce Modern Moment: Camp, Postmodernism, and the Films

of Kenneth Anger." Juan Antonio Suárez also discusses the latter two, together with Jack Smith, in terms of camp in his study of 60s gay avant-garde culture, where he stresses "their reworkings of mass cultural products [...] most often informed by gay identifications and desires, and by the gay remotivations of cultural artifacts knows as 'camp'" (xvii).

6. See Ken Feil, "Ambiguous Sirk-Camp-Stances: Gay Camp and the 1950s Melodramas of Douglas Sirk" and Ryan Powell, "Putting on the Red Dress: Reading Performative Camp in Douglas Sirk's *All That Heaven Allows.*"

7. In addition to naming only some of the most prominent "camp filmmakers," I have also limited the list to those from the US. Camp in cinema is one of the few areas, on investigation, that frequently include other national contexts, as for example in the films of Rainer Werner Fassbinder (see Moltke; Babuscio) and Pedro Almodóvar (see Ziermann)

8. Anecdotal evidence by Benshoff and Griffin supports the claim that the "structural bias" extends beyond the realms of filmmaking into the field of reception and critique: "An excellent example of New Queer Cinema form and content, *Watermelon Woman* is a pseudodocumentary that selfconsciously mixes fact and fiction. [...] Sadly, it remains relatively unknown outside of queer film circles. *Variety* pronounced it 'scarcely more substantial than a doodle,' a preposterous assertion that reveals that racist, sexist, and homophobic biases can still be found in Hollywood" (242).

9. Her examples include *Me and Rubyfruit* (1989, Dir. Sadie Benning), *It Wasn't Love* (1990, Dir. Sadie Benning), and *Age 12: Love with a Little L* (1991, Dir. Jennifer Montgomery).

10. "Unpleasure" is here defined as solely on the part of the audience, as Barbara Hammer in particular focuses a majority of her movies on the explicit depiction of female (sexual) pleasure, see for example *Nitrate Kisses* (1992).

11. As in "going camping in the countryside."

12. Some directors were seemingly more aware of their lineage than Rich gave them credit for; *Watermelon Woman* links its story to a Dorothy Arzner-like figure, the director whom Judith Mayne credited with introducing lesbian irony to the silver screen (114–23).

13. While these characters are not "out," films like *Touch of Evil* (1958, Dir. Orson Welles), and *Children's Hour* show that a more open treatment of women's sexuality does not equal a less daunting one: the first shows the lesbian character participate in a gang rape; and the latter merges the scenes depicting the main character's outing with those implying her suicide (at a boarding school, no less).

14. Among the most prominent North American lesbian feature films of the 1990s are *High Art* (1998, Dir. Lisa Cholodenko), *The Incredibly True Adventure of Two Girls in Love* (1995, Dir. Maria Maggenti), *Bar Girls* (1994, Dir. Marita Giovanni), and *When Night is Falling* (1995, Dir. Patricia Rozema).

15. "Sweeps week lesbianism" is an ongoing marketing strategy in which some form of "girl on girl" action is introduced into the series just in time for the bi-annual Nielsen ratings.

16. For scholarly explorations of the camp potential of these examples see: Yvonne Keller on "Pulp Politics: Strategies of Vision in Pro-Lesbian Pulp Novels, 1955–1965;" Elizabeth Whitney on performances in *Grrrly Shows: Camping up Feminism*; Joanne Morreale on *Xena* as feminist camp; and—though the author does not use the term camp itself—Julia Scanlon's "*The L Word*—Producing Identities through Irony."

17. Clichés of boarding schools as the breeding ground for lesbianism, for example, have already been lampooned by the performance group The Five Lesbian Brothers in their Off-Off-Broadway play *BRAVE SMILES... Another Lesbian Tragedy*, see https://www.lisakron.com/bravesmiles.html.

18. Two of the few fictional butches at the time were Cleo, played by Queen Latifah, in *Set it Off* (1996, Dir. F. Gary Gray) and Corky, played by Gina Gershon, in the neo-noir thriller *Bound* (1996, Dir. The Wachowskis). For an analysis of Corky's role in connection to lesbian chic, see Kessler. Today, Ellen DeGeneres is the most well-known lesbian—and butch—celebrity in the US. Yet while DeGeneres has become more outspoken about her sexuality, gender identity, and her marriage with actress Portia De Rossi, none of her numerous magazine spreads has a similarly erotic component. The closest to a successor to k.d. lang's *Vanity Fair* cover would be Rachel Maddow in a crisp shirt and suspenders on the cover of *Advocate* in November 2008—even here, however, despite the niche market *Advocate* addresses and Maddow's well-established public butch persona—her status as "serious news anchor" (and as one half of a monogamous relationship) preclude the overt sexual references permissible for lang.

19. For an analysis that further considers ageism and racism, see Rosalind Gill's "Beyond the 'Sexualization of Culture' Thesis."

20. That is not to say that there are not still countless instances of dead lesbians, particularly on TV. Among those most vocally criticized at the time were Tara on *Buffy: The Vampire Slayer*, who—to add insult to injury—was shot the morning after the first semi-explicit sex scene with her girlfriend Willow after three seasons as a couple, and Sandy on *Emergency Room*, who died shortly after her girlfriend's lengthy struggle with coming out.

21. Stacey uses the term "Lesbian disaster movies" to describe the majority of Hollywood movies depicting lesbian romance in which the relationship between the two protagonists is—unlike films with straight lovers—obstructed not by romantic incompatibility, misunderstandings, class issues, or ex-lovers, but rather by "heterosexual men, suicide, murder, neurosis, isolation, depression, homophobia and fear of discovery" (72).

22. The main exception from this genre in his oeuvre is *I'm Not There*, which translates New Queer Cinema's historic constructionism and gender play into one of the most traditional Hollywood genres, the biopic. Haynes updates the genre via the use of collage aesthetics favored by New Queer Cinema and its effort to deconstruct normative identity formations by splitting the different facets of Bob Dylan's life and career into different stories that lack any final merging.

23. McWilliam and I both look at *But I'm a Cheerleader* from a camp perspective, which leads to some similar conclusions concerning certain aesthetic choices. And while I find many of McWilliam's insights to be very useful, there are significant differences in our approach, as her inquiry starts from a genre perspective and includes the notion of camp in this analysis, while my project takes its cue from an inquiry into the relation of camp to contemporary lesbian culture and looks at the genre only as an expression of this camp sensibility. Furthermore, I am more interested in a historically precise placement of *But I'm a Cheerleader* within a larger context of lesbian representation, which includes aspects such as space, stereotypes, and sound omitted in McWilliam's study.

24. I borrow the term from a *New York Times* retrospective on New Queer Cinema by Dennis Lim.

25. Admittedly, it does *Boys Don't Cry* and its New Queer Cinema-style independent production a disservice to be lumped together with big studio productions and their award-guaranteeing stars like *Milk* (2008, Dir. Gus Van Sant) and *Brokeback Mountain* (2005, Dir. Ang Lee). In this case, the description as a "liberal prestige film" is most definitely made a posteriori. Considering the attention the film received from academics and award ceremonies, and the meteoric rise of its Oscar-winning star, Hillary Swank, and the fact that it is almost always mentioned in one breath with other films within this category, the description seems adequate nonetheless.

26. McWilliam makes a similar observation: "The use of camp in these two films [*It's in the Water* and *But I'm a Cheerleader*] is particularly interesting given that they represent the only diegetic uses of camp within the films" analyzed in her study (97).

27. *D.E.B.S.* extends its gender swap to the supporting cast by introducing Lucy Diamond's male straight best friend as instrumental to the queer

love story. It thus picks up the trope of the "gay best friend" introduced to straight romances such as *My Best Friend's Wedding* (1997, Dir.
P.J. Hogan), *The Object of My Affection* (1998, Dir. Nicholas Hytner), or
(more recently, and less conventionally) *Easy A* (2010, Dir. Will Gluck),
and even the lesbian romantic comedy *April's Shower* (2003, Dir. Trish
Doolan). Suzanna Danuta Walters characterizes this trope as one variety
of the "incidental queer" favored by 1990s media. The main purpose,
Walters describes, is "to unite heterosexual couples, or to provide solace
to heterosexuals sufferings from the slings and arrows of wayward affec-
tions" (155). Lucy Diamond's straight male confidante and co-mobster
reverses this trope. Additionally, as one of the only straight men in the
movie with a noticeable amount of screen time, he would be in a privileged position to form a threat to the lesbian relationship—instead he
actively supports it, thus also contradicting the competition between lesbian women and straight men established in Classical Hollywood cinema
as much as lesbian chic. Moreover, by representing him without a trace of
voyeuristic pleasure in relation to the central lesbian romance, his character is used to contain the threat of exploitative voyeurism associated with
visual representations of lesbian sexuality.

28. Katharina Lindner contests that most romantic comedies with lesbian pro-
    tagonists do not question the "heterosexualized generic conventions,"
    and therefore add little in terms of challenging the heteronormative
    impetus of Hollywood cinema. Consequently, she looks at films without
    explicitly queer female characters, which—she argues—are nonetheless
    more significant concerning lesbian representability: movies about female
    athleticism (278). For Lindner, romantic comedies lack critical poten-
    tial due to their reliance on conventional narrative patterns, and—even
    more importantly—because they look and sound almost exactly the same
    as their straight counterparts. While I understand Lindner's concerns, a
    more nuanced reading of romantic comedies will, at least in some cases,
    reach different conclusions.

29. Katharina Glitre notes the queer subtext of sex comedies' central couple
    Rock Hudson and Doris Day. Glitre points not only to the presence of
    Tony Randall, who co-starred in all three collaborations and "compli-
    cated [...] the dynamics of this coupling," but also to the open secret of
    Rock Hudson's homosexuality and rumors about Doris Day's sexuality,
    which "add another dimension to the sex comedy's themes of masquer-
    ade and identity" (159).

30. For an analysis of how the conventions of the romantic comedy change
    when non-white ethnicity is introduced, see Karen Bowdre's "Romantic
    Comedies and the Raced Body," which argues that due to black bodies'
    overdetermination as comic and sexual, romantic comedies with black

protagonists differ drastically from the Hollywood norm. Concerning the rise of romantic comedies centered on older women in the 2000s, see Jermyn.

31. The term was coined by Mike Bygrave in his *Guardian* article "Farewell Rambo, Hello Romeo," in which he discusses how several hitherto accepted forms of meeting/first interaction between the future couple, such as a boss complimenting his secretary, would today be considered sexual harassment and hence neither "romantic" nor "cute."

32. Halberstam elaborates on the power of names in creating relations to gender and sexuality in *Female Masculinity* (8).

33. The name references another famous Russian spy from Hollywood's history: the titular character from Ernst Lubitsch's 1939 comedy *Ninotchka* played by lesbian icon Greta Garbo.

34. Frank Krutnik observes a trend of intensified hybridization of the romantic comedy ("Conforming Passions" 131–34), which places *D.E.B.S.* within a general trend.

35. The significance of the graduation is discussed below.

36. McWilliam reads this dominance of non-lesbian specific spaces for the "girl meets girl" moment as a way to make lesbian love seem like an "ordinary" occurrence in contrast to the "supernatural mobilisations of lesbian desire" in film through body swapping and disguise narratives (94), which were the most frequent cinematic opportunities for lesbian desire within Hollywood narratives prior to the "new wave of lesbian feature films" noted by Berenstein. While this reading is convincing within the scope of her argument, within the tradition of lesbian chic and New Queer Cinema, the obscuring of specifically lesbian experiences through the avoidance of queer spaces becomes more troubling than progressive, as it implies the policing of non-normative sexualities as not suitable for public display.

37. Pramaggiore refers to a distinction originally made in Sedgewick's *Epistemology of the Closet*: "universalizing discourse of acts" vs. "minoritizing discourse of persons" (57).

38. For a commentary on the casting's significance for the film's intertextual potential, see Penney (133–34).

39. For an analysis of the *Charlie's Angels* remake in the context of girl culture, camp appropriation, and the development of the female (girly) action hero, see Jacinda Read.

40. Ladenson contends that the books paint a more nuanced picture of lesbian identity, for example, by including the character of Tilly Masterson who seems to be a young tomboy in love with Pussy Galore, thus encouraging a less tragic reading of her gay persona (421–22).

41. Prominent examples include the central lesbian couples in *The L Word* (2004–2009), *Glee* (2009–2015), and *Grey's Anatomy* (2005–). For Elyce Rae Helford, *Xena: The Warrior Princess'* lesbian coding as representing a butch-femme relationship is to a large extent evoked by the visual contrast between tall, toned, dark Xena, and smaller, slimmer, blonde Gabrielle (149).

42. Another moment in which Amy's reaction adds to and dismantles the "evil lesbian" trope is when she admits to writing a thesis about Lucy with elaborate psychoanalytical explanations for her actions—unaware of her homosexuality. Via her (failed) attempt at rationalizing Lucy's actions *D.E.B.S.* pokes fun at the psychoanalytical explanations often given for queer characters' behavior and mannerisms in Hollywood movies, which ignores the most obvious one, their queerness.

43. *D.E.B.S.'* Jordana Brewster plays head cheerleader in the same film.

44. As New Queer Cinema happened mainly on the festival circuit, the MPAA's ratings system was initially a minor concern. Once the films gained popularity beyond LGBT festivals, the rating system could no longer be evaded. Hence, the explicit depiction of (non-straight) sexuality became a liability to investors who hoped for revenue from regular cinemas. *D.E.B.S.'* status as the first LGBT movie to receive a PG 13-rating therefore could be considered a defeat against commercialism as much as a success for its producers as well as its (young) audiences, depending on one's point of view. However, given the sexually more explicit content of the original short—by now available on DVD, but originally meant mainly for festival distribution—by the same director, it is obvious that the low rating was a conscious effort. On the MPAA nebulous rating techniques, see *This Film Is Not Yet Rated* (2006, Dir. Kirby Dick), which includes an interview with Jamie Babbit on her fight against censorship in *But I'm a Cheerleader*.

WORKS CITED

Age 12: Love with a Little L. Dir. Jennifer Montgomery. Women Make Movies, 1990.

Aaron, Michele. "The New Queer Spectator." *New Queer Cinema: A Critical Reader*. Ed. Michele Aaron. Edinburgh: Edinburgh University Press, 2004. 187–200.

Allen, Dennis. "Why Things Don't Add Up in 'The Sum of Us': Sexuality and Genre Crossing in the Romantic Comedy." *Narrative* 7.1 (1999): 71–88.

American Pie. Dir. Paul and Chris Weitz. Universal Pictures, 1999.

April's Shower. Dir. Trish Doolan. Regent Releasing, 2003.

As Good as It Gets. Dir. James L. Brooks. TriStar Pictures, 1997.

Babuscio, Jack. "Camp and Gay Sensibility." *Camp Grounds: Style and Homosexuality.* Ed. David Bergman. Amherst: University of Massachusetts Press, 1993. 19–37.

Bailey, Steve, and James Hay. "Cinema and the Premises of Youth: 'Teen Films' and Their Sites in the 1980s and 1990s." *Genre and Contemporary Hollywood.* Ed. Stephen Neale. London: BFI, 2002. 218–235.

Banks, Amy Ellen. *'Look at the Woman I've Become': Camp, Gender and Identity in Rainer Werner Fassbinder's* The Marriage of Maria Braun *and John Cameron Mitchell's* Hedwig and the Angry Inch. MA Thesis, University of North Carolina at Chapel Hill: 2007. 20 Oct 2014 http://dc.lib.unc.edu/cdm/ref/collection/etd/id/1560.

Bar Girls. Dir. Marita Giovanni. Orion Classics, 1994.

Barsanti, Chris. *"D.E.B.S.* Review." *Contactmusic.com.* 8 Apr. 2013 http://www.contactmusic.com/movie-review/debs.

Basic Instinct. Dir. Paul Verhoeven. TriStar Pictures, 1992.

Benshoff, Harry M. "Camp: Introduction." *Queer Cinema: The Film Reader.* Ed. Harry M. Benshoff. New York: Routledge, 2005. 119–120.

———, and Sean Griffin. *Queer Images: A History of Gay and Lesbian Film in America.* Lanham: Rowman & Littlefield, 2006.

Berenstein, Rhona J. "Where the Girls are: Riding the New Wave of Lesbian Feature Films." *GLQ: A Journal of Lesbian and Gay Studies* 3.1 (1996): 125–137.

Better Than Chocolate. Dir. Anne Wheeler. Trimark Pictures, 1999.

Bitch Slap! Dir. Rich Jakobson. Summit Entertainment, 2009.

Black Narcissus. Dir. Michael Powell and Emeric Pressburger. Universal International, 1947.

Born in Flames. Dir. Lizzie Borden. First Run Features, 1983.

Bound. Dir. The Wachowskis. Gramercy Pictures, 1996.

Bowdre, Karen. "Romantic Comedies and the Raced Body." *Falling in Love Again: Romantic Comedy in Contemporary Cinema.* Eds. Stacey Abbott and Deborah Jermyn. New York: Palgrave Macmillan, 2009. 105–116.

Boys Don't Cry. Dir. Kimberly Peirce. Fox Searchlight Pictures, 1999.

Bringing Up Baby. Dir. Howard Hawks. RKO Radio Pictures, 1938.

Brokeback Mountain. Dir. Ang Lee. Focus Features, 2005.

Bronski, Michael. "The Queer 1990s: The Challenge and Failure of Radical Change." *The Wiley-Blackwell History of American Film.* Vol. IV. Eds. Lucia Cynthia, Roy Grundman and Art Simon. Oxford: Wiley-Blackwell, 2012. 272–295.

Brook, Vincent. "Puce Modern Moment: Camp, Postmodernism, and the Films of Kenneth Anger." *Journal of Film and Video* 58.4 (2006): 3–15.

Brown, Jeffrey A. *Dangerous Curves: Action Heroines, Gender, Fetishism, and Popular Culture.* Jackson: University Press of Mississippi, 2011.

But I'm a Cheerleader. Dir. Jamie Babbit. Lionsgate, 2000.

Buffy: The Vampire Slayer. Creat. Joss Whedon. The WB / UPN, 1997–2003.

Bygrave, Mike. "Farewell Rambo, Hello Romeo." *Guardian* 6 June 1991, 30.

Caged. Dir. John Cromwell. Warner Bros., 1950.

Camp. Dir. Todd Graff. IFC Films, 2003.

Castle, Terry. *The Apparitional Lesbian: Female Homosexuality and Modern Culture.* New York: Columbia University Press, 1993.

Charlie's Angels. Creat. Ivan Goff and Ben Roberts. ABC, 1976–1981.

Charlie's Angels: Full Throttle. Dir. Joseph McGinty Nichol. Columbia Pictures, 2003.

Ciasullo, Ann M. "Making Her (In)Visible: Cultural Representations of Lesbianism and the Lesbian Body in the 1990s." *Feminist Studies* 27.3 (2001): 577–608.

Clark, Danae. "Commodity Lesbianism." *Popular Culture: Production and Consumption.* Eds. C. Lee Harrington and Denise D. Bielby. Malden: Blackwell, 2001. 80–93.

Cleto, Fabio. "Camp." *Routledge International Encyclopedia of Queer Culture.* Ed. David A. Gerstner. New York: Routledge, 2006. 121–124.

Cohan, Steven. *Incongruous Entertainment: Camp, Cultural Value, and the MGM Musical.* Durham: Duke University Press, 2005.

Codependent Lesbian Space Alien Seeks Same. Dir. Madeleine Olnek. Pro-Fun Media, 2011.

Cruel Intentions. Dir. Roger Krumble. Columbia Pictures, 1999.

Davis, Glyn. "Camp and Queer in the New Queer Director: A Case Study – Gregg Araki." *New Queer Cinema: A Critical Reader.* Ed. Michele Aaron. Edinburgh: Edinburgh University Press, 2004. 53–67.

DeAngelis, Michael. "The Characteristics of New Queer Filmmaking: Case Study – Todd Haynes." *New Queer Cinema: A Critical Reader.* Ed. Michele Aaron. Edinburgh: Edinburgh University Press, 2004. 41–52.

D.E.B.S. Dir. Angela Robinson. Screen Gems, 2004.

Desert Hearts. Dir. Donna Deitch. Samuel Goldwyn Company, 1985.

Doty, Alexander. *Flaming Classics: Queering the Film Canon.* New York: Routledge, 2000.

Dracula's Daughter. Dir. Lambert Hillyer. Universal Studios, 1936.

Driver, Susan. *Queer Girls and Popular Culture: Reading, Resisting and Creating Media.* New York: Lang, 2007.

Dry Kisses Only. Dir. Jane Cottis and Kaucyila Brooke. Women Make Movies, 1990.

Dyer, Richard. "Stereotyping." *Media and Cultural Studies: Keyworks.* 2nd ed. Eds. Meenakshi Gigi Durham and Douglas M. Kellner. Chichester: Wiley-Blackwell, 2012. 275–283.

Easy A. Dir. Will Gluck. Screen Gems, 2010.

Eating Out. Dir. Q. Allan Brocka. Ariztical Entertainment, 2004.

Ellen. Creat. Ellen DeGeneres. Disney, 1994–1998.

Far From Heaven. Dir. Todd Haynes. Focus Features, 2002.

Feil, Ken. "Ambiguous Sirk-Camp-Stances: Gay Camp and the 1950's Melodramas of Douglas Sirk." *Spectator* 15.1 (1994): 30–49.

First Wives Club. Dir. Hugh Wilson. Paramount, 1996.

Foxy Brown. Dir. Jack Hill. American International Pictures, 1974.

Friends. Creat. David Crane and Marta Kauffman. NBC, 1994–2004.

Frith, Simon. "Mood Music: An Inquiry into Narrative Film." *Screen* 25.3 (1984): 78–88.

From Russia with Love. Dir. Terence Young. United Artists, 1963.

Fuchs, Cynthia. "Thinking Pink: Review of *But I'm a Cheerleader.*" *Nitrate Online.* 28 Jul 2000. Nitrate Productions. 9 Jan 2012 http://www.nitrateonline.com/2000/rcheerleader.html.

Garwood, Ian. "Must you remember this? Orchestrating the 'Standard' Pop Song in *Sleepless in Seattle.*" *Screen* 41.3 (2000): 282–298.

Gill, Rosalind. "Beyond the 'Sexualization of Culture' Thesis: An Intersectional Analysis of 'Sixpacks', 'Midriffs' and 'Hot Lesbians' in Advertising." *Sexualities* 12.2 (2009): 137–160.

Girltrash! Creat. Angela Robinson. ourchart.com, 2007.

Girltrash: All Night Long. Dir. Alex Kondracke. Power Up Films, 2014.

Glee. Creat. Ryan Murphy, Brad Falchuk, and Ian Brennan. Fox, 2009–2015.

Glitre, Kathrina. *Hollywood Romantic Comedy: States of the Union, 1934–65.* New York: Palgrave, 2006.

Go Fish. Dir. Rose Troche. Samuel Goldwyn Company, 1994.

Gray Matters. Dir. Sue Cramer. Freestyle Releasing, 2006.

Grey's Anatomy. Creat. Shonda Rhimes. ABC, 2005–.

Goldfinger. Dir. Guy Hamilton. United Artists, 1964.

Halberstam, J. *Female Masculinity.* Durham: Duke University Press, 2003.

Hamer, Diane, and Belinda Budge. "Introduction." *The Good, the Bad and the Gorgeous: Popular Culture's Romance with Lesbianism.* Eds. Diane Hamer and Belinda Budge. London: Pandora, 1994. 1–14.

Hankin, Kelly. *The Girls in the Back Room: Looking at the Lesbian Bar.* Minneapolis: University of Minnesota Press, 2002.

Hedwig and the Angry Inch. Dir. John Cameron Mitchell. Fine Line Features, 2001.

Helford, Elyce Rae. *Fantasy Girls: Gender in the New Universe of Science Fiction and Fantasy Television.* Lanham: Rowman & Littlefield, 2000.

High Art. Dir. Lisa Cholodenko. October Films, 1998.

Hollinger, Karen. "From Female Friends to Literary Ladies: The Contemporary Woman's Film." *Genre and Contemporary Hollywood.* Ed. Stephen Neale. London: BFI, 2002. 77–90.

Home Movie. Dir. Jan Oxenberg. Frameline, 1973.

I Can't Think Straight. Dir. Shamim Sarif. Regent Releasing, 2008.
Imagine Me and You. Dir. Ol Parker. Fox Searchlight Pictures, 2005.
I'm Not There. Dir. Todd Haynes. The Weinstein Company, 2007.
It Happened One Night. Dir. Frank Capra. Columbia Pictures, 1934.
It's in the Water. Dir. Kelly Hard. Pocket Releasing, 1997.
It Wasn't Love. Dir. Sadie Benning. Pixelvision, 1990.
Itty Bitty Titty Committee. Dir. Jamie Babbit. Pocket Releasing, 2007.
Jermyn, Deborah. "Unlikely heroines? 'Women of a Certain Age' and Romantic Comedy." *CineAction* 85 (2011): 26–33.
Kalinak, Kathryn. *Film Music: A Very Short Introduction.* New York: Oxford University Press, 2010.
Kasindorf, Jeanie Russel. "Lesbian Chic: The Bold, Brave New World of Gay Women." *New York Magazine,* 10 May 1993: 30–37.
Kassabian, Anahid. *Hearing Film: Tracking Identifications in Contemporary Hollywood Film Music.* New York: Routledge, 2001.
Keller, Yvonne. "Pulp Politics: Strategies of Vision in Pro-Lesbian Pulp Novels, 1955–1965." *The Queer Sixties.* Ed. Patricia Juliana Smith. New York: Routledge, 1999. 1–25.
Kessler, Kelly. "Bound Together: Lesbian Film That's Family Fun for Everyone." *Film Quarterly* 56.4 (2003): 13–22.
Klinger, Barbara. *Melodrama and Meaning: History, Culture, and the Films of Douglas Sirk.* Bloomington: Indiana University Press, 1994.
Kissing Jessica Stein. Dir. Charles Herman-Wurmfeld. Fox Searchlight Pictures, 2001.
Krutnik, Frank. "The Faint Aroma of Performing Seals: The 'Nervous' Romance and the Comedy of the Sexes." *The Velvet Light Trap* 26.3 (1990): 57–72.
———. "Conforming Passions? Contemporary Romantic Comedy." *Genre and Contemporary Hollywood.* Ed. Stephen Neale. London: BFI, 2002.
Ladenson, Elisabeth. "Lovely Lesbians; or, Pussy Galore." *GLQ* 7.3 (2001): 417–423.
Lim, Dennis. "When 'Poison' Was a Cinematic Antidote." *New York Times* 5 Nov 2010. The New York Times Company. 23 Aug 2013 http://www.nytimes.com/2010/11/07/movies/07poison.html?_r=1&.
Lindner, Katharina. "'In touch' with the Female Body: Cinema, Sport and Lesbian Representability." *The Handbook of Gender, Sex and Media.* Ed. Karen Ross. Oxford: Wiley-Blackwell, 2011. 277–293.
Lister, Ruth. *Citizenship: Feminist Perspectives.* New York: New York University Press, 1998.
Lost and Delirious. Dir. Léa Pool. Lions Gate Entertainment, 2001.
Love, Heather. *Feeling Backward: Loss and the Politics of Queer History.* Cambridge: Harvard University Press, 2009.
Loving Annabelle. Dir. Katherine Brooks. Wolfe Releasing, 2006.

Mädchen in Uniform. Dir. Leontine Sagan and Carl Froelich. Bild und Ton, 1931.

Mayne, Judith. *The Woman at the Keyhole: Feminism and Women's Cinema.* Bloomington: Indiana University Press, 1990.

McDonald, Tamar Jeffers. *Romantic Comedy: Boy Meets Girl Meets Genre.* London: Wallflower, 2007.

McWilliam, Kelly Ann. *Girl Meets Girl: Lesbian Romantic Comedies and the Public Sphere.* PH.D. Thesis, Brisbane: 2006. QUT ePrints. 11 Apr 2014.

Me and Rubyfruit. Dir. Sadie Benning. Pixelvisoin, 1989.

Mernit, Billy. *Writing the Romantic Comedy: From "Cute Meet" to "Joyous Defeat" How to Write Screenplays that Sell.* New York: HarperResource, 2001.

Meeting of Two Queens. Dir. Cecilia Barriga. Women Make Movies, 1991.

Milk. Dir. Gus van Sant. Focus Features, 2008.

Miles, La'Tonya Rease. "American Beauty: The Cheerleader in American Literature and Popular Culture." *Women's Studies Quarterly* 33.1/2 (2005): 224–232.

Mizejewski, Linda. *Hardboiled and High Heeled: The Woman Detective in Popular Culture.* New York: Routledge, 2004.

Mockus, Martha. "Queer Thoughts on Country Music and k.d. lang." *Queering the Pitch: The New Gay and Lesbian Musicology.* Eds. Philip Brett, Elizabeth Wood, and Gary Thomas. New York: Routledge, 1994. 257–271.

Moltke, Johannes von. "Camping in the Art Closet: The Politics of Camp and Nation in German Film." *New German Critique* 63 (1994): 76–106.

Moonstruck. Dir. Norman Jewison. Metro-Goldwyn-Mayer, 1987.

Morocco. Dir. Josef von Sternberg. Paramount Pictures, 1930.

Morreale, Joanne. *"Xena: Warrior Princess* as Feminist Camp." *The Journal of Popular Culture* 32.2 (1998): 79–86.

Morrison, James. "Still New, Still Queer, Still Cinema?" *GLQ: A Journal of Lesbian and Gay Studies* 12.1 (2006): 135–146.

Mulkey, Annemarie. *Queering Culture: Confounding and Troubling Heteronormativity through Critical Queer Identities in Literature, Film, and Music.* M.A. Thesis, University of Texas at San Antonio: 2010. ProQuest.

My Best Friend's Wedding. Dir. P. J. Hogan. TriStar Pictures, 1997.

Neale, Steve. "The Big Romance or Something Wild? Romantic Comedy Today." *Screen* 33.3 (1992): 284–99.

Ninotchka. Dir. Ernst Lubitsch. Metro-Goldwyn-Mayer, 1939.

Nitrate Kisses. Dir. Barbara Hammer. Strand Releasing, 1992.

Out at the Wedding. Dir. Lee Friedlander. Paramount Home Entertainment, 2007.

Paris is Burning. Dir. Jenni Livingston. Miramax Films, 1990.

Penney, Renée. *Desperately Seeking Redundancy? Queer Romantic Comedy and the Festival Audience.* M.A. Thesis, Vancouver: 2010. Scribd. 9 Jan 2012.

Peraino, Judith Ann. *Listening to the Sirens: Musical Technologies of Queer Identity from Homer to Hedwig*. Berkeley: University of California Press, 2006.

Pick, Anat. "New Queer Cinema and Lesbian Films." *New Queer Cinema: A Critical Reader*. Ed. Michele Aaron. Edinburgh: University Press, 2004. 103–118.

Poison. Dir. Todd Haynes. Zeitgeist Films, 1991.

Powell, Ryan. "Putting on the Red Dress: Reading Performative Camp in Douglas Sirk's *All That Heaven Allows*." *Forum Journal* 4 (2007). University of Edinburg. 10 July 2014 http://www.forumjournal.org/article/view/583.

Pramaggiore, Maria. "Fishing for Girls: Romancing Lesbians in New Queer Cinema." *College Literature* 24.1 (1997): 59–75.

Read, Jacinda. "'Once upon a time there were three little girls...': Girls, Violence and *Charlie's Angels*." *New Hollywood Violence*. Ed. Steven Jay Schneider. New York: Palgrave, 2004. 205–229.

Rebecca. Dir. Alfred Hitchcock. United Artists, 1940.

Reichert, Tom, Kecin R. Maly, and Susan C. Zavoina. "Designed for (Male) Pleasure: The Myth of Lesbian Chic in Mainstream Advertising." *Sexual Rhetoric: Media Perspectives on Sexuality, Gender, and Identity*. Eds. Meta G. Carstarphen and Susan C. Zavoina. Westport: Greenwood, 1999. 123–134.

Rich, B. Ruby. "Goings and Comings." *American Independent Cinema: A Sight and Sound Reader*. Ed. Jim Hillier. London: BFI, 2001. 92–97.

———. "New Queer Cinema." *New Queer Cinema: A Critical Reader*. Ed. Michele Aaron. Edinburgh: Edinburgh University Press, 2004. 15–22.

———. *New Queer Cinema: The Director's Cut*. Durham: Duke University Press, 2013.

———. "Out at Sundance." *The Advocate: 2* March 2004: 22.

———. "Queer and Present Danger." *Sight & Sound* (March 2000): 22–25.

Rodman, Ronald. "The Popular Song as Leitmotif in 1990s Film." *Changing Tunes: The Use of Pre-Existing Music in Film*. Eds. Phil Powrie and Robynn Jeananne Stilwell. Burlington: Ashgate, 2006. 119–136.

Rüll, Lisa M. "A Soundtrack for Our Lives: Chick-Flick Music." *Chick Flicks: Contemporary Women at the Movies*. Eds. Suzanne Ferriss and Mallory Young. New York: Routledge, 2008. 79–91.

Safe. Dir. Todd Haynes. Sony Pictures Classics, 1995.

Saving Face. Dir. Alice Wu. Sony Pictures Classics, 2004.

Scanlon, Julia. "*The L Word*: Producing Identities through Irony." *The Handbook of Gender, Sex, and Media*. Ed. Karen Ross. Malden: Wiley-Blackwell, 2012. 226–40.

Schwichtenberg, Cathy. "Charlie's Angels. The Cheryl Ladd Special: A Patriarchal Voice in Heaven." *Jump Cut: A Review of Contemporary Media* 24–5 (1981). 4 Apr. 2013 http://www.ejumpcut.org/archive/onlinessays/JC24-25folder/CharliesAngels.html.

Seinfeld. Creat. Larry David and Jerry Seinfeld. NBC, 1989–1998.

Set it Off. Dir. F. Gary Gray. New Line Cinema, 1996.

Sex and the City. Creat. Darren Star. HBO, 1998–2004.

Sleepless in Seattle. Dir. Nora Ephron. TriStar Pictures, 1989.

South of Nowhere. Creat. Thomas W. Lynch. The N, 2008–2008.

Stacey, Jackie. "'If You Don't Play, You Can't Win': *Desert Hearts* and the Lesbian Romance Film." *Immortal, Invisible: Lesbians and the Moving Image.* Ed. Tamsin Wilton. London: Routledge, 1995. 67–87.

Stein, Arlene. "All Dressed Up But No Place to Go? Style Wars and the New Lesbian World." *Out in Culture: Gay, Lesbian, and Queer Essays on Popular Culture.* Eds. Corey K. Creekmur and Alexander Doty. London: Cassell, 1995. 476–484.

Stuller, Jennifer K. *Ink-stained Amazons and Cinematic Warriors: Superwomen in Modern Mythology.* London: I.B. Tauris, 2010.

Suárez, Juan Antonio. *Bike Boys, Drag Queens & Superstars: Avant-garde, Mass Culture, and Gay Identities in the 1960s Underground Cinema.* Bloomington: Indiana University Press, 1996.

Swoon. Dir. Tom Kalin. Fine Line Features, 1992.

Tasker, Yvonne. "Pussy Galore: Lesbian Images and Lesbian Desire in the Popular Cinema." *The Good, the Bad and the Gorgeous: Popular Culture's Romance with Lesbianism.* Eds. Diane Hamer and Belinda Budge. London: Pandora, 1994. 172–183.

The Children's Hour. Dir. William Wyler. United Artists, 1961.

The Faculty. Dir. Robert Rodriguez. Miramax Films, 1998.

The Incredibly True Adventure of Two Girls in Love. Dir. Maria Maggenti. New Line Cinema, 1995.

The Kids Are All Right. Dir. Lisa Cholodenko. Focus Features, 2010.

The Killing of Sister George. Dir. Robert Aldrich. Cinerama Releasing Corporation, 1968.

The L Word. Creat. Ilene Chaiken. Showtime, 2004–2009.

The Object of My Affection. Dir. Nicholas Hytner. 20th Century Fox, 1998.

The Truth About Cats & Dogs. Dir. Michael Lehmann. 20th Century Fox, 1996.

The Watermelon Woman. Dir. Cheryl Dunye. First Run Features, 1996.

This Films Is Not Yet Rated. Dir. Kirby Dick. IFC Films, 2006.

Tinkcom, Matthew. *Working like a Homosexual: Camp, Capital, and Cinema.* Durham: Duke University Press, 2002.

Touch of Evil. Dir. Orson Welles. Universal Pictures, 1958.

Vesey, Alyx. "Bechdel Test Canon: *D.E.B.S.*" *BitchMagazine.* 23 Dec 2011. Bitch Media. 10 Jan 2012 http://bitchmagazine.org/post/bechdel-test-canon-debs.

Wallace, Lee. *Lesbianism, Cinema, Space: The Sexual Life of Apartments.* New York: Routledge, 2009.

3 THE GREAT DYKE REWRITE: LESBIAN CAMP ... 109

Walters, Suzanna Danuta. *All the Rage: The Story of Gay Visibility in America*. Chicago: University of Chicago Press, 2001.

Weiss, Andrea. "Transgressive Cinema: Lesbian Independent Film." *Queer Cinema: The Film Reader*. Repr. Ed. Harry M. Benshoff. New York: Routledge, 2005. 43–52.

When Harry Met Sally. Dir. Rob Rainer. Columbia Pictures, 1989.

When Night is Falling. Dir. Patricia Rozema. First Distributors, 1995.

Wild Things. Dir. John McNaughton. Columbia Pictures, 1998.

White, Patricia. *UnInvited: Classical Hollywood Cinema and Lesbian Representability*. Bloomington: Indiana University Press, 1999.

———. "Lesbian Minor Cinema." *Screen* 49.4 (2008): 410–425.

Whitney, Elizabeth. *Grrrly Shows: Camping up Feminism*. Ph.D. Thesis, Ann Arbor: 2002. ProQuest.

———. "Pop Culture Princess." *Text and Performance Quarterly* 26.2 (2006): 199–207.

Wings. Dir. William A. Wellman. Paramount Pictures, 1927.

Xena: The Warrior Princess. Creat. Robert G. Tapert, John Schulian. Universal Television et al., 1995–2001.

Young Man with a Horn. Dir. Michael Curtiz. Warner Bros., 1950.

You've Got Mail. Dir. Nora Ephron, Warner Bros., 1998.

Ziermann, Bernd. "'Camp' und die Auflösung der Geschlechtergrenzen im Kino von Pedro Almodóvar." *GeschlechterDifferenzen*. Eds. Katharina Hanau, Sylvia Setzkorn, Anja Schliemann, Volker Rivinius. Bonn: Romanistischer Verlag, 1999. 165–171.

TV in/vs. Postfeminism: Feminist Camp in *30 Rock*

As the first female head writer of *Saturday Night Live* (1975–), the face of its *Weekend Update*, coiner of the phrase "Bitches get stuff done" and writer of the cult hit *Mean Girls* (2004, Dir. Mark Waters), Tina Fey had become "Hollywood's Token Feminist" (Mizejewski "Feminism") long before the premiere of her sitcom *30 Rock* on October 11, 2006 on NBC—a status further reinforced during the show's run by the publication of her autobiographical book *Bossypants* in 2011 and her special appearances on *Saturday Night Live* during the 2008 presidential campaign as vice-presidential nominee Sarah Palin. In keeping with this perception of the star behind their central character, Liz Lemon, *30 Rock*'s first moments introduce her as she hops down the streets of Manhattan, hands out "150 bucks worth of wieners" to strangers, and finishes this upbeat performance with a familiar looking twirl in an homage-cum-parody of *The Mary Tyler Moore Show*'s (1970–1977) iconic opening sequence. The scene underscores the parallels between Liz Lemon and feminist icon Mary Tyler Moore beyond their common identity as single women in their 30s working behind the scenes of a television show and trying to "make it" in the big city.

Far from being an exception, the reference is only the first of many instances in which *30 Rock* places itself and its protagonist in the lineage of female-centered or feminist comedy, of which Lauren Rabinovitz in her article "Ms-Representation: The Politics of Feminist Sitcoms" considers *The Mary Tyler Moore Show* the starting point. As a reason for the creation of such sitcoms in the mid-1970s Rabinovitz pragmatically

© The Author(s) 2017
K. Horn, *Women, Camp, and Popular Culture*,
DOI 10.1007/978-3-319-64846-0_4

111

cites the emerging insights into audience demographics, through which "'feminism' became an important strategy because it served the needs of American television executives who could cultivate programming that could be identified with target audiences whom they wanted to measure and deliver to advertising agencies" (146). The state of feminism, however, has changed since the 1970s almost as much as its cultural currency; whether feminism still holds the potential to "be identified with target audiences" in a cultural climate defined by a postfeminist sensibility alternating between an anti-feminist backlash and the insistence on gains achieved by second-wave feminism, is as much up for debate as the question of what a "feminist sitcom" would look like today. Numerous scholars have therefore pointed to postfeminism's ambivalence, that is its "double-entanglement" (McRobbie 255–6) or "double address" (Tasker and Negra 108), which complicates the evaluation of contemporary cultural products with the traditional tools of feminist media studies. Tasker and Negra summarize this issue poignantly with their question: "If postfeminist culture tends to produce highly ambivalent pleasures, how do we make that ambivalence a wellspring for effective critique?" (108).

30 Rock offers an answer to this question. This uneasiness about what makes a cultural program feminist, is central to *30 Rock*'s frequent engagement with questions of gender, sexuality, and feminist politics, among others, achieved through the citing and referencing of established examples of a feminist media corpus. *30 Rock*'s embeddedness in the history of female-fronted sitcoms comes to the fore in multiple ways, ranging from stylistic borrowings like the pilot's homage to *The Mary Tyler Moore Show*, to treatments on the plot level such as the episode "Rosemary's Baby," in which Liz Lemon meets one of her icons, a second-wave feminist who "broke barriers for her" when working as a (fictional) writer on the (real) NBC show *Laugh-In* (1967–1973). Other examples include short intradiegetic references such as the *Designing Women* (1986–1993) marathon in a season one episode titled "The C Word" as well as almost every scene in the two live broadcasts in seasons five and six—both of which offered a tour de force through the history of television—restaging sketches from *I Love Lucy* (1951–1957) and referencing *The Carol Burnett Show* (1967–1978) and its infamous on-screen breaking, respectively, as well as ridiculing the overt sexism and racism of early news broadcasts. Finally, *30 Rock* incorporates paratextual elements for historicizing purposes such as the title of episode 6x17, "Murphy Brown lied to us!"—a sitcom especially noteworthy in its contrast to *30 Rock*, as Rabinovitz points out: only a few months after its premiere and after winning three Emmy Awards "*Murphy Brown* had achieved all the criteria associated with 'quality' and an uncompromised status as a feminist product" (156). *30 Rock* on the other hand, garnered seven Emmy nominations for its first season with two wins, one in the important category "Outstanding Comedy Series," and rose to a record-breaking 22 nominations at the 2009 Emmy ceremony, quickly ascending to a status of "quality" program as equally uncontested as *Murphy Brown*'s.[1] Yet, despite its creator's reputation, the comedy series' status as a "feminist product" remains everything but "uncompromised."

Rather, reviews attest to a widespread skepticism concerning the show's feminist potential, even among those who generally consider *30 Rock* "a step in the right direction for feminist comedy," such as *Bitch* magazine's Kelsey Wallace, who in the same article admits that when "it comes to answering the question of whether or not Lemon is a feminist, [...] the answer might be no, or maybe on a good day." The show and its lead character have been plagued, among other things, by unfavorable comparisons to Tina Fey's fellow SNL alumna and *Baby Mama* (2008, Dir. Michael McCullers) co-star Amy Poehler in her role as the ever-optimistic city-level government employee Leslie Knope in *Parks & Recreation* (NBC, 2009–2015) (Dailey). Additionally,—and often more devastatingly—*30 Rock* has been judged by critics who read it alongside older TV texts deemed groundbreaking for their progressive portrayal of single, working women—exactly those texts to which the show refers so frequently itself. Joanne Morreale for example concedes that *30 Rock* is often cited "for its progressive take on gender politics embedded within a broader critique of the entertainment industry" ("Do Bitches" 485). She herself remains suspicious of a reading of *30 Rock* as feminist, arguing that the show's progressiveness stems largely from Tina Fey's position as its creator and her status within the industry. Liz Lemon on the other hand fails as a positive role model not only due to her constant reliance on her male boss' intervention and guidance, but also because of the supposed negation of her liberal politics within the show:

> *30 Rock*'s adherence to comedic conventions and familiar tropes of femininity work to negate the threat posed by a "woman on top" [...] social inadequacies—in this case, unattractiveness, awkwardness, and insecurity—are made laughable. In the process, the cultural values that form the

backdrop against which Liz's failures are measured and affirmed rather than questioned. (Morreale "Do Bitches" 486)

Writing for *Slate* magazine in 2009 under the headline "I Want to GOP to There: *30 Rock*'s Weird Conservative Streak," Jonah Weiner voices similar concerns and asks, "Flawed people are funny, sure, but why does Liz Lemon have the traditionally gendered flaws she does?" He continues by comparing Liz Lemon to Murphy Brown (Candice Bergen), whom Weiner considers a "strong, feminist-friendly [character] and funny, to boot":

> Murphy Brown is a funhouse-mirror image of Liz. She works in TV, wants to be a single mother, rolls her eyes at the cleavage-flashing coquetry of her bimbo co-worker, Corky, and embarks on a love-hate relationship with a right-winger, Jerry Gold. But she's also confident, ambitious, and doesn't run to her boss for guidance so much as bully him constantly.

The idea of the "funhouse-mirror image" is quite a useful one, only not in the way Weiner applies it. He judges the characters of Liz Lemon and Murphy Brown in isolation, as if their context was either negligible or identical. Yet, while their characters are similar, their respective shows, *30 Rock* and *Murphy Brown*, are not. To look at *30 Rock* as a whole, as opposed to singling out Liz Lemon, leads to strikingly different conclusions about her and firmly establishes her as the "funhouse-mirror image" of the Murphys and Marys that came before her. The series' form, content, and references all emphasize *30 Rock*'s connection to the above-mentioned examples of US feminist sitcoms, but another genre of comedy is equally relevant to understanding the show's form and function, the sketch variety show. *30 Rock* infuses the sitcom genre with elements from sketch comedy, thereby distancing itself from the "sitcom proper" in which Murphy Brown and Mary Tyler Moore existed, instead stressing its own reflective and intertextual, rather than realistic, qualities. It is essential to take sketch comedy's anti-realist impetus seriously to understand *30 Rock*'s difference from earlier feminist sitcoms (and their representational politics), as it enables and enhances the camp qualities of the show's two female protagonists, who additionally expand the sitcom's constellation of lead sidekicks to explore the fringes of narrative possibility. Through these stylistic deviances *30 Rock* rejects the empowerment through representation that characterized earlier examples of feminist sitcoms, and instead positions itself as a show which functions as cultural analysis and critique, as hyperbole of and (funhouse-) mirror to media trends, most prominently among them being postfeminism.

1   CONTEMPORARY SITCOMS AND METAREFLECTION

30 Rock depicts its gender politics, as Morreale points out, "embedded within a broader critique of the entertainment industry" ("Do Bitches" 485). In fact, these comments on the entertainment industry and entertainment as an industry are so central to the show's style, plot, and appeal that it has been dubbed by popular feminist blog *Jezebel* the "most meta of shows" (Traister). As such, *30 Rock* serves as a prime example of the characteristics and the development of the US American sitcom, which, according to Lauren Bratslavsky,

> has escalated its humor to a level containing self-aware jokes and reflexivity, such as acknowledging genre conventions, television structure, […it] has emerged as a potential site of social critique, commenting on everything from current events and politics to reflecting on popular culture. (2)

The show's premise makes it perfectly suited to do just that. Liz Lemon is the head writer of fictional *The Girlie Show* (usually referred to as *TGS*), a live variety program not only reminiscent of The Carol Burnett Show (1967–1978), but also Fey's former workplace *Saturday Night Live*, produced just like *30 Rock* by NBC, which is in turn owned by General Electrics (GE), creating a veritable mise en abyme of the TV industry.[2] The complicated business models of GE and the mutual entanglements of the different company subsidiaries are the object of frequent snubs. The personification of GE, Liz Lemon's socially as well as fiscally conservative boss and opponent, when it comes to defending "her show" against the demands of a multi-billion/multi-national/multi-corporations business is Jack Donaghy, played by Alec Baldwin. Their friendship and their employee–boss relationship forms the dramatic, or rather, comic center of the show, as they discuss various topics ranging from their respective private lives to questions of artistic integrity, audience demographics, product placement, and struggles with so-called Standards—the legal department which tries to keep GE from being sued over politically incorrect jokes on the fictional *Girlie Show*—while *30 Rock* itself has earned yet another "most," namely that of "most unethical workplace-show on TV [for] routinely violating ethics in the workplace" (*CBS*). This focus on backstage activities enables *30 Rock* not only to comment on current incidents in popular culture and politics, but also to incorporate such events as NBC merging with other companies and struggling to come up with new show ideas. Little time is spent on showing footage from *TGS*. What we do see, however, serves mainly to underline the low quality of the program, which Jack describes as "skits mocking our president to fill time between car commercials" (1x05 "Jack-Tor"). Such self-reflective jokes about *TGS*, which extend to an ongoing commentary on *30 Rock*, NBC, and TV more generally, elevate the show's insider gags to the level of metareferentiality, a form of self-reflexivity that extends beyond the artwork to the whole media system in which it exists. This "medium-awareness," as Werner Wolf calls it, renders "mediality or representationality [...] an object of more or less active awareness" for audiences (28).

Media products are not solely shaped by monetary demands and industrial structures, but also by tropes, discourses, and sensibilities—in this case, first and foremost, postfeminism. Referencing the latter is therefore just as important for the show's self-reflexivity and humor as are its TV show within a TV Show jokes. It is in this context that camp as "an invasion and subversion of other sensibilities [that] works via parody, pastiche, and exaggeration" (Dollimore 224) becomes central to *30 Rock* and the metaquality of its gender politics.[3] As a female-centered sitcom *30 Rock* is a particularly fitting space for the investigation of postfeminism through metareferences: the genre not only has a history of camp used as feminist critique (Schuyler; Robertson 144–46), but has also been pointed out as the primary locus of postfeminist media beside the romantic comedy and TV drama (Tasker and Negra 107). Furthermore, the female-centered sitcom is "the television genre most consistently associated with feminist heroines and with advocating a progressive politics of liberal feminism" (Rabinovitz 145).

Central to the show's metareferences to feminism, yet often forgotten in critiques of *30 Rock*'s gender politics, is its second major female character, Jenna Maroney. Portrayed with great gusto for the excessiveness of her character and even greater comic timing by *Ally McBeal*'s Jane Krakowski, Jenna is the blonde, outgoing, drinking, sex crazy, attention craving, and bursting into song entertainer, constructed as the opposite of brunette, prude, socially awkward writer Liz. The critics' neglect of this character, who fulfills almost every stereotype of the dumb blonde and thus could be considered an even "worse" example of media representation of women than Liz Lemon, makes perfect sense if you are looking for positive role models.[4] In light of *30 Rock*'s metamechanisms and its camp politics, however, snubbing Jenna is a substantial oversight.

Her intricate connection to Liz is introduced in the pilot's opening sequence that also aligns Liz with Mary Tyler Moore. Whereas the latter establishes historic context, Jenna's appearance launches the show's comic dynamics. After Liz Lemon's twirl a swift cut to the rehearsal for *The Girlie Show* introduces audiences to *30 Rock*'s backstage characters and Jenna, whom audiences first encounter wearing a sparkly pink fat-suit in a (as they later learn) recurrent *TGS* sketch about "Pam—The Overly Confident, Morbidly Obese Woman." The two scenes are connected by the background song's continuation, which transforms from extradiegetic allusion, to *The Mary Tyler Moore Show*'s credit sequence, to intradiegetic stage performance at the same time as the lyrics evolve from a Mary Tyler Moore-like innocence ("Who's that kickin' it down the street?/Causing a stir/Who's that?/I know that you're wondering"), into a more obviously parodic ("She's like a summer sky/a slice of cherry pie/the rarest butterfly"—as a description of Pam) and overtly sexual tone ("Who flaunts her feminine magic?").

Here, *30 Rock* not only introduces its comic pattern—in which metacommentary and comedy based on a vast knowledge of TV tropes and current affairs are juxtaposed with visual gags and cheap one-liners ("This fat-suit smells like corn chips")—it also establishes the two female leads as closely linked to these two aspects of the show's humor and to each other. In this particular scene, the full meaning of the intertextual link to *The Mary Tyler Moore Show* becomes legible in the interplay between the two female leads, a strategy that is kept up through the series, both playing on and parodying known patterns of the sidekick–lead dynamic. In this case, the contrast between Mary Tyler Moore and Liz Lemon, as well as its comic potential, unfold after Jenna enters the picture to finish the parody started by Liz. The original *The Mary Tyler Moore Show*'s theme song "You Can Make It After All" is emblematic of TV's emerging focus on women taking on the challenges of work and private lives (Rabinovitz 146). Jenna translates the song and its sentiment for a twenty-first-century audience accustomed to media's focus on celebrities and reality TV stars "flaunting their feminine magic," as the song puts it, rather than "making it." The phrasing implies that the song is referring not only to the contemporary obsession with beauty and

femininity, it is also invoking the "flaunting" of "crotch shots" and stripper aesthetics, representative of what Judith Regan has called "porno-ization of the culture" (qtd. in Levy 19).

Thus introduced as complementing each other on levels of plot, character, appearance, and behind/in front of the camera position, Liz and
Jenna are inextricably linked in the show's depiction of gendered flaws,
TV tropes, and feminist ideas and ideals. This opposites attract strategy
of matching the lead with a complementing female sidekick has been a
common feature of female-centered sitcoms to balance different portrayals of femininity. Examples range from: *The Mary Tyler Moore Show*'s
Mary and Rhoda Morgenstern (Valerie Harper); Susan Keane (Brooke
Shields) and Vicki Groener (Kathy Griffin) in *Suddenly Susan* (1996–
2000); to Grace Adler (Debra Messing) and Karen Walker (Megan
Mullally) in *Will & Grace* (1998–2006). In *30 Rock* Jenna poses as the
"unruly woman" (Rowe) intent on "making a spectacle of oneself"
(Russo 12). She represents the excess of femininity, the frivolous camp
character contrasted with Liz's supposed lack of femininity as a "New
York third-wave feminist, college educated, single and pretending to be
happy about it, over-scheduled, under-sexed" (1x01 "Pilot").

While *30 Rock* thus stays within the tradition of the feminist sitcom by
pairing a central female character with a secondary character drastically
different in her gender representation, it also fundamentally diverges
from this traditional lead–sidekick dynamic by associating *both* characters
with tropes of comic seconds, which foregrounds their meta-, and thus
camp, characteristics. How and to what end Liz and Jenna are paired off
in this unique manner is best understood through the lineage of sitcoms
30 Rock places itself in. The following short look at earlier programs also
fosters a clearer comprehension of the interconnectedness of feminism
and the female-centered sitcom, which helps grasp *30 Rock's* relation to
postfeminist issues.

2   LEGACY OF THE FEMINIST SITCOM

Arguably one of the most iconic feminist TV texts in the US and major
influence on *30 Rock* is *Murphy Brown*, which was known to "thread
topical relevancy into its narratives and comedy" (Rabinovitz 160). A
particularly striking example for this occurred when Murphy Brown's
on-screen pregnancy and decision to raise her child as a single parent
became the topic of heated off-screen debates in the 1992 election, after

vice president Dan Quayle made the following statement during a campaign speech in California:

> It doesn't help matters when prime-time TV has Murphy Brown, a character who supposedly epitomizes today's intelligent, highly paid professional woman, mocking the importance of fathers by bearing a child alone and calling it just another lifestyle choice.

A few months later Murphy Brown responded to a clip of this speech in the fifth season's pilot: "Perhaps it's time for the vice president to expand his definition and recognize that, whether by choice or circumstance, families come in all shapes and sizes."[5] This direct attack on a prominent political figure caused a media frenzy with coverage in major newspapers on the controversy dubbed "Murphy's revenge" and "the surrealistic Quayle-Brown waltz" (*The Register Guard*, see Robinson) or "the Murphy Brown Feud" (*New York Magazine*, see Walls) and developed into one of the most widely publicized instances of a sitcom integrating real-life events and feminist issues.

Among the noteworthy predecessors is *Maude* (1972–1978), which highlights female-centered sitcoms as particularly willing to function as sites of "social critique, commenting on everything from current events and politics to reflecting on popular culture" (Bratslavsky 2). In November 1971, several months prior to Roe v. Wade, the show devoted a two-episode arc ("Maude's Dilemma") to the titular character's (Bea Arthur) unwanted pregnancy and subsequent abortion. In 1991 *Designing Women* (1986–1993) had its cast discuss the Anita Hill vs. Clarence Thomas hearings concerning sexual harassment allegations against the Supreme Court nominee in "The Strange Case of Clarence and Anita." The episode ends with a plea for women's rights presented by one of the protagonists dressed for a community theater production as the Bette Davis-character from *Whatever Happened to Baby Jane* (1962, Dir. Robert Aldrich), which became one of the show's most well-known and widely discussed scenes (see Jeremy G. Butler; Robertson; Doty). Six years later "The Puppy Episode" in season four of the sitcom *Ellen* (1994–1998) made headlines for outing its main character Ellen Morgan—making her the only gay lead character on US TV at the time—simultaneously with its star's, Ellen DeGeneres, public coming out.

30 Rock's most well-known extradiegetic references, which place the show in this tradition, include the season six episode "Idiots are People Too." Here the show engages with the aftermath of a homophobic statement made by the fictional *Girlie Show* actor Tracy Jordan, played by Tracy Morgan who had spent the season break apologizing for his non-fictional homophobic rant during a stand-up routine. Not quite as directly linked to the *30 Rock* cast, but still closely connected to the show's politics, the season five episode "TGS Hates Women" offered a thinly veiled treatment of the controversy between the popular feminist blog *Jezebel* and James Stewart's fake news program *The Daily Show*, in which the former accused *The Daily Show* of sexist bias in its casting choices. In the *30 Rock* episode *TGS* is similarly attacked by the blog *Joan of Snark* for its portrayal of women—exemplified by a flashback to a *TGS* scene in which Amelia Earhart crashes into the ocean because she gets her period. Liz's response:

> That is an ironic reappropriation. Kch. I don't know anymore. This started as a show for women, starring women. At the very least we should be elevating the way women are perceived in society. Augh, my period! You're all fired!

Despite Liz's later insistence "You're wrong. I support women. I'm like a human bra," the episode remains ambivalent about the validity of her feminist beliefs. "TGS Hates Women" combines self-reflexive comments such as the one quoted above with allusions to real-life female TV personalities like Courtney Thorne-Smith, a former colleague of Jane Krakowski's on *Ally McBeal* (1997–2002), and comedienne Sarah Silverman, who has become one of the most controversial female comedians due to her excessively naïve stage persona and tendency towards sexual crudeness. Additionally, Jenna and Liz are once again contrasted in their behavior, as their newly hired colleague, Abby Flynn, is perceived by them as "pity project" and a threat, respectively. Likewise, the episode depicts different reactions to Abby Flynn's persona—described by Jenna as "hot and doing baby talk"—in great detail, ranging from Jenna feeling threatened, to all male staff members being immediately smitten with her. The episode furthermore features a subplot about Jack's feud with a teenage girl he considers his rival in the corporate hierarchy—one who outsmarts him by using his own (business) strategies against him. "TGS Hates Women" thus is not only an example of the genre's tendency to be topical, but also exemplifies how historically the sitcom—including those examples of feminist sitcoms already mentioned—has been and continues to be "obsessed by how men and women behave" (R. White 355).

2.1 Female-Centered Sitcoms and the Politics of Gender

A case in point illustrating this obsession with gender is *Murphy Brown*, again. In season ten, two episodes before its finale, the show takes a time-out from the loose ends of the season's (and series') overarching storylines, such as Murphy's single parenting and her cancer treatment, to devote an entire episode to a screwball-like farce about gender performances. In the episode titled "A Woman and A Man" the *FYI* team consisting of news anchors Jim Dial (Charles Kimbrough), Frank Fontana (Joe Regalbuto), Corky Sherwood (Faith Ford), Murphy herself and producer Carter-Shepley (Lily Tomlin) try to gain information on a scandal involving a senator's relation to a prostitute, whom he supposedly had sex with in front of the Lincoln Memorial and who, reputedly unbeknownst to the senator, was a transvestite. After Corky, a former beauty queen and the show's arbiter of femininity, shares a story about her uncle "Melanie," much to the amusement of the rest of the team, and Frank points out that there is always a "tell," (e.g., Adam's apple or big hands), the anchors all agree that the senator must have known he was dealing with a man. Only the show's producer Kay challenges the notion that an individual's biological sex is always instantly recognizable.

To prove her point Kay dresses up as Rick, flirts with Murphy over lunch, and goes on to fool the rest of the team, as she passes as a man right up to the point that Frank starts a fight with him/her for coming on to Murphy. After her identity is revealed and Murphy and the rest admit that they did indeed fall for Kay's act, the unexpected declaration of love by Kenny, one of her informants, makes Murphy introduce the still dressed in drag Kay as her boyfriend, which leads to several Shakespearian misunderstandings over the course of the episode. Though "A Woman and A Man" is structured as a stand-alone episode without narrative ties to the final season's continuing issues, audiences and Frank alike might have picked up on a particularly bothering throwaway line in a past episode. Here, having put Murphy in a compromising position by setting her up with a former classmate, the FYI team tries to flee the scene upon realizing their mistake.

Corky: She's gonna kill us.
Kay: Not me. I've got a passport and a fake mustache in the car.

Such playful engagement with masculinity, however, is rare in the female-centered sitcom and in the context of *Murphy Brown* best explained by the show's tendency to include famous guest stars in its final episodes. With appearances in her comedy special *Lily: Sold Out* leading to a performance at ABC's *Happy Birthday Elizabeth: A Celebration of Life* in 1997, Lily Tomlin's drag act, sleazy "composite of all the Las Vegas singers she has ever seen" (Laurent), Tommy Velour becomes a guest star in its own right, playing off his iconicity as the character Rick in the same vein as Rosie O'Donnell as the overly enthusiastic Broadway fan, or Bette Midler as the Jewish diva in their cameos as Murphy's short-lived secretary aspirants.[6]

The figure of the diva on the other hand is almost synonymous with camp (Griffin 157) and "feminine excess as comic"—unlike masculinity—"is a regular practice in feminist sitcoms" (Rabinovitz 148). Rabinovitz cites Blanche (Rue McClanahan) in The Golden Girls, Suzanne Sugarbaker in *Designing Women*, and Corky in *Murphy Brown* as major examples. More recent embodiments of female excess can be found in *Cybill*'s Maryann Thorpe (Christine Baranski), *Absolutely Fabulous'* Patsy Stone (Joanna Lumley), Vicki (Kathy Griffin) in *Suddenly Susan*, or Karen (Megan Mullally) in *Will & Grace*, all of whom are sidekicks or secondary characters rather than the shows' central protagonists—a tradition upheld by *30 Rock*'s Jenna. Despite Jenna's "typical" depiction as the excessively feminine secondary character, however, her relation to the show's supposed lead Liz, and in turn Liz's relation to excess and the sidekick, constitute a break with the tradition of the feminist sitcom that fundamentally alters how affective attachment and critical detachment are produced in *30 Rock*.

2.2   Comic Seconds, Wisecracks, and Female Excess

Beginning her analysis with such women's film classics as *Mildred Pierce* (1945, Dir. Michael Curtiz) and *All About Eve* (1950, Dir. Joseph L. Mankiewicz), Roof argues that the comic second's re-emergence in TV after their waning importance in film after 1960 can be traced back to Agnes Moorehead's character Endora in *Bewitched* (1964–1972) (166–67). Historically, as Roof claims, "female comic secondary characters are

degendered, masculinized, or queered [... hinting] at perverse alternatives of nonmarriage, independence, and business success" (10) and they
therefore "can do 'unfeminine' things in unfeminine ways because they
aren't presented as sufficiently womanly" (13). The implied queerness of
the female sidekick is also noted by Patricia White, who—among others,
referring also to Agnes Moorehead—describes their appearance as "different versions of femininity than that of female stars" and their subtextual potential as drawing "the image of 'woman' embodied in the female
lead, with whom they are contrasted iconographically, into a lesbian
economy" (*UnInvited* 173). In terms of lead–sidekick dynamics, the
elements of "nonmarriage, independence, and business success" clearly
are among Liz's characteristics. Additionally, the queer potential of her
character is repeatedly pointed out. She gets called out on her "bi-
curious shoes," she is advised to, "for once," buy something in a "*wom-
en's* clothing store" by Jack, and falsely identified as "an adorable little
lesbian" while still in a baby stroller (1x03 "Blind Date"), accepted into
the writers' room "boys club," and promoted as an author in China as
Lesbian Yellow-Sour-Fruit (4x05 "The Problem Solvers"). The definition of the comic second therefore fits her, the show's ostensible lead
character, much better than hyper-feminine Jenna. An additional, almost
metareferential function of the comic second, which is equally applicable to Liz, is described by both Michael Bronski and Judith Roof in
their respective assessments that the "sidekick's role was generally to act
as a confidante and to give the audience a pungent analysis of the plot"
(Bronski 102) and that in "their position as wise fools, female comic secondary characters provide alternative perspectives" (Roof 18). The role
is thus capable of "coming close to breaking filmic diegesis," alerting the
audience to what they implicitly already know and hence emphasizing or
even enabling dramatic irony (18).

Liz's association with the comic second, despite her central role in the
narrative, is supported by Roof's observation that the role of the sidekick
changes in the 1980s and 1990s, when "the female comic second either
disappears into the group or becomes even stronger and more central"
(159). Roof cites Ellen Morgan in *Ellen* and several roles by Whoopi
Goldberg as instances of this movement of the classic comic second to
the center of the story, where these characters "convey an outsiderness, a
sense that they have always been audience to a story in which they might
appear only as interlopers from outside" (159). This development in turn
creates room at the margins for secondary characters who are excessively

gendered instead of "degendered [and] masculinised," queered through the "feminine excess" Rabinovitz defines as a standard trope of the feminist sitcom (148).

Especially from the mid-1990s onwards secondary characters like Maryann (*Cybill*), Karen (*Will & Grace*), and ultimately Jenna are depicted as figures marked by feminine excess—"excess being the engine of critical reflection" (Cleto 5)—and thus employing the strategy of female masquerade. In her study of feminist humor, Kathleen Rowe describes female masquerade as essential to female comedy, since as "a form of self-representation, masquerade retains the distance necessary for critique, but a distance that is Brechtian and politicized, created by the subject between herself and various forms of representation available to her" (*Unruly Woman* 6–7). Michael T. Schuyler also emphasizes this strategy's effect in his article on the camp value of *Absolutely Fabulous* (1992–2012). Schuyler praises the show for its critical engagement with "the image of woman (more precisely, the male-imposed image of woman) that is simultaneously hyperbolized and inverted in an effort to shake up the status quo by unmasking the social norms imposed on womanhood" (12). Judith Roof also detects this strategy as a characteristic trait in comic seconds Patsy (*Absolutely Fabulous*) and Maryann (*Cybill*), and claims that through feminine masquerade both are "more assertive and influential than the shows' ostensible stars" (167).

The female second's influence, however, is more restricted than the classical wisecrack's as "their knowledge does not produce any dramatic irony or site of epistemological identification because their knowledge seems to come from out of a drunken stupor" (Roof 167). The trope of drunken stupor is taken up again in Karen (and to a lesser extent later Jenna), who is rarely seen without either a drink in hand or pills within reach. In fact, in their analysis of Karen as the central camp element of *Will & Grace* (rather than the show's two gay male protagonists), Shugart and Waggoner emphasize the "cartoonish qualities of Karen's aesthetic of excess," which are mirrored in her behavior, as "her addiction to alcohol and prescription drugs is a staple feature of her character" (*Making* 87). Danielle Mitchell even proposes *Will & Grace*'s female sidekick as the show's queerest figure. Basing her argument in Annamarie Jagose's definition of queer as that which is not only non-straight, but destabilizes established notions of "the normal" (97), Mitchell claims that "Karen creates a rhetorical and ideological space for such destabilization [which makes] room for the production of counterdiscourses" (89). Mitchell concludes that while she is "not a title character, Karen is responsible for much of the program's electricity" (89), a status comparable to Jenna's.

Despite Roof's reservation about "drunkard" characters, Mitchell's statement supports the idea that unrelated to the comic second's relative insignificance for plot development, she is a crucial factor in setting the mood of the narration as well as guiding the audience's attitude towards the central characters' actions. Her character is therefore in many instances more interesting and rewarding for feminist media scholars than the female protagonists, who due to their central status in the narrative and its almost inevitable heteronormative romance, lack the same leeway for less restrictive gender presentation and ironic distance to the plot. Schuyler's exploration of *Absolutely Fabulous*, Mizejewski's discussion of Kathy Griffin's role in *Suddenly Susan* (*Pretty/Funny* 30–58), or Shugart and Waggoner's chapter on *Will & Grace*'s Karen all exemplify these qualities and stress camp's importance to the sidekick–protagonist equation.

Yet, as mentioned before, Liz is a decisively unusual choice for a protagonist and thus opens additional narrative space for camp interventions. One of the parallels between a 1990s sitcom that supposedly changed the representation of queer characters on American TV, *Will & Grace*, and a contemporary show constantly under scrutiny due to its links to feminist debates, *30 Rock*, then, is the strengthening of the excessive comic second running parallel to the deconstruction of the female lead. Looking at the dynamic in a sitcom which also featured an excessive comic second and aired only a few years prior, *Suddenly Susan*, this shift—and its implications—become even more apparent. While the dynamic between Vicki and Susan is defined by Susan's unquestionable attractiveness (she is played by Brooke Shields after all), the tense relationship between Karen and Grace is marked by the latter's (perceived) lack of femininity for which other characters tease her constantly. Nevertheless, *Will & Grace* shies away from allowing Grace's on-screen appearance to be anything but flattering and conventionally attractive. Furthermore, while Grace might not be "good" at heterosexual romance, her approach to the topic is far from non-normative and her status is rarely that of the perceptive "outsider" to the narrative. The third lead in this line, Liz Lemon, is depicted as the bespectacled mousy woman with bad hair days, unflattering clothes that do not fit properly, and a thus "masculinized" screen personality, who through her quick-witted responses and disillusioned ideas on marriage and romance personifies Bronski's claim: "Too smart ever to get the man, sidekicks had to settle for being funnier than everybody else" (102). Despite Tina Fey's appearance on magazine covers and her capacity to carry a movie, there is little doubt about Liz Lemon's lackluster performance of desirable normative femininity—a "failure" mirrored at the other end of the spectrum by excessive Jenna. Additionally, Liz is repeatedly shown as either close to or breaking the fourth wall (though she is not the only one to do that within the context of series); for example, she directly addresses the camera to ask for money after a particularly blatant product placement for Verizon (2x06 "Somebody to Love"); or ends a telephone conversation in the season five premiere, "The Fabian Strategy," by saying "Ok, season five, here we go." Furthermore, several storylines, especially as the show progresses, put her in the position of the "wise" onlooker guiding audience perception of extra- as well as intradiegetic developments, which range from Jack's love life to NBC's new hit program, *MILF Island*, GE's merger activities, and US American women's obsession with Oprah Winfrey.

In a unique manner, *30 Rock*'s female characters Liz and Jenna thus depict both the original comic second elevated to the status of protagonist and the transformed comic second now characterized by female excess. This enables the show to incorporate both strands of humor as well as the ironic distance provided by the different, usually separated tropes: the "unfeminine" outsider, whose wisecracks border on "breaking filmic diegesis"; and the secondary character marked by gendered excess, whose female masquerade debunks clichés of femininity and whose "eccentricities [...] provide a fertile ambiance in which everything becomes funny" (Roof 167). Without a female lead character in the traditional sense, *30 Rock* is free to continuously explore the fringes of narration, and to comment rather than show. The series can put wisecracking and eccentricity front and center without having to put them in relation to a more restrained, but ultimately stronger primary plot focused on a relatable female character whose personal development towards (hetero-)normative romance dominate the story. Though Liz's screen time makes her the central character, and Jenna's status as the star of the show-inside-the show make her a potential lead character, from the perspective of tropes of female comedy neither qualifies as a female protagonist. With this attention to the liminal, the show becomes a particularly fruitful ground for camp's denaturalizing, questioning, and critiquing impulses towards sexual mores, gender relations, and ideals of femininity. The show is thus uniquely equipped to address the ambiguous perils and pleasures of US media's changing attitudes towards and representations of women and feminism over the past 20 years, often referred to as postfeminism. As *30 Rock* comments on them and depicts different (post)feminist positions in their complexity and incongruity, the show becomes a metareferential postfeminist text.

3 POSTFEMINISM IN US (MEDIA) CULTURE

3.1 Elements of a Sensibility

The term postfeminism is highly contested and, like camp, often insufficiently defined. It can refer to a broad range of connected as well as contradictory phenomena in Anglo-American media, culture as well as theory. With developments labeled as postfeminist ranging from the incorporation of queer and postcolonial inquiries into feminist theory, to the rise of "raunch culture" in media and society on the one hand, and the celebration of motherhood on the other, the only agreed upon feature of postfeminism seems to be its pervasiveness. Rosalind Gill differentiates four major changes regarding feminism that might invite the post prefix. Among these, she proposes a definition of postfeminism as a sensibility as the most relevant to pop-cultural depictions of gender and feminism; media texts influenced by this sensibility are shaped by both pro- and anti-feminist motives, and are characterized by "relatively stable features that together constitute a postfeminist discourse" ("Postfeminist" 148).

Contextualizing *30 Rock* within this inconsistent discourse not only helps to explain the show's own partially contradictory politics, but also accounts for the disparity critics perceive between *30 Rock* and its predecessors more univocally cherished as feminist texts. While *30 Rock* engages with many of the media clichés that define postfeminist discourse, the sensibility's overarching issue of double entanglement emerges as particularly significant. Hence, to reduce *30 Rock*'s multi-layered engagement with gender and sexuality merely to Liz Lemon's supposed failure as a role model in comparison to the likes of Murphy Brown and Mary Tyler Moore, does justice neither to the series nor its reception. Nonetheless, its limitations with regard to (third-wave) feminist goals are readily apparent in its cast and setting, which reflect a larger issue Amanda Lotz observes in postfeminist media: "white, heterosexual, upper-middle-class women remain the norm in many of these series" (114).[7] Yet, speaking of the series only in terms of a backlash and its shortcomings, inevitably falls short of the complexities of this metareferential and highly self-reflexive text, which constantly alerts audiences to its awareness of tropes and trends, including the state of feminist debate, and its willingness to engage with, rather than reiterate them.

To explain the conflation of feminist and anti-feminist views and demands in postfeminist texts, Yvonne Tasker and Diane Negra point to TV and film producers who, by the late 1990s, had to accept that "representational verisimilitude required an acknowledgment of feminism as a feature of the cultural milieu" (107). The effect, however, is not that feminist gains and goals are universally agreed upon and unchallenged, but rather the opposite. McRobbie, for example, explains that precisely because of the widespread acceptance of the principles of feminism as "a form of Gramscian common sense," its potentially more radical politics and demands are easily discredited and written off as outdated (255). Tasker and Negra furthermore note that feminist issues such as economic and political equality or sexual freedom have been reimagined as connected purely to "individualism and consumerism" (107).

In such instances of commodified feminism, irony is often emptied of its critical potential and instead used to discredit feminist politics via the mock evocation of a "post-gender" context. Simon Critchley, who generally argues for the liberating power of humor, warns against the reactionary potential of humor that "seeks to confirm the status quo," for which he explicitly cites sexist humor as one example (*On Humour* 11–12). His assertion that humor depends on "a consensus about the world we inhabit" ("On Humor") reflects Hutcheon's definition of the discursive community, who shares certain values and codes as the basis for irony. In the scenarios described by McRobbie, and Tasker and Negra this "consensus" is a superficial acceptance of commodified feminism in a post-discrimination age. Irony here is exploited as "a way of 'having it both ways,' of expressing sexist or homophobic or otherwise unpalatable sentiments in an ironized form, while claiming this was not actually 'meant'" (Gill, "Postfeminist" 159).

30 Rock explicitly addresses this mechanism in the Amelia Earhart/ menstruation sketch. It functions like the postfeminist texts from the 1990s Angela McRobbie has analyzed and which she describes as contextualizing exploitative images of women in such a way as to imply a "knowing wink": even such a degrading depiction of Amelia Earhart should not be taken to task, because it presents a form of "ironic reappropriation" and surely no one working at *TGS* is truly so sexist as to assume menstrual cramps would make an accomplished pilot steer her plane into the ocean. *30 Rock* reflects on the hollow quality of the *TGS* sketch through Liz Lemon's growing doubt about the show's empowering potential, especially when the same episode confronts her with the spousal abuse of one of her (momentary) co-workers. *TGS* as representative of the ironic mode of postfeminist sensibility, which perpetuates rather than intervenes in sexist representations and harmful stereotypes, is thus framed by *30 Rock*, which uses humor and irony instead to discredit the postfeminist "knowing wink" in a manner that critiques the easy rejection of responsibility for the presented image and its implications.

The reactionary potential of humor and irony is not the only consequence of this form of "acknowledging feminism." The premise that feminism has somehow achieved its goals and is thus not politically relevant anymore, influences most of postfeminism's "stable" features:

> the notion of femininity as a bodily property; the shift from objectification to subjectification; an emphasis on self-surveillance, monitoring and discipline; a focus on individualism, choice, and empowerment; the dominance of a "makeover paradigm"; a resurgence of ideas of natural sexual difference; the marked sexualization of culture; and an emphasis on consumerism and the commodification of difference. (Gill 147)

In accordance with the order in which Gill names these features, "subjectification" is at the root of many of these trends, especially "makeover paradigm" and "marked sexualization of culture."[8] The increase in sexualized imagery and jargon is best captured in Ariel Levy's analysis of the "rise of raunch culture" in her bestseller *Female Chauvinist Pigs*, in which she argues, among other things, that to be an "empowered woman" in contemporary culture is inevitably linked to an acceptance and celebration of the exploitation of the female body, be it in pole dancing classes for housewives who want to please their husbands or in professional women who accompany their colleagues to strip clubs. This trend paradoxically thrives alongside a growing stress on virginity (Press 110), and on glamorized narratives of marriage and motherhood

(Mizejewski, *Pretty/Funny* 78), again underlining the contradictory nature of postfeminist discourse.

Gill defines subjectification as exploitation "in which the objectifying male gaze is internalized as to form a new disciplinary regime" ("Postfeminist" 151–52) and interpreted as a liberating expression of an individual woman's choice. The emphasis on choice as the litmus test of empowerment can be traced to postfeminism's entanglement with neoliberal thought, which relies on "the autonomous, calculating, self-regulating subject" as much as postfeminism imagines an "active, freely choosing, self-reinventing subject" (Gill and Scharff 171). This fosters a cultural environment in which, as described by Levy, almost any "choice"—whether to participate in *Girls Gone Wild*, move into the Playboy mansion, or undergo plastic surgery—is labeled "empowering."

The language of neoliberal choice, which codes surveillance as an expression of free will, is also at play in a far less sexualized, yet equally problematic context; the postfeminist trend defined of "retreatism," where "a well-educated white female professional displays her 'empowerment' and caring nature by withdrawing from the workforce (and symbolically from the public sphere) to devote herself to husband and family" (Tasker and Negra 108). This further complicates the question of what constitutes feminism—and feminist media representations—today. Most romantic comedies to feature this trope, such as *Sweet Home Alabama* (2002, Dir. Andy Tennant) and *The Stepford Wives* remake (2004, Dir. Frank Oz)—starring Nicole Kidman and a dangerous combination or irony and nostalgia—usually end without addressing the consequences of retreatism. One of postfeminist TV's most high-profile series, *Desperate Housewives*, however, is concerned with this postfeminist ideal, its long-term and ultimately darker consequences, and addresses them through camp. In addition to *Desperate Housewives*, the series *Ugly Betty* and *Sex and the City* have been analyzed as queer and/or camp interventions in the postfeminist sensibility. They create an important background and contrast to *30 Rock*'s engagement with the outlined issues and the question of how to effectively challenge postfeminism's "ambivalent pleasures" (Tasker and Negra 108).

3.2 Contemporary TV: Postfeminist Concerns, Queer Readings

The ABC dramedy *Desperate Housewives* (2004–2012) dismantles, rather than celebrates, the ideals of marriage, family, and content housewives connected to retreatism. It incorporates violent themes such as suicide, murder, and (sexual) abuse into its storylines and thus relocates them from crime shows and major cities to a drama series and the suburbs, the typical scenery of the women's film (or melodrama). The melodrama is the Hollywood genre most closely linked to the domestic, feminine, and trivial to explore contemporary cultural issues. It is also a genre historically associated with camp—a connection never more apparent than in the work of Douglas Sirk, icon and iconoclast of 1950s melodrama. Accordingly, *Desperate Housewives* quotes well-known aspects of Sirk's iconography, such as the pilot's deceiving establishing shot which, like the one in *All That Heaven Allows* (1955, Dir. Douglas Sirk), is as comforting in its inconspicuousness as it is unsettling in its artificiality. Other aspects of Sirk's distinct style enhance this initial feeling of artificiality, such as the use of mirrors to underline the multiplicity of characters and the importance of playing social roles as opposed to "being" someone, of jarring colors in the mise en scène and costume to provide implicit characterization, and a soundtrack that provides commentary as much as it transports emotions. In combination with *Desperate Housewives'* melodramatic storylines and focus on women trapped by social expectations and their own high standards, these stylistic choices create an atmosphere in which camp is used as a distancing device from the moral norms portrayed. The style of the series thereby enables and enhances the show's "satir[e of] bourgeois domesticity," which Niall Richardson observes in his reading of *Desperate Housewives* (160). For Richardson, it is first and foremost the character of Bree van de Kamp (Marcia Cross) through which the series expresses its "feminist politics and [...] queer agenda" (157), namely its rejection of postfeminist ideals of natural gender differences, heteronormativity, and celebration of marriage and motherhood. Bree's "campiness" is achieved by her conscious performance of a retro-femininity evocative of the feminine mystique, yet confronted with and placed in a decisively modern, postfeminist social order. Her flawless, highly stylized appearance, perpetual smile, and embrace of traditional gender roles, contrasted with a rather unfeminine insistence on having things her way, connects her to the camp trope of the high-maintenance diva. This attention to the artifice of her femininity not only contradicts the postfeminist sensibility's tendency to see gender as a natural bodily property, but also, Richardson claims, tarnishes her heterosexual relationships and their claims to "normality" (167–68).

Richardson's queer reading employs parts of the same language I have outlined as problematic, namely Bree's "knowing wink at the audience" (165). Through the show's sinister tone, however, its "common sense" is explicitly not one of achieved equality and utopian possibilities, but of repressed desires and oppressive structures. Therefore, the effect of irony is decisively different from what McRobbie and Tasker and Negra have found fault with; instead of precluding critique, irony and camp become instruments of critique, ensuring that rather than celebrating retreatism or the new momism, "*Desperate Housewives* asserts the *desperate* need for ongoing feminist politics" (Richardson 168, emphasis in the original).

Desperate Housewives is not the only postfeminist text to rely on tactics such as camp style and the queering of central characters or relationships, yet it is exceptional in its sole focus on the suburban. Negra and Tasker's claim about retreatism, in its purest sense of women leaving the work-force and the hectic metropolis, holds mainly true for cinema and real-ity TV, whereas TV packages this issue in a different way. For Amanda Lotz fictional TV series set themselves apart from other media outlets by focusing on women in different positions of and relations to (economic) power and by examining "contemporary struggles faced by women and feminists" (115–16). Many examples in recent TV programming, from *Ally McBeal*, to *Sex and the City*, its "successors" such as *Cashmere Mafia* (2008) or *Lipstick Jungle* (2008–2009), and any number of crime and medical shows—most prominently *Grey's Anatomy* (2005–)—as well as sitcoms such as *Parks & Recreation* and *30 Rock* itself demonstrate a growing interest in women's careers and their depiction as accomplished professionals. In these "pro-feminist" narratives, a "backlash" in the form of the retreatist trope nonetheless resurfaces as part of the recurring "dilemma of 'having it all'" (Genz, "Singled" 98).

Genz describes this dilemma as critical for the postfeminist woman, "as she endeavors to reconcile her experiences of being female, feminine, and feminist" ("Singled" 98).[9] If Genz is right in her assumption that the desire (and inevitable failure) "to have it all" is indeed the proto-postfeminist idea, Liz Lemon steps forward as the perfect candidate. After she rejects the "retreatist scenario" in season one by deciding to stay in New York rather than move to Cleveland, Liz wants to resolve her issues with her ex-boyfriend Floyd as he visits New York in season two. Rushing through the airport to catch him before he leaves New York again—re-enacting the same scene from almost every romantic comedy ever produced (a trope already addressed in Ellen's infamous coming out moment at an airport)—Liz is not stopped by an alternative love interest, but by a TSA agent and the sandwich and dipping sauce in her carry-on.

Liz:	No, look. I just need to catch up with this guy, before he gets in a plane to Cleveland.
TSA Agent:	That's sort of a cliché. […] Just leave the sandwich and go through.
Liz:	Leave the sandwich? Leave the sandwich?
Over Speakers:	Final boarding call for Flight 254 to Cleveland.
TSA Agent:	You're choosing a sandwich over a guy? Hmm. That is less clichéd.
Liz:	I can do it. [Starts eating the sandwich] I can have it all! (2x14 "Sandwich Day")

Liz devours her sandwich in record (real) time, the TSA agent yells at her in disgust that she is "eating foil," but despite it all Liz achieves her goal and runs through security, before her ex boards his flight, giving them the chance to reconcile. The clichéd romantic background music and close-ups, however, are reserved for Liz and her sandwich, while the talk with her ex-boyfriend passes almost uneventfully—squeezed in between scenes depicting the romance between Liz and food, and Liz and her workplace. As the episode ends and fades to black over a news anchor's report on Jack Donaghy's departure from GE to a government position blasting from a TV, Floyd's role in the series and Liz's life fade equally abruptly.

Not all of *30 Rock*'s treatments of postfeminism's peculiar attributes are quite so literal, yet both the obviousness of the episode itself, and the amount of attention it received underscore the prominence of the "have it all" dilemma in contemporary media.[10] In her analysis of *Sex and the City* as *the* defining TV text of postfeminism Jane Gerhard even calls the fearful realization that "being liberated is not all we were told it would be," especially not when it comes to romance, the fundamental "post-feminist angst" (46).

Like *Desperate Housewives*, *Sex and the City* focuses on four female friends in their 30s and early 40s, yet the similarities end there. Rather than the fictional suburban Wisteria Lane, *Sex and the City*'s fifth pro-tagonist is metropolitan Manhattan. The difference in location is reflected in a difference in atmosphere; despite the lingering "postfemi-nist angst," *Sex and the City* is, for the most part, celebratory, light in tone, and hedonistic in its appraisal of the city's potential for its affluent protagonists. The women's mutual affection is portrayed as unwavering, their several "sex-capades" trigger small talk and laughter, rather than the dread which is caused by infidelities in *Desperate Housewives*, their shopping sprees are signs of their financial independence, while fashion and sex pose as forms of empowerment. As such, *Sex and the City* has been the focal point of much discussion on postfeminist TV, with consumerism, sexualization, individualism, and surveillance of female bodies all represented in the series almost "by the book." The women are seldom portrayed eating, their bodies are almost impossibly slim, political activism is not talked about ("The women's movement? Jesus Christ, I haven't even had coffee yet!"—4x07 "Time and Punishment"), instead sex seems to be a constant factor in their conversation and lives. All four protagonists are successful in their respective careers, enjoying the advances of second-wave feminism, while feminism is indeed the proverbial, never to be mentioned, "f-word," and at least for two of the protagonists marriage and kids raise the question of living the "retreatist scenario" (though in the case of Miranda, played by Cynthia Nixon, the retreat would mean a move to Brooklyn rather than the countryside).[11] The quest for Mr. Right (or at least Mr. Big) remains central, even as all other aspects of their lives seem far removed from any previous incarnations in TV series. Despite this conservative streak, the series has been perceived as progressive, especially in its frank portrayal of female sexuality, aided by its openness to queer discourses. As Gerhard elaborates,

> Carrie and her friends live in a world where they enjoy the company of their gay male friends, meet potential sex partners in clubs, bars, and parks, and pledge everlasting love to each other. Even as the main characters are "straight," the narrative queerness of the show alters the representations of their heterosexuality, drawing it out from the shadow of its hegemonic closet. (42–3)

The central "postfeminist angst" is "mitigated" through this queer potential for alternative kinds of kinship (46). In addition to the narrative queering of the women's various relationships and the portrayal of their friendship in ways traditionally reserved for romantic couples (42–3), Jane Arthurs highlights the show's "appropriation of camp as a style" (138). While this argument can convincingly be made for a show so invested in fashion, femininity, and excess of all kinds, *Sex and the*

City has not taken its camp aesthetics to quite the extremes that another fashion-focused "dramedy" has.

Ugly Betty (2006–2010) became a rare phenomenon on American TV, when it introduced an ethnic, working class, overweight (for TV standards) female character with braces as its protagonist. The ABC series tells the story of Betty Suarez (America Ferrera), the family's first college graduate and aspiring journalist, as she enters the world of *Mode*, *Vogue*'s fictional equivalent within the series, and learns to adapt to Manhattan, the fashion industry, and severe changes in her family's situation. For all its differences from other postfeminist texts—most obviously its diversion from the norm of "the white, heterosexual, upper-middle-class" protagonist (Lotz 114)—*Ugly Betty* is firmly embedded in the postfeminist sensibility. Among the employed stable features is the makeover paradigm, which structures the series as well as Betty's own journey, since her character for most of the series looks like the typical "before" picture of a TV makeover. Other postfeminist features include the setting within a highly professional and competitive environment, which features women in several different positions of power within *Mode*. Additionally, the series regularly invokes questions about consumerism, sexualization, as well as bodies and their regulation.

More so than any other scripted series at the time *Ugly Betty* distinguished itself through camp via its aesthetics and narrative style, which aid the protagonist's outsider perspective in supporting the series' critique on postfeminism. Based on a Colombian telenovela, *Ugly Betty* is free to explore even the most melodramatic and absurd soap opera storylines, such as one male arch nemesis' return as a woman after a secret sex-change, and her continued flirtation with her brother's love interests.[12] Due to its setting in a fictional fashion magazine on the one hand, and an excessively "ethnically-styled" Queens on the other, the series has ample opportunity to enrich its aesthetics with bright colors and over-the-top sets, which are additionally supported by the show's equally colorful credits. More importantly, "the wholehearted embrace of camp" manifests itself on the level of storytelling and the series' signature "mixture of tone," which allowed for melodramatic moments in a series "generally comedic in tone" (Rowe, *Unruly Girls* 210). Through camp's distancing qualities, in short, *Ugly Betty* could base its story on the stable features of postfeminism without endorsing them.

4   *30 ROCK*'s DIVERGENCES IN COMIC FORMAT
AND NARRATIVE FORMULA

Through their openness to alternative discourses and stylistic experimentation, these three texts thus distinguish themselves from most postfeminist texts, in which the "real uncertainties and ambivalences embedded in
postfeminist fiction [are] most often subject to easy and artificial modes
of textual resolution" (Negra 90). In contrast, *30 Rock*, while certainly
and consciously "artificial" in its plot turns and problem solutions, complicates rather than placates the issues depicted and it does so not only
through its choice in content, but also its reliance on stylistic make-up to
support its reading as a meta-postfeminist text. The decision, for example, to shoot *30 Rock* as a single-camera show without the laugh track,
supports its "complication." Besides a more cinematic quality of the
recorded image (as scenes are lit differently for each camera angle) and
greater flexibility with regard to settings, the missing laugh track is the
most notable feature of current "quality comedies" like *Modern Family*
(2009–), *Parks and Recreation*, and *30 Rock* itself. This omission adds to
the visual flexibility of these sitcoms by allowing for faster editing and a
much higher joke per minute ratio, as laugh tracks inevitably slow down
the narration when actors must wait for the laughter to die down before
continuing their dialogue. In addition to this stylistic innovation, the
missing laugh track enables—but also forces—audiences to determine
themselves which part of the series to regard as funny, and to a certain
degree whose side to take in arguments between characters who often
present different political or ideological ideas. While *30 Rock* employs
musical cues, camera movement, and other subtle stylistic indicators to
alert audiences to jokes, the missing laugh track underlines the series'
narrative non-closure and openness to different interpretations, and thus
its insistence on "exploring the messy ways feminist ideals actually play
out in institutions and in popular culture" (Mizejewski "Feminism") and
its refusal to partake in easy textual resolution.

4.1   *Flashbacks of Spit Takes: Sketch Comedy in* 30 Rock

In addition to the missing laugh track and the show's innovative combination of comic seconds, *30 Rock* distinguishes itself by infusing the
sitcom format with elements from another tradition of televised comedy, the sketch or variety show. Similarly to the way *Desperate Housewives*

reworks the classical Hollywood melodrama and how *Ugly Betty*'s characters and aesthetics are influenced by the series' roots in telenovelas,
30 Rock's depiction of its characters, its character development, and its
narrative and visual style are rooted not only in the sitcom genre, but
also pay reference to variety shows like *Laugh-In*, *The Carol Burnett
Show*, or *Saturday Night Live*. *30 Rock*'s ties and references to this comedy format are numerous: *TGS with Tracy Jordan* is itself a (low-quality)
sketch comedy show; *30 Rock*'s cast and crew is full of *Saturday Night
Life* alumni (ranging from head writer Tina Fey, to cast member Rachel
Dratch, to executive producer Michael Lorne, director Beth McCarthy-
Miller, and repeated host Alec Baldwin); Liz Lemon's boyfriend in later
seasons, played by Matt Damon, is named Carol Burnett after one of
the USA's most successful female comedians; and allusions to famous
sketches and sketch shows range from *Laugh-In* re-enactments (2x04
"Rosemary's Baby"), to tributes to The Carol Burnett Show's trademark
breaking, and the *SNL* scandal of Sinead O'Connor ripping apart a picture of the pope during the live broadcast in October 1992 (6x19 "Live
from Studio 6H").

Rather than simply referencing sketch comedy, however, *30 Rock*
abounds with examples of comedic tropes established in sketch rather
than situational comedy, "such as vaudeville performances, direct address
to the camera, a disregard for plot and a refusal to create characters distinct from the performer's personalities" (Mills 35). Beside the casting
of Tracy Morgan more or less as himself in the role of Tracy Jordan, and
the repeated inclusion of actors, news anchors, and other celebrities as
themselves (such as Conan O'Brian as Liz's ex-boyfriend and Al Gore
as NBC's Green Week sponsor), which constitutes Mills' "refusal to create characters distinct from the performer's personalities," the direct
address of the audience—already mentioned in connection to comic seconds who tend to break the fourth wall—is among *30 Rock*'s most overt
disregards for the sitcom's genre conventions. These occurrences range
from short off-hand comments and looks into the camera, to whole tags
framed as direct address, such as the end of "What Will Happen to the
Gang Next Year?" (6x22), in which Kim Jong Ill (Margaret Cho) muses
over the fate of *30 Rock*'s protagonists in the following season. While the
latter is an example of dealing with intradiegetic developments, the former is moreover connected to metareferential comments, which include
either industry conventions, such as Liz turning around after a particularly blatant product placement to ask "Can we have our money now"

(2x06 "Somebody to Love"), or addressing Tina Fey's own reputation in "Hardball" (1x15). Here Liz Lemon winks into the camera, after a patriot themed episode of *TGS* causes Jack to compliment her on "doing a good job," to which she replies: "Why do you sound so surprised? I love America. Just because I think gay dudes should be allowed to adopt kids and we should all have hybrid cars doesn't mean I don't love America." In this case, the direct address further underlines the many parallels between Liz Lemon and Tina Fey and thus the sketch trope of neglecting to differentiate between character and actor.

Additionally, "Hardball" (1x15) also serves to exemplify how short glimpses into the sketches from *TGS with Tracy Jordan*, formerly known as *The Girlie Show*, are among *30 Rock*'s recurrent sketch-inspired elements. The earliest of these instances is the "Pam, the Overly Confident, Morbidly Obese Woman" sketch starring Jenna in a sparkling pink fatsuit. Other recurring motives include a fart machine, animal costumes, and celebrity parodies. Overall, the tone of *TGS* can be described as carnivalesque due to its employment of a humor mainly based on bodies and bodily functions on the one hand and the mocking of powerful figures such as Oprah Winfrey, Barack Obama, and Hillary Clinton on the other (Gerigk). "As a site of insurgency" (Russo 64), *TGS*' carnivalesque mode of humor additionally embeds *30 Rock*'s storylines and characters, in and of themselves already invested in the uprooting of tradition and norm, within an atmosphere that mocks social mores.

Beside the "show within the show" setup, another important variety show element in *30 Rock* are the frequent flashbacks to several characters' (often absurd) pasts. They function as mini-sketches inserted into the narrative and give *30 Rock* an additional opportunity to comment on the series' ongoing events or simply to add to its carnivalesque tone. Prominent examples include an eating contest, in which page Kenneth Parcell—the show's take on religiously fanatic hillbillies—must eat his father figure, a pig named Harold, to earn the money to leave for New York, or Jack Donaghy's recollection of his school-play failure as a protein (both in 5x09 "Chain Reaction of Mental Anguish") and his secret life as a prize-winning cookie jar collector (2x03 "The Collection").

Moreover, a heavy reliance on intertextuality, unmatched frequency of guest stars, and casting of the same actor in different roles characterize *30 Rock*. According to Brett Mills a coherent narrative and a stable set of characters are the most important features to distinguish the sitcom from other forms of TV comedy, as sketch shows do not have a narrative and characters are only stable inasmuch as sketches are picked up in later episodes (37). Similarly, Jason Mittell emphasizes that even highly episodic shows still maintain a consistent set of characters and that it is subsequently "rare for a program to violate such serialized characters and world-building" and noteworthy if such disturbances occur (par. 10).[13] In *30 Rock*, the coherent story world is most frequently disrupted by the casting of Rachel Dratch, the original Jenna Maroney from the discarded pilot, as a cat trainer and janitor for *TGS*, as Barbara Walters and Elizabeth Taylor, as well as the little blue monster Liz and Tracy see on different occasions (during seasons one and five) under the influence of prescription drugs, a gas leak, and hunger respectively. Other examples include John Anderson playing Liz Lemon's almost-date on her ex-boyfriend's wedding, her dream boyfriend Astronaut Mike Dexter, her mother's 1960s boyfriend Buzz Aldrin, and TV anchor for Jack's "Porn for Women" channel. On the other hand, the same character is repeatedly played by different actors. Jack's younger selves, for example, are played by Alec Baldwin himself, a CGI version of a younger Alec Baldwin from *The Hunt for Red October* (1990), and Jimmy Fallon, whereas Liz Lemon is played most often by Tina Fey—even in flashbacks in which she is nine—but also by Tina Fey's daughter, several child actors (Michal Antonov and Marcella Roy) as well as Julia Louis-Dreyfus and Amy Poehler in the two live episodes.

This fusion of styles has consequences not only for the kind of humor favored by the show, but more importantly it also changes the way in which characterization and narration work in *30 Rock* in comparison to traditional sitcoms. For all its ability to comment on current affairs and to bring humor to common concerns, the sitcom is bound—like all serial storytelling—to a certain amount of verisimilitude and narrative coherence. Variety formats in contrast are marked by "sequential segmentation and direct address" (Neale and Krutnik 179). Moreover, sketch comedy has a long tradition of employing a "markedly 'self-reflexive' style" (201), with a humor based on mocking and parodying other formats and programs rather than creating a unique narrative that results in a punch line or funny situation. Thus, Neale and Krutnik remark on the metareferential qualities of variety TV shows that their

> effect is not just to expose the limits of conventional formats but to link their absurd arbitrariness to institutions and representatives of institutional

power, [mocking] the powers of the broadcasting institutions (a mocking
which nevertheless recognizes that these powers are real). (201–2)

30 Rock's trademark status as the "most meta of shows" (Traister) is
hence partially created by its blending of sitcom and sketch comedy,
as the genre mixture introduces new ways of engaging with metareferentiality. Additionally, Neale and Krutnik's phrasing mirrors Pamela
Robertson's claim that (feminist) camp "depends on our simultaneously
recognizing stereotypes as stereotypes" and understanding the "power
those stereotypes have over us" (142). This dual connection of sketch
comedy's characteristics to *30 Rock*'s metaqualities and Robertson's definition of camp's mechanisms is not incidental. Rather, *30 Rock*'s structural porousness, created by its indebtedness to sketch comedy, is as
fundamental to its camp quality as the feminist sitcom tropes of feminine excess and manly wisecrack outlined above. The show's meta and
camp qualities mutually enhance the other's parodying and criticizing
effect, which strengthens the show's ability to deal with stereotypes and
to comment on gender representations.

It is crucial to remember these characteristics of *30 Rock*'s style when
commenting on its female protagonists, as the sketch or variety show has
no interest in character depth and development, just as the comic second
is almost never meant to be the fictional figure the audience is invited to
identify with or imagine as a role model. Through this complex formal
and comedic setup, *30 Rock*'s female protagonists gain immense leeway
to position themselves in contemporary postfeminist discourses as mocking comment rather than willing participant. Thus, they resist easy textual resolution in favor of a humor that challenges contemporary fables
of ideal women and empowerment. Understanding Liz and Jenna's
function as not only comic seconds, but also as occasional sketch character, helps first to grasp how their depiction can be far from positive
yet still enjoyable: the success of Tina Fey's *SNL* impersonation of Sarah
Palin does not hinge on her representation of positive traits, neither does
SNL's menstruation medication spoof, "Annuale," starring among others Tina Fey as a pink-axe wielding incarnation of PMS induced craziness. Second, it clarifies why certain forms of feminist criticism do not
adequately address the issues raised by *30 Rock*.

4.2   Sweeps Week Sexualities

Frequent flashbacks, as indicated before, are one of *30 Rock*'s comedic trademarks and essential to its blurring of lines between sitcom and variety show. The prominent status of Liz Lemon's flashbacks in particular is reflected in NBC's decision to use a montage of her flashback sequences as a promotional tool for *30 Rock*'s final season.[14] In her case, however, the flashbacks fulfill an additional function. While some of these sketches are used to shed light on Liz Lemon's early career—most notably her early forays into acting, such as her appearance as Bijiou in a phone sex company commercial (3x16 "Apollo, Apollo")—the majority of flashbacks to Liz's youth and adolescence serve the purpose of illuminating her gender transgressions. They thus strengthen *30 Rock*'s deviation from the sitcom's (and TV's) standard depiction of postfeminist femininity and heteronormative sexuality, which the series achieves through several characters' association with queerness.

Liz's transgressions in terms of gender and sexuality are established as early as her appearance in a baby stroller, which is commented on by an older lady with the observation "My, what an adorable little lesbian" (1x03 "Blind Date"). Such allusions to Liz's failure to perform heterosexual femininity rely heavily on clichés, many of which might be regarded as offensive. At the same time, however, they are part of her comic second (queer) persona and crucial for the show's assessment of sexualities, as they underline that both sexiness and heteronormativity rely on performances, rather than being the "bodily property" postfeminist sensibility portrays them as.

In addition, Liz's "lesbian issue" is framed from the beginning in a way which makes it clear that even Jack Donaghy, *30 Rock*'s epitome of conservatism, and foremost contemporary (as opposed to the flashbacks' retrospective) source of critique of Liz's appearance, is relying on stereotypes he himself knows not to be true. This distinction is clarified as early as episode four of the premiere season, titled "Blind Date," when *30 Rock* opts for a story arc usually reserved for sweeps week of later seasons (supposedly shortly before or coinciding with "jumping the shark").[15,16] In the episode, Jack sets up Liz on the eponymous blind date with a woman without any prior discussion of her sexuality and dating behavior.[17] Alexander Doty explains the necessity for female-centered sitcoms and dramas "such as *The Golden Girls*, [...] and *Designing Women* [which] point toward lesbian readings through double entendres; oblique, displaced, or jokey references to lesbianism" (*Making* 43) to incorporate episodes in which the "lesbian menace" is addressed. This trend is continued in postfeminism's defining texts, such as *Ally McBeal* (2x07 "Happy Trails," 2x09 "You can never tell," 3x02 "Buried Pleasures"), *Desperate Housewives* (5x17 "The Story of Lucy and Jessie"), and *Sex and the City* (3x04 "Boy, Girl, Boy, Girl").

Lesbian representation on *30 Rock* works differently from these TV shows, particularly concerning the "containment" of the "charge of lesbianism [...] the series has accumulated around its regular cast" (43). While the "adorable little lesbian" flashback, which also features a teenage Liz being comforted by her high school volleyball teacher for being different from other girls and addressed as "young man" by her dentist at kindergarten age, is indeed featured on "Blind Date" (the lesbian episode), these mini-sketches are shown only after Liz is already on her date and without any prior jokey references to lesbianism that needed to be diffused. Instead, *30 Rock* changes the timeline and introduces the lesbian charge via the special episode rather than "detaining" it through the very same. Quite the contrary, future episodes and seasons feature repeated references to lesbians, such as Jenna's observation that "the best way for a lady to get heat in this industry is to either record a country album or have a lesbian relationship" (4x01 "Season 4"). Jenna's willingness to "go lez" with Liz, when they both attend a wedding without a male date (4x22 "I do do") is another instance reminiscent of the sweeps week trope. On the other hand, Jack's continuing mocking of Liz's clothing style as "lesbian Mario brothers" (5x07 "Brooklyn Without Limits") and Liz's own slip-ups, such as her phonetically suspicious explanation of her newly developed problem-solving philosophy Lizbeanism and her interest in seeing one of Jack's girlfriends (Salma Hayek) naked, supplement the never fully contained "charge of lesbianism."[18]

Besides the change in time line and the sheer number of jokes including lesbian clichés, *30 Rock* furthermore clearly deviates from the trope's established rationale of devaluing representations of lesbians by casting actress Stephanie March as Lemon's blind date Gretchen Thomas, who represents the exact opposite of the unfashionable and unfeminine stereotype Jack uses as a foil for his critiques of Liz Lemon's appearance. Jack's fondness of Gretchen personally and the relaxed manner in which he sets her up on a blind date with Liz speak of a far less prejudiced stance on gayness than his teasing of Liz implies. Furthermore, Liz reacts to the misunderstanding not by being offended, but rather with a matter of fact flashback to previous instances of confusion about her gender representation to which she did not take offense either. Overall, her staff's positive reaction, Liz's comfort with the situation, plus an ending in which the joke (being dumped) is on Liz not Gretchen, make for one of the least offensive and most enjoyable "one-week" lesbian stunts primetime TV has had to offer in recent years—of which there are plenty, as sweeps week lesbians have become a TV trope worthy of discussion even in major publications such as *The New York Times*—in its Critic's Notebook, Virginia Heffernan works through the criteria of a "good sweeps stunt," which include being visually spectacular, inexpensive, controversial, reversible, and concluding that "the lesbian kiss […] hits all four." The Gretchen–Liz storyline reflects on this tiring TV trope. Several characters talk about Liz's date with Gretchen in exactly the terms used in sweeps weeks stunts, assuming that Liz could switch sexualities and do so instantly. In the end, however, she turns the tables on Pete, hoping to expose the offensive assumptions about female sexuality implicated in the trope:

Liz: So what are you saying, Pete, I should just be a lesbian?
Pete: Oh, I'm not saying it would be easy. You know, get drunk first.
Liz: Why do guys think that women can just flip a switch like that? What if I said to you, go be with Frank now?
Pete: Ah, I would be honored. Frank is a very tender, beautiful man.

The dialogue manages to walk the fine line between validating women's sexuality, yet being open to sexual fluidity and queer desires, and still keeping the tone comic, as the camera cuts to Frank—the show's trucker-hat-wearing expert on porn, computer games, and slacker chic—eating shrimp off the floor. More importantly, while Liz's endeavor fails on the intradiegetic level, as Pete is, in fact, open to the idea of a gay male sweeps week stunt, extradiegetically the inversion works. Precisely because of the lack of offense at Liz's suggestion, the audience must confront its own surprise at Pete's bi-curiousness, usually a taboo for male TV characters, and the unusually sexualizing camera position used for Pete's point-of-view shot of his co-worker Frank, which draws attention to the double standard of sweeps week lesbians.

This reversal of media's obsession with women's sexuality is picked up again in a later episode in which Liz starts dating a man 17 years younger than her, *TGS*' coffee boy Jamie (2x07 "Cougars"). Upon meeting the 20-year old, Frank instantly falls for him. One of the other writers, Lutz, whose sexuality remains a puzzle to his co-workers throughout the series and who is usually at the receiving end of "gay jokes," starts teasing him about wanting to kiss Jamie.[19] The joke falls flat, however, as Frank is not the least disturbed or hurt by the implication and instead of trying to defend himself, admits in an uncharacteristically flamboyant manner "maybe I am gay, for that little peach." At the end of the episode, while enjoying his time at a gay bar and despite his openness to the idea of being gay, Frank, however, realizes that he, in his own words, is indeed "just gay for Jamie"—contradicting Liz's earlier statement that "You can't be gay for one person. Unless you are a lady and you meet Ellen [DeGeneres]."

Given the frequent conflation of the character Liz Lemon and the actress Tina Fey, who has "met Ellen," such comments further blur the lines of normative sexuality on *30 Rock*. They thus mirror the effects which sketch elements have in creating a carnivalesque environment on the story level in relation to gender and sexualities, insofar as Rowe defines "transgression and inversion [...], sexual reversals, [...] and the leveling of hierarchies" as central themes of the carnivalesque (*Unruly Woman* 8). Therefore *30 Rock* not only deviates from the sweeps week trope outlined above, but more generally from the sitcom characteristic of "patrol[ing] the borders of gendered behavior" (R. White 355). While *30 Rock* falls in line with what White has described as defining the sitcom, namely "satirizing socially endorsed boundaries" of stereotypical male and female behavior (355), the series refrains from portraying deviance from such sexual norms as dangerous, which usually complements gender satire in sitcoms.

Equally unusual is the show's employment of unresolved sexual tension, another TV trope relating to sexuality, which—as the show points out in the season six finale via Kim Jong Ill's commentary—has been made famous by *Moonlighting* (1985–1989). In *30 Rock* this tension is tellingly not built up between the two straight lead characters Liz and Jack, but rather between Jack and his gay male business nemesis Devin Banks (Will Arnett). Their rivalry is depicted as one of the driving forces behind their respective careers, yet their interactions are marked by lengthy takes of them staring at each other's lips and their exchange of innuendo-laden dialogue:

Devin: If there's one thing I learned from you, Jack... it's keep your friends close. And your enemies so close... that you're almost kissing. (3x01 "Do-Over")

Devin: Jack Donaghy taking welfare? It would kill you.

Jack: But with so many jobs at stake...

Devin: You'd have to take it. I'd make you. I'd make you take it all.

Jack: And I'd roll over and let you give it to me.

Devin: I'm honestly not trying to make this sound gay. (4x02 "Into the Crevasse")

Jack: I will not gay set you up again. So, I'll be very clear. You'll be under me, and if there's one slip-up, your ass is mine.... Damn it. (5x18 "Plan B")

This built-up of sexual tension between characters of the same sex puts the gay couple in the dramatic "Will they, won't they" position, which is not only usually upheld by straight couples, but is often also the central draw of a sitcom, as in the cases of *Moonlighting* or *Who's the Boss?* (1984–1992). In addition to this alignment of a non-central gay couple with the narrative function of central straight couples, the gay flirtation complicates Jack's portrayal of conservatism and further questions his position as the arbiter of correctly gendered behavior which he inhabits towards Liz Lemon.

Other references to gay couples are snuck into the season six finale "What will Happen to the Gang Next Year," in which Jack realizes that Liz has officiated at a lesbian wedding after obtaining the license online and thus could also serve during his "vow renewal ceremony." This introduces a quick—and again heavily cliché reliant—sketch insert of the couple Liz wedded, as one partner sits on a couch while the other yells at her "congrats on turning into your father," when she refuses to go to the Container Store on a Saturday. Through Liz's explanation that "[she] married Becky and Dee, [b]ecause love is love and there is no reason they shouldn't experience the joy of marriage like any other couple," however, the meaning of the sketch changes. By underscoring clichés related to unhappily married (straight) couples, the scene potentially unfolds as an intervention in the current obsession of activists and politicians with gay marriage from a queer perspective of non-conformity which—as the series so often does—questions the value of normality and offers a biting comment on the sanctity of marriage. On a more unambiguously positive note Liz experiences a day dream about her future child (for which she and her boyfriend Criss use the code word, plant) during the same episode, in which she happily raises a gender-ambivalent gay plant kid. Other instances of *30 Rock*'s inclusive approach to gay individuals and couples include the episode "Kidney Now" (3x22), which depicts Liz telling an elderly gay couple "I think you guys are gonna make it" during a talk show appearance, in which she had hitherto announced everyone else's relationship issues to be "dealbreakers" (the most recent and most successful catch phrase from a *TGS* sketch).

Similarly to Anne Gerigk's claim that audiences' perceptions of antifeminist jokes uttered on the character level are "over-ridden" by *30 Rock*'s metareferential framing, the show also gets away with its often politically incorrect references to gay characters and queer sexualities.[20] The sketch-inflected metareferential structure marks such jokes as a commentary on media representations of LGBT people in the USA and on homophobia more generally rather than as expressions of the show's own homophobia. Furthermore, individual comments that could be read as homophobic are balanced—much like Jack's through his personal friendship with and appreciation of Gretchen Thomas and his glee in passing as a "daddy bear, a prize in the gay community" (5x01 "The Fabian Strategy")—against the inclusion of celebratory moments of queerness. *30 Rock*'s is thus established, similarly to earlier quality (and camp) postfeminist texts such as *Ugly Betty*, as a show invested in more than just a middle-class, heteronormative postfeminist sensibility. Even without a gay lead character, *30 Rock* becomes a "queer space" in accordance with Jennifer Reed's definition of the "queer persona" of comics who are not necessarily gay themselves, but whose "body of work over an extended period of time [...] creates a queer public presence" ("Sexual" 767). And while the queer public presence of *30 Rock* can be traced to many more jokes, storylines, and moments than those outlined above, it mainly hinges on its female leads, Liz and Jenna.

Despite the frequent inclusion of LGBT stories, characters, and allusions, which align *30 Rock* with other postfeminist texts characterized by a growing "queer visibility" (Gerhard 42–43), recurring gay male characters are marginal in *30 Rock* compared to their role in *Ugly Betty*, *Sex and the City*, and *Desperate Housewives*. The sidelining of gay male characters as friends and confidantes on the character level extends to a fundamentally different symbolic meaning of male homosexuality compared especially to that in *Sex and the City* and *Desperate Housewives*. In these two series, critics often read the female protagonists as substitutes for gay male characters, "stand-ins" for the out gay creators of the series (see Gerhard 42–43). This characterization of unconventional female characters as "gay men in disguise" limits the spectrum of femininity represented and representable on TV (and other media). *30 Rock* avoids this issue of devaluing its female protagonists as mere ersatz-gays. Rather than relying on male dominated discourses of camp, *30 Rock* instead evokes earlier feminist camp texts such as *Absolutely Fabulous* and *Cybill*, in particular their play with feminine excess and their juxtaposition of fleshed-out female characters, with Liz and Jenna as two complementary sides of the same (camp) coin unfolding their potential to intervene in the postfeminist discourse.

5 "I Want to Go to There!": The Camp Routes of *30 Rock*'s Leading Ladies

Prior to delving into Jenna's and Liz's contrasting strategies, it should be noted that these two are linked by more than comedy dynamics and postfeminist influences, namely their friendship which—despite its unusual presentation—offers an affective component essential to their respective comedic (and critical) functions. Their friendship not only predates the series' premiere episode, but also the beginning of *TGS* and thus any other relationship depicted in *30 Rock*. While it is not presented as centrally (and sentimentally) as it is in other (post)feminist shows, such as *Absolutely Fabulous*, *Cybill* or *Sex and the City*, Liz's and Jenna's friendship is essential to both women's private lives and careers, as they have lived, and more importantly worked, together long before their breakthrough in TV—resulting in nothing less than *The Girlie Show* itself, which despite its depiction in *30 Rock* as low quality has been on national television for five years and is able to sustain an income for three stars, two producers, several writers and a whole crew of make-up artists, camera men, and technicians. The only barely functional, yet somehow still successful *TGS*, which has long verged from its idealistic beginnings can indeed be read as a fitting metaphor for the development of Liz's and Jenna's relationship more generally. Their interactions only bear a fleeting resemblance to more idealistic versions of women's friendship on TV. Nonetheless, the unlikely pairing of diva-esque star and nerdy writer provides them with at least a modicum of emotional support and the occasional reason for much-needed introspection in many of the rather absurd situations they regularly face.

In an episode specifically dedicated to their problematic friendship (6x04 "The Ballad of Kenneth Parcell"), *30 Rock* uses the narrative and stylistic characteristics of the romantic comedy genre to frame how the two find each other again after an initial fallout. Used by Jenna as a diversionary tactic for a PETA attack, Liz sets out to find "someone like her" to befriend instead—which she does at the Barnes & Noble Bookstore, with another introvert named Amy—while Jenna decides to spend her time with other egomaniacal B-celebrities. After walking ten minutes around the block with Amy, berating everything from the state of the American family to Ethiopian food, Liz realizes:

> Oh brother, hanging out with me is awful. Amy, we can't both be the negative, judgmental one [...] you're supposed to be so vacant and self-absorbed that you just let me vent without piling on... I need Jenna!
>
> [Dramatic music sets in during the close-up on Liz's face as she turns to run]

In a sequence parodying the formulaic ending of romantic comedies (much like the fake movie *Martin Luther King Day* Jenna is trying to promote during this episode), Liz and Jenna finally admit their feelings for each other and the failure of their potential friendships with people more like themselves. Upon meeting on the studio floor, they smile at each other, as the first chords of a generic pop-rock song set in to accompany the shot-reverse-shot of their overly expressive faces:

> Jenna: I never should have treated you the way I did, Liz! I need some-
>   one who has so little going on in her life, she lets me get all the
>   attention.
> Liz: And I need someone in my life who doesn't listen to a word I say.
> Jenna: [Touching her hair] Thank you. I just got it cut. [The volume is
>   turned up as the song's lyrics begin]

By contrasting the nonsensical dialogue with the conventional cues of cinematic romance, the scene lays bare the emotionally manipulative devices of romantic comedy. Through this emotionally charged refer-ence—even if it is a parodic one—the scene, however, also foregrounds their relationship and thus highlights *30 Rock*'s engagement with the "primacy of women's friendship" (Thornham 78) that is prevalent in postfeminist texts as much as in feminist sitcoms and its persona of the comic second. More specifically, "The Ballad of Kenneth Parcell" exemplifies the underlining sincerity which characterizes the depiction of Liz's and Jenna's friendship and interactions throughout *30 Rock*, even as the series and its humor revel in its unlikelihood and weirdness: egomania and despondence are, after all, exactly what the two need from each other.[21] This variation on the friendship trope ties in with *30 Rock*'s camp potential, which stems less from the harmonious relationship between the two comic seconds and instead feeds off their construction as different to the point of being polar opposites. The presentation of Liz and Jenna as best friends enhances their effect as oppositional comic seconds by putting their respective points of view and actions on a par and in dialogue with each other.

The doubling of the comic second in the carnivalesque and queered version of a postfeminist environment gives the series the chance to offer dissenting views on the topics discussed and, more importantly, to tackle many of the issues defining postfeminism from the deviant perspectives of both the "too much" and the "too little" (femininity, feminism, self-surveillance, etc.). By presenting not only two contrasting positions, but also presenting them as connected through the emotional bond of the two comic seconds, the series achieves a balance which underscores that there is no right way to approach postfeminism's most salient issues (nor a right way to be a woman). Contributing to this balance is the series' refusal to establish a normative viewpoint in its central character, Liz. Thus, *30 Rock* can make fun of Jenna without devaluing her in contrast to Liz, and vice versa. In this way, Jenna's and Liz's characterizations are used in relation to the postfeminist sensibility to much the same effect as the metareferential aspects of *30* Rock are used to create a distinct connection to TV, while also establishing a distance; they expose the limits of conventional femininity, while they link the absurd arbitrariness of its characteristics and demands to a postfeminist ideology, which is mocked at the same time as its powers are recognized as real.

Consequently, most of Liz's and Jenna's central storylines not only include the main issues affected by postfeminism, but also mirror each other over the course of the series, sometimes within the same episode. Among the themes prominent in both of their storylines are relationships with younger and/or professionally less successful men, concerns

about pregnancies and motherhood, career aspirations and inequality at
the work place, concerns about beauty standards, bodily surveillance and
aging, their respective relation to feminism, as well as—probably most
prominently—their vastly different stances on femininity, female sexuality, and the sexualization of culture.

In some of these matters, such as motherhood, the difference between
Liz and Jenna could not be more apparent. On Liz's part there is a
lengthy adoption storyline (including an unintentional kidnapping,
mistaking a little person for a young boy and subsequently dating him
to cover up that mistake), and the memory loss of an adoption agency
employee (played by Megan Mullally of *Will & Grace*), who has been hit
over the head during a studio tour, as well as later the continued effort
to have a kid with her boyfriend Criss. This endeavor is supported and
even assisted by Jack, who sets Liz up on a blind date with a colleague,
so Liz will meet his pre-teen daughter Kate. Via a quick-witted back and
forth, typical once again of the romantic comedy, Kate instills in Liz the
renewed conviction that she wants children.[22] Jack's reason for his intervention, namely that "your country needs more Liz Lemons" (6x18
"Murphy Brown Lied to Us") is among their kindest and most endearing interactions (even as Jack snubs the US manufacturing industry in
its lead-up), thus establishing this second attempt at motherhood as distinctly different from Liz's baby crazy phase in season three; this time
it is about her connection to children rather than her fuzzy ideas about
biological clocks.

Jenna on the other hand, by default—"she's the show's unhinged id"
after all (Blake)—never gets beyond her crazy phase, which is reflected
in her attitude towards motherhood and children, to whom she refers as
"condom accidents" (6x11 "Standards & Practices"). Bereft of the sentimentality and glamorization which usually accompany pregnancies and
motherhood in postfeminist texts, Jenna's thoughts on the subject are
clearly framed by an economic rationale—reversing the logic of having
it all, where a job gives the woman an opportunity to start a family, to a
baby just being the means to an end concerning the progress of Jenna's
career. Her hysterical pregnancy in "100" (5x20/21), for example, is
caused by her realization that "a baby gets you attention."

> Jenna: I just feel like I'm at a point in my life where I'm starting to have
> this real desire to nurture… my career. I think pregnancy would
> be a great PR move.

Liz: Oh my God you want a baby to help your career?

Jenna: Look, *TGS* may be going away. Being pregnant is a great excuse for why I stopped working instead of the truth: I'm in my 40s, very difficult, and not that good at playing "la réalité."

The pregnancy ends as quickly as it began, however, when Kabletown boss Hank Hooper offers her a job as a talk show host:

Hank: Why couldn't you be a mother and do a daytime talk show?

Jenna: Well, because the talk show would be my baby. I'm not going to be held back by some uterus turd. Let's call my agent.

Similarly, when Jenna's plan to cry on *America's Kidz Got Singin'* is halted by the inebriation of the contestants and she is forced to find other ways to connect with her audiences, she explains to Liz:

Jenna: The whole point of the cry was to humanize me, to change public perception. But what else humanizes a monster? Motherhood!

Liz: Oh God, don't adopt. That child is better off in Somalia. It could be a pirate or a warlord's concubine.

The decisive twist turns out to be that Jenna does not need to adopt, since she has several biological children. Reworking the sperm donor storyline in vogue at the time—see *The Kids Are All Right* (2010, Dir. Lisa Cholodenko), *The Switch* (2010, Dirs. Will Speck and Josh Gordon) or *Starbuck* (2011, Dir. Ken Scott)—with reversed genders and a heightened lack of emotional attachment, Jenna clarifies

Jenna: This is better than adopting. Remember that old money making scheme back in Chicago? [...] I'm talking about when I donated my eggs.

Liz: Hang on, are you saying you have a kid?

Jenna: [sadly] No, I don't. [Turns around and opens the door to her dressing room revealing five almost identical blonde girls, one blonde guy and one brunette girl] I have six kids.

Jessica: [inside the dressing room] Gerome, share the bronzer, you slut!

Liz: Oh God.

Liz's shock is validated by the unfolding story of Jenna's spawn turning the tables on her and using their relation to a TV star to make themselves D-list stars in a reality show from which Jenna is excluded:

Jessica: You're so much older than the rest of us. So, we're thinking the show's more like *The Girls Next Door*, and you're that old boat captain that shows up sometimes.
Jenna: That's Hugh Heffner, Jessica.
Jessica   Yeah, we have no idea who that is, so you're kinda just proving our point.

The perception of playboy bunnies as independent agents serves as a camped up postfeminist empowerment dream come true idea. More importantly, however, the scene realizes Jenna's fears connected to motherhood, which her boyfriend Paul summarizes as "what if we had a child that was prettier than us? We'd have to leave it in a desert" (5x20/21 "100"). When Liz's dream of motherhood finally becomes reality, the result is similarly disillusioned.

After her attempts to conceive fail, Liz and Criss decide to marry to improve their chances of adoption. Diverging from the norm of postfeminist TV texts like *Sex and the City*, their marriage does not conclude the season or the series, nor is the first meeting with their adoptive twins the emotional climax at the show's end. Instead Liz and Criss pick up the two six-year-old siblings from the airport at the end of the penultimate episode, thus leaving room in the final double-episode to explore the issues the couple encounter as recent parents. Even more important, however, is the characterization of the children as younger versions of Liz's "work-children," Jenna and Tracy, through looks, wardrobe, and attitude. Their adoptive son Terry, clad in Tracy's signature red leather jacket, greets his new parents by stating that he will not make it to school the next day due to issues with his lizard (one of Tracy's favorite excuses at work), while their daughter Janet, in a T-shirt that spells DIVA in glitter, reacts to Criss' attempt to take pictures of their first moments together by schooling him on her "good side" and mispronouncing "camerahh" the way Jenna has continuously done. This scenario at first seems to smash her dream of a private life that counterbalances her work life, yet Liz happily and with tears on her eyes states "that seems about right." It is right, in fact, not only for Liz, who can finally start the family she has hoped for for the last four years, but also for the series,

which can give her a happy ending—and thus take her emotional journey seriously—without resorting to formulaic clichés of happiness—and
thereby conforming to conservative values. Rather, the end to her adoption storyline rejects retreatism, but embraces (non-biological and non-
traditional) motherhood. Despite the vastly different outcomes, Liz's
and Jenna's motherhood storylines are closely connected by their shared
absurdity, which distances them from the supposedly empowering—yet
prescriptive—postfeminist frameworks of career woman and retreat-
ing mother respectively. In their shared liminality, their arcs are used to
highlight two distinct aspects of the same issue, and avoid the endorse-
ment of normative solutions. Other postfeminist issues are addressed not
through contrast but through explorations of the grey areas between two
(supposed) extremes, which nonetheless serves *30 Rock*'s intervention in
discourses of normativity, as pinpointing the normal becomes effectively
impossible.

5.1   *Alter Egos, Alternative Voices*

As a show that seldom deals in subtlety, *30 Rock* has equipped both of
its leading comic seconds with pop-cultural alter egos that can be understood as literalizations of their characteristics. Liz's adoration of *Star
Wars'* Princess Leia is alluded to throughout the series and is already
established by season one, where her status as a fan of a science fiction is
depicted as a sort of arrested development in her female sexuality, when
Jenna has to explain to her that attractive men do not enjoy *Star Trek*
references.[23] Liz's agitation (later fittingly coined as nerd rage in 7x03,
"Stride of Pride") about the mix-up of *Star Trek* and *Star Wars* further
aligns her with the increasingly prominent TV trope of the (male) nerd;
the perpetual pre-teen boy who has become the center of attention,
for example, in the hit series *The Big Bang Theory*. As such, Liz as Leia
embodies a different form of the "girling" defined as a characteristic of
postfeminist representations in which "the competent professional adult
woman [...] is made safe by being represented as fundamentally still a
girl" (Tasker and Negra 109), and summarized by Liz Lemon as "society's demand [from women] to infantilize [themselves]" (5x16 "TGS
Hates Women"). As mentioned in connection to the episode "TGS
Hates Women," the appearance of Abby Flynn, the new female cast
member described by Jenna as "being hot and doing baby talk," highlights this issue. The episode thus underscores that the girling effect is

not only to make a powerful woman appear "safe," but is also highlighting her sexual availability. In contrast to this, Liz's nerd allusion represents a decisive twist by "boying" rather than girling her, which includes her repeatedly verbalized disinterest in and uneasiness about sexual relations. The reiteration of the girling trope in this tomboy/nerd version, however, not only ridicules the idea of the "thinking man's (= nerd) sex symbol" applied to both Carrie Fisher (the original Princess Leia) and Tina Fey (the original Liz Lemon so to speak) as a supposedly less degrading version of the objectified female body, but also lampoons the sexualization of a pre-sexual figure.

While Liz's problematizing of girling is based on the gender reversal of this specific trope—a strategy used quite often, as detailed below—Jenna exposes girling's inherent paradox by taking it to its logical extremes. Her reaction to Abby Flynn's baby talk is the insistence that "I invented that! Summer of '98 I took it to a whole new level," which introduces a flashback to Jenna and Liz at a bar surrounded by admiring guys, with Jenna making "Uhhh goo gaa!" baby noises.

The competitiveness apparent in this response is one of Jenna's recurring characteristics and is usually realized as an excessive cattiness towards other women, presented with a high level of consistency in both urgency and form, even in her reactions to comparisons that are hypothetical or negative:

> Frank: You may be the most high-maintenance bitch in Hollywood!
> Jenna: Maybe. Who's more? Who is she? (7x04 "Unwindulax")
> Frank: [to Lutz] Another way to meet damaged women is to hang out with actresses.
> Jenna: Actresses? Where? How young are they? I'll do nudity." (6x06 /07 "Hey Baby, What's Wrong")
> Danny: I can't even imagine you pregnant. A picture of you in US Weekly next to Natalie Portman in the same maternity outfit. "Who Wore It Best?"
> Jenna: I did. I wore it best. (5x20 "100")

One of the most poignant of such comparisons over the course of the series is the "Who Wore It Best" magazine spread, in which Jenna loses to Miss Piggy wearing an identical pink outfit by 84% of readers' votes (3x15 "The Bubble").[24] While 30 Rock has been reviewed as the live-action version of The Muppets more generally (see Chee), Jenna's similarities to Miss Piggy are not only particularly obvious, but also gain special significance in light of Kathleen Rowe's discussion of Miss Piggy as an example of the comedic type of the "unruly woman" and her "potential for feminist appropriation" for which she draws on Mary Russo's analysis of the female grotesque:

> The unruly woman points to new ways of thinking about visibility as power. Masquerade concerns itself not only with a woman's ability to look, after all, but also with her ability to affect the terms on which she is seen. (*Unruly Woman* 11)

Considering Miss Piggy's appeal more specifically, Rowe describes characteristics which are easily applicable to Jenna as well:

> for her, femininity is a masquerade, a costume like any other, which she can relish—or wallow in, if you will—but discard in an instant. Feminine passivity and weakness are artificial ploys, tools to utilize toward her own ends [...] she mobilizes laughter against the posturing and illusoriness of a femininity that encourages such silliness as [...] girlish ways for full-sized, fully grown women. (30)

Jenna's "baby talk as flirtation"-flashback is a striking instance of the latter. More surprisingly maybe, another trait Jenna shares with Miss Piggy is her ability to discard her feminine passivity instantaneously. This comes to the fore most often in her fights with the self-pronounced pranksters, *TGS* writers Frank, Toofer, and Lutz, who repeatedly have to admit defeat in their struggle to out-prank Jenna, whose ruthlessness combined with resourcefulness belie the dumb blonde stereotype she seemingly represents.

In a different context, Jenna's ability to shed her feminine façade is proven in the season five premiere "The Fabian Strategy." Due to thinking ahead farther than any of her partners during the process of negotiating her initial *TGS* contract, which resulted in a clause that guarantees her the status of executive producer after five years, Jenna joins the ranks of Liz and Pete as decisionmakers behind the scenes. Jenna's mastering of a traditionally masculine connoted business savviness is exemplified in her successful contract negotiation and underscored when she turns out to excel at her new duties. Her excellence is based on the very same characteristics that marked her daily confrontation with "non-stars," her "Listen up, fives, a ten is speaking!" attitude (5x19 "I Heart Connecticut"), for which she is usually resented in contexts that highlight her femininity, but earns admiration (especially Pete's) when applied to business interactions. Jenna's unruly woman thus plays on the combination of incongruous gendered character traits with an excessively gendered behavior she can discard at will, to ridicule not her femininity but its supposed limitations.

5.2   Fetishes

The relation between camp and the unruly woman is equally evident in Jenna's sexuality and her seemingly insatiable sexual appetite, which ties her not only to Miss Piggy, but also to the comic second's tradition of the loose woman. Roof describes her as a transformation of the middle character's excess "into fool or quasifool characters," which can easily be incorporated into Hollywood (and one might add, network TV) verisimilitude (17). Jennifer Reed further clarifies that female comedians were often "reduced to a battle of the sexes" in their material, yet the "most important feminist cultural work done by massmediated women comedians of the last generation has been a result of their subversions of heteronormativity" ("Sexual" 762, 764).

While Liz's and Jenna's handling of sex and sexuality is very different, both offer subversions of heteronormativity. The mirroring of their sex lives creates a larger whole, which is among contemporary network TV's kinkiest and most playful engagement with female sexual needs (cable and streaming, obviously, offer different pleasures). Its combined effect is exactly the dethroning of the normal essential to camp. Whereas Jenna's numerous past relationships, one-night stands, and other sexual escapades—most often with other D- to B-list celebrities[25]—are the basis for several throwaway lines, in Liz's case the lack of a sex life, indicated early by her nerd status, is a continuous source of mocking, particularly by Jenna and Jack. Engaging either too much or too little in postfeminism's obsession with female sexuality, Jenna and Liz nonetheless emerge sexually triumphant in the end (albeit in very idiosyncratic definitions of triumphant).

A significant episode that highlights their differing women's approach to their own and other's sexuality is "Leap Day" (6x09), in which Jenna challenges Liz to a "slut off" for the attention of a billionaire, who used to have a crush on Liz (or rather "the Young Nazi Boy in the unlicensed version of *The Sound of Music*" Liz played in a school production). In a reversal-cum-exaggeration, Jenna inverts the stereotypical "yawning and putting arm around shoulders" move into "yawning and hugging a billionaire with her leg," thereby transforming a traditional sign of masculine assertiveness in male dating behavior into a satire of social norms of courting by conflating this trope with the promiscuous gold digger. To add to the absurdity of the scene, Liz reacts by performing parts of her school theater act (once again aligning herself with the pre-pubescent boy rather than girl). While Liz's gender-bending musical act wins over Jenna's display of adult sexuality (one with the added twist of usurping a male position of power), Jenna warns Liz against "Models waking up from their coke binges, multi-ethnic bartenders with daddy issues, former ballerinas who had to quit because their boobs got too big. Click, click. That's their stilettos." Despite Jenna's allusions to models' drug addiction and supposed sluttiness (which, however, never make her belittle the threat posed by these women), the scene does not play out to support Liz's feeling of superiority. Her assumption that models could never be as quick-witted as her is quickly falsified, when Liz gets "burned" by supermodel Karolina Kurkova and subsequently admits defeat on the gold digger front.

Such direct opposition in sexual matters between the friends is rare. Instead their interaction—at least concerning their final relationships in the series—is informed by mutual respect. Looking more closely at their respective storylines, especially as they are progressing in later seasons (roughly four to seven), additionally reveals how *30 Rock* equips its female protagonists with far more complexity than a simple opposition between ferocious sexual appetite and awkward rejection of physical intimacy. The most important relationships in this regard are Jenna's relationship with "gender dysmorphic bi-genitalia pansexual" Paul (Will Forte), the female impersonator she met at a "Jenna Maroney impersonator contest, at which [she] came in fourth" (4x19 "Argus"), and Liz's commitment to Criss (James Marsden), owner of a hot-dog van named after *Dawson's Creek* star James van der Beek. Both underscore how *30 Rock*'s treatment of gender "deviants" differs from the sitcom tradition of regulating genders after moments of transgression.

30 Rock shows its deviation from sitcom rules in favor of sketch-inspired openness to gender parody, drag, and sexual playfulness, when Liz and Pete, and with them the audience, are first introduced to Paul (4x19 "Argus"). According to Marjorie Garber's study on cross-dressing and cultural anxiety in film, cross-dressing protagonists usually "embrace transvestism unwillingly, as an instrumental strategy rather than an erotic pleasure and play space" (70). While there is a financial necessity implied in Paul's work at a drag-themed restaurant, the focus on his cross-dressing lies in its impact on his relationship with Jenna, since both are depicted as deriving (sexual) pleasure from Paul's female impersonation, and from role play more generally. Through role play Jenna can additionally contest the notion that men "masquerading as female [...] provide more fertile ground" for comedy (King 141), as her uber-masculine interpretations of male characters highlight the "marking" of specific types of contemporary masculinity vis-à-vis maleness as a supposedly "unmarked norm" (141).

In sharp contrast to other sitcoms, the audience is not asked to identify with the Liz's initial discomfort with the revelation that Jenna is dating one of her impersonators. Rather, Liz gets called out for her "judgmental badger face." Moreover, the episode's narrative framing emphasizes the relative normalcy of Jenna's relationship. The episode's B-plot consists of Jack talking to a peacock he thinks is his reincarnated boss and which is trying to mate with Liz, and it culminates in the following encounter at the studio buffet:

Liz: Jack. I just found out that Jenna is dating a guy who does a drag show. As her.
Jack: Lemon, what is with this food layout? Kenneth says he needs some sumac bark and shrub yellow root to make a poultice for Argus.
Liz: How is your thing weirder than mine?

Not only is Jack's thing weirder, Liz's thing turns out to not be weird at all, as over the course of the remaining series Jenna and Paul are depicted as the most stable relationship—even as they do not try to assimilate to gain (audience) acceptance. Instead, the storylines of Paul and Jenna question the logic of the normal, thereby fulfilling camp's most important cultural work. In this endeavor, *30 Rock* supports the couple by surrounding them with more traditional relationships which either fall apart or reveal their queerer side over time, such as Jack's assessment of his warped marriage to Avery Jessup (Elizabeth Banks) that "playing psycho-sexual mind games is our normal" (6x21 "The Return of Avery Jessup").

Returning to the scene of Jenna and Paul's outing, it should be noted that while the scene remains comic in tone overall and the make-up is designed to underline the artifice of Paul's appearance—even considering how natural a drag act based on the impersonation of a biological women who herself is heavily influenced by drag impersonations of divas could ultimately be—the content picks up one of the serious threads of *30 Rock*, the dethronement of Liz as the arbiter of good (feminism). The series repeatedly rejects any claim to superiority by Liz's a-political white postfeminism as opposed to either Jenna's and Cerie's anti- or retro-feminist use of their femininity and conventional attractiveness, or the more radical approaches implied mostly by Liz's alignment with other feminist traditions, either through music or TV.[26] When Jenna calls Liz out for her "judgmental badger face" and asks her to "be a friend," the circumstances might once again seem absurd, the sentiment, however, is heartfelt and Liz comes around to support her friend. Approaching Paul in drag after initially mistaking him for Jenna, Liz starts to apologize to her best friend, yet quickly changes strategies to investigate Paul's ulterior motives. As he convinces her that he "would never tuck his penis again, if Jenna asks him to," Liz encourages the approaching Jenna: "This situation is empirically weird. But I'm glad you're happy." As Paul and Jenna kiss, "the visual image presenting two women locked in an embrace,"[27] Liz's trademark discomfort with public displays of affection gets the upper hand—she blurts out "Ew, Jenna, why are you grabbing his boobs?"—but tellingly this is not the last word. Rather, after the credits the audience is treated to a duet by Paul and Jenna singing "All by Myself," with Tracy as their single audience enthusiastically stating, "This is awesome," thereby condoning their shared relationship and individual diva personalities.

This focus on Jenna and Paul as an "empirically weird," but happy couple is not limited to the beginning of their relationship and special (sweeps week) episodes, but is picked up regularly over the following three seasons and continues to be central to their affective, rather than only comic, contribution to the series. Paul and Jenna are repeatedly used to defamiliarize the normal, in three cases quite literally so. This destabilizing quality stems as much from their weirdness as individuals as it results from being taking seriously (by fellow characters and the series overall) as a couple. In "Chain Reaction of Mental Anguish" (5x09), for example, Paul confronts Jenna "Why can't we just paint each other's toenails, watch vintage pornography, and then go to bed in our swing like a *normal* couple?" Paul and Jenna's claim to normalcy here—combined with the obvious rejection of what the majority perceives as normal—is one important factor in *30 Rock*'s continued effort to question value judgments. In the same episode, and also centered around the struggle between Paul's definition of moving forward in their relationship as introducing Jenna to his parents from the suburbs versus Jenna's suggestion of shooting a sex tape (reversing the trope of the commitment-phobic man), Jenna's highly ironic phrasing of her complaint to Liz is telling in its parodying of postfeminism's obsession with marriage and its upholding of traditional gender roles despite (or because) of an obvious change in the lived reality of most couples:

> Jenna: I'm the one trying to make this relationship work. Which is why I'm going to have to be the one to propose the sex tape. Call me old fashioned but I think that's the man's job.

After a temporary break-up (and a celebrity breakdown to win Paul back) the couple once again must confront the notion of normal gender roles and relationships, when Jenna is to become "the new celebrity face of wool" in the season five finale "Respawn" (5x23). While she charms the Wool Council (comprising among others of a sheep) with a song about the many uses of sheep products, their director is concerned about whether Jenna is the right person to reflect wool's wholesome image. He points to an article titled "Hooray for Hollyweird?" accompanied by a photo of Jenna walking Paul like a dog, and reminds Jenna that her "contract includes a morality clause [… which requires her] to conduct [her] personal life in a manner which is consistent with the values of this industry." Jenna, convinced that her relationship with Paul is "everything that wool is about. Love, warmth, chafed skin," hosts a dinner party at her place, during which Wool Council Director Eugene, and his wife U. Jean, will have the opportunity to meet Paul. Using clichés of gendered behavior to connect their relationship to other TV couples, while at the same time underscoring and celebrating its unconventionality, the dialogue between the hosting "wife" Jenna and her reluctant "husband" Paul and the subsequent dinner comprise a tour de force of exaggerating the average beyond recognition.

Paul: So, what, we can't be ourselves?
Jenna: Just not in public. We can do whatever we want here. Except
        tonight. Mr. Gremby is coming over for dinner.
Paul: Eugene Gremby from the Wool Council? Tonight?
Jenna: I just want him to meet you and see us together. Then he'll get it.
        He'll understand what we have. But, the Gremby's are pretty con-
        servative. Maybe you should change.
Paul: Really? This is a conservative top, Jenna. And I hate to be the
        stereotypical man, but this is my home and I want to wear this
        blouse.

During dinner, with Paul in male drag "passing" as a conservative straight man, the party is interrupted by a "sitter," a little person in fairytale dwarf clothes Paul and Jenna usually have over to sit on them as foreplay, whom Paul pretends not to know, and throws out claiming, "We are good people who have no interest in being sat on. [...] We're normal! And being normal is American and it's respectable and it makes us... happy." The obvious hypocrisy is rewarded with a contract for Jenna. The next day at the photo shoot, however, Jenna for once puts honesty before her economic interest and need for attention. As Eugene approaches the couple dressed in conservative clothes to welcome them into the "Wool Family," Paul and Jenna turn around to reveal their matching drag outfits: him in a blonde wig and a woolen dress; her with a fake beard in a wool turtleneck. In front of a stunned Eugene, Jenna finally takes a stance saying: "You want us to be normal? Well this is our normal!" before Paul passionately bites her beard. With appropriations such as these, Paul and Jenna's relationship becomes a camp commentary upon family values and traditional gender roles, changing "the 'natural' and 'normal' into style and artifice" (Bronski 42–3). Their camp intervention into restrictive norms of gendered behavior and heterosexual relationships works so effectively because they do not mock the underlying sentiment of love— Jenna is, after all, putting somebody else's feelings before her economic interest for once—while they expose the performative and deceptive nature of the normal. At the same time, the scene indicates, through the beard-biting, another way in which *30 Rock* turns the normal—in keeping with postfeminism's penchant for sexualization—into a special kind of stylized artifice, namely the epitome of liminal pleasures, the sexual fetish.

For Jenna, this occurs during "The Tuxedo Begins" (6x08), when Paul returns from a drag cruise to find Jenna on the bed in a negligee, waiting for "all the Thai STDs [his] penis is gonna give [her]," and instead of "unpacking... the sex monkey [he] bought in Jakarta" he falls asleep. The next morning both wake up alarmed with the "what happened last night" typical of TV depictions of a one-night stand. Realizing in panic that they slept together (and nothing else), Paul wonders "Did we mix up our days and accidentally both roofie each other?" Refusing to believe that they are just like any normal couple without hating it, Jenna finally suggests: "It's a whole new fetish called 'normalling'." Over the course of the episode, they take their new fetish to its extremes, such as:

Jenna: I just had the sickest idea: to go out as a couple to *Bed, Bath and Beyond*, and shop for home necessities in front of everybody.
Paul: [surprised, but also aroused] Normalling in public?

The sad truth of his reaction to Jenna's suggestion of acting like a regular couple is, of course, that for most non-straight couples even such a regular activity as shopping for their shared home together can be as alienating to others as if they were practicing their fetish in public. More importantly, however, Paul and Jenna's copying of regular couples in this manner—as one review fittingly put it, "It's so regular, it's perverse!" (Abramovitch)—illustrates Judith Butler's claim that the "loss of the sense of 'the normal' [...] can be its own occasion for laughter" (*Gender* 138–9).

Another such occasion occurs in *30 Rock*'s final season, when Liz's sex life is overhauled by appropriating the normal for presumably unintended objectives. Criss and Liz decide to have a child together and, despite Liz's aforementioned reluctance towards all things sexual, to have it themselves rather than adopt. To spice things up, Criss writes love songs for Liz and surprises her at work. This kind of spontaneity is brought to an abrupt halt, however, when Criss enthusiastically clears Liz's office desk to have sex there, and Liz—instead of appreciating this supposedly passionate gesture—panics because "there was a system!" Once again Liz's love of rules is underlined, the first characteristic of hers established in the series, when she calls out the guy who cuts the hot-dog line. Yet, against all clichés it is precisely this compulsivity that, instead of ruining Liz's sexual pleasure, dramatically improves it. The success of her show during the presidential campaign and its subsequent upgrade from weekly to daily, combined with the need to consider her cycle to maximize her chances to conceive, force Liz to schedule sex with Criss based on an intricate color-coded system. Putting together this chart, Liz almost climaxes just from thinking about all the planning that will go into it and barely makes it home to Criss, where she announces that what "was missing from my sex life was organization!"—thereby also contradicting Jack's patronizing assessment of her, and "New York Third-Wave Feminists" generally, when he described her in the pilot as "over-scheduled, under-sexed" (1x01). Liz realizes that scheduling and office supplies, exactly those things that supposedly kill not only the postfeminist women's libido, but also her relationship (putting her job before her man, the refusal of retreatism), are her major turn-ons—illustrated in a soft-porn montage of Liz and Criss experimenting at a Staples, where they perform a parody of the famous clay sequence from *Ghost* (1990, Dir. Jerry Zucker), as well as several re-enactments of "sexy" themes, such as pouring things (paper clips instead of milk, whiteout instead of wax) over each other. The episode complements Jenna's and Paul's storyline of making the normal a kinky turn-on and thus decidedly less normal.

The montage at Staples serves another purpose. It reminds audiences of the reversal of traditional gender roles in Liz's relationships by depicting Criss as the receiving partner and thus tying in with other allusions to sexual role play that feature Liz in the male position of power. A prominent example is the dialogue that occurs between Criss and Liz when he renovates her apartment's upper level, which quickly turns into a gay porn re-enactment:

Liz: I'm Brent. I'm the new guy in the crew.
Criss: I'm Rod. I'm the boss and what I say, goes... I've never been with
         a man before.
Liz: Looks like I'm the boss now.

As with Jenna's leg hug the scene's humor depends on its conflation of expected male and female behavior. The re-enactment of this specific kind of porn can further be understood as an ironic participation in the postfeminist "porno-ization" of culture, which thrives on presenting sexual fantasies that celebrate the powerlessness of women by either victimizing them, fetishizing their lower social status in nurse and maid outfits, or showing them in primarily passive positions and scenarios. Contrary to such glorifications of female objectification, Liz's re-enactment of gay porn is presented as the more egalitarian approach to gender equality (in the bedroom) for a straight couple, once again begging the question of who imitates whom, and which "original" can lay claim to being regular and natural. On the other hand, one might argue that Liz as a comic second can "do 'unfeminine' things in unfeminine ways because [she isn't] presented as sufficiently womanly" (Roof 13). While this might partially account for the freedom Liz's character is allowed, *30 Rock* deviates from this stereotype, as the quote further reads "among men, they are reluctantly maternal or aunt-like crosses between buddies and moms who are definitely out of the mating game." This is precisely not true for Liz, whose successful participation in the mating game happens not despite, but because of her willingness to embrace her less conventional traits and dreams. Her sex life—a major aspect of postfeminist media—is representative not of neo-traditional ideologies, but rather of "taking queer pleasure in perceiving if not causing category dissonance [...] in representations of heterosexual normality," which Cohan describes as camp's affect (*Incongruous* 18), and which in significant aspects mirrors Jenna's function and appeal in *30 Rock*.

5.3   Food

Another excessive appetite that characterizes the unruly woman—like Jenna's figurative sexual appetite—is also noteworthy in outlining how *30 Rock* critically engages with postfeminist myths and demands, a craving for junk food. Beside the sexualization of culture, the disciplined female body is among the chief features of the postfeminist sensibility. This self-surveillance comes to the fore in a stress on exercise routines—which ties in neatly with the makeover trend—and the treatment of food. In postfeminist contexts eating is presented in many clichéd forms: the stress eating of the professional woman; the giant ice-cream box to get over a heartbreak; or the elaborate dinner at a date. Food, however, is equally marked by its curious absence from those day-to-day routines that do not fall under these cliché categories. While cooking shows make up a sizable portion of reality TV programming, fictional series such as *Sex and the City* are characterized much more by what their protagonists do not eat than by what they do eat. Yet (bodily) discipline is not only connected to quantity, but also to quality. In her assessment of postfeminist culture, *What a Girl Wants*, Diane Negra stresses how "the well-kept body" as an index "of achieved adult femininity in America" (118) is inherently connected to "luxury consumerism" (125), thus once again inscribing neoliberalism into the postfeminist discourse. (Luxury) food, furthermore, becomes not only a marker of femininity, but also of class, as Negra points out. It takes time, money, and skill to prepare food that is not the "non-nutritious and low-status processed foods" associated with the working class (134).

30 Rock reflects on the constant surveillance of the female body and chastisement of women for being too thin, too big, or in any other way non-conforming, through the recurring commentary on Liz and Jenna's bodies by themselves, as well as by Jack and other (male) characters. Importantly, however, this obsession is lampooned as the two comic seconds illustrate the issue by embodying the uber-feminine "too much" and the unfeminine "too little." The connection to Miss Piggy's tradition of the unruly woman is in this case not represented in Jenna—whose relation to food is nonetheless noteworthy—but in Liz, whose obsession with unhealthy food is a recurring motif throughout all the seasons. From Liz's very first appearance in line at a hot-dog vendor to the very last episode, in which she is cheered on by her fellow writers as she prepares a "cupcake sandwich," Liz is repeatedly indulging in highly processed food. By thus refusing constant bodily surveillance, she follows Miss Piggy's example of giving up women's magazines' "deferred gratification in favor of the pleasure principle" (Rowe, *Unruly Woman* 29). Food thus becomes one of the markers of Liz's personality, which underscores her excess—albeit not traditionally feminine—rather than Jenna's, and one activity which links her to the aesthetics and logic of sketch comedy more than sitcom.

While Liz seems to agree with Jack's early observation that she buys "any magazine that says 'healthy body image' on the cover" (1x01 "Pilot"), her actions throughout the series do not imply that she has body image issues. Liz repeatedly comments on her lack of athletic ambition and discipline, for example with "Why are my arms so weak? It's like I did that pushup last year for nothing!" (7x06 "Aunt Phatso vs. Jack Donaghy"). Yet, when it comes to showing her—supposedly untrained and thus unattractive—body in public, she is immensely self-confident, whether it is ripping her shirt open to dance at a GE event or oiling her stomach at a fake-pregnancy photo shoot (3x09 "Retreat to Move Forward" and 5x13 "¡Qué Sorpresa!" respectively). Reversing the trope of women who console themselves with comfort food when they cannot have sex, Liz often prefers food over sex or seems to be at least equally passionate about food. In "The Ones" (3x19), for example, Jack comes to Liz's place late at night to seek relationship advice. Rather than interrupting a date, he finds her on the couch enjoying a plate of cheese, and serenading said cheese with her cover of Bob Seger's 1976 sex-themed single "Night Moves" by singing "working on my night cheese."

Yet serenades of sexy love songs are not the most outrageous things Liz does for and with food. In her discussion of Miss Piggy's character in *The Kermit and Piggy Story* (1985, Dir. Peter Harris), Kathleen Rowe draws attention to the depiction of her romantic dinner with Kermit, which serves to underline the differences between the two characters and Miss Piggy's insistence on self-gratification. While he slowly eats a salad, Miss Piggy's meal consists of a giant serving of spaghetti and meatballs, which gets smaller every time the camera returns to it, either from a flashback or a shot of Kermit (*Unruly Woman* 29). In an exaggerated version of this appetite-stressing scene, Jack invites Liz to his office to watch her eat a steak in front of him since his recent heart attack forces him to abstain from red meat. The scene (especially through Jack's voice) suggests an erotic component to the "shared" meal:

Jack: I would like you to eat it here. Right now.
Liz: You want to watch me eat this steak in front of you?
Jack: That's what I want.

Liz's excitement over the "$54 steak" quickly breaks the spell and she simply responds to Jack's highly suggestive tone with "OK," before she enthusiastically sits down to eat it. While Jack tells her about his hopes for the current CEO's retirement, because he read an interview in a magazine, Liz is seen eating in the background and half-heartedly following the conversation. When Jack after only a few sentences turns around, he is visibly stunned and exclaims "You ate the whole thing." Liz simply shrugs (2x02 "Jack gets in the Game"). The relatively short scene highlights the conflation of eating and sex by hinting at Jack's sexual excitement over watching Liz, while the same connection is reversed for her, as Liz once again puts food on a higher rank when she refuses to acknowledge the erotic element. Their interaction furthermore turns the tables on sitcom's usual gender relations concerning the preparation of food, where the male protagonist quickly finishes his meal, while his wife/girlfriend, who cooked for him, tells him about some magazine article she read. The scene is one of many which underscores not only Liz's love for food, but also exaggerates her eating habits beyond the sitcom's verisimilitude. In another such instance Jack and Pete want to watch Liz "shotgun a beer"—their excitement again drawing attention to the sexualized relationship between women and food/drinks. Liz instead opts for "shotgunning" the pizza. Pete's voice-over scream after the cut to the credits, "Nooo, she's unhinging her jaw!," emphasizes the grotesqueness of the scene, but cannot deny the joy in Liz's face that reflects the genuine, Miss Piggy-like glee Liz takes in her self-gratification rather than satisfying Pete's and Jack's voyeurism (5x08 "College").

Beyond the introduction of this larger theme, the scene in "Jack gets in the Game" also sets the tone for an episode specifically dedicated to (unhealthy) food and "America's body image madness," as Liz calls it. The episode, however, does not focus on Liz's issues, such as her ham-grease stained wedding dress, but the parallels between Jack's heart-attack induced foray into healthy living and Jenna's parallel experimentation with extreme weight-loss options, including bone shaving and organ reduction. Starring in a Broadway musical named *Mystique Pizza* between *TGS* seasons, Jenna gained several pounds from eating numerous slices of pizza during the daily performances (twice on Sunday) and struggles with her new (body) image. While Jack puts pressure on her to lose weight so she can be the show's star again, his storyline is similarly constructed around his need to appear healthy despite his heart attack to keep his chances of becoming GE's CEO in the face of younger competition. For Jack this means watching other people (women) eat his favorite food, while Jenna resorts to the Japanese Porn-Star Diet—explained as "I only eat paper, *but* I can eat all the paper I want, so ..."

Jenna's experimentation with several extreme forms of dieting and medical procedures to reduce her weight produces a stark contrast to Liz's acceptance of her own body, yet mirror the widespread cultural obsession with bodies that exhibit "slenderness, youthfulness, and extreme sexualization, packaged and positioned as entirely available for consumption by the male gaze" (Shugart and Waggoner, "A Bit Much" 76). Jenna's exaggerated reaction to being temporarily overweight thus illuminates "America's body image madness" Liz had previously decried. Jenna only overcomes her anxieties, when she falls on stage during a rollerblade sketch, ripping down the curtain, and—to relieve the tension in the studio and cover up her mistake—uses the catchphrase suggested by Frank, yet rejected by Liz for being demeaning: "Me Want Food."

Jenna's use of that phrase oscillates between humiliation and self-determination. The audience reacts with uproarious laughter, and Jenna realizes that being overweight gets her attention, her own T-Shirt at the NBC merchandise store, and new job opportunities. She subsequently embraces her weight, gets complimented on her looks by Jack, and lands an exclusive contract with Enorme, "the number one fragrance for plus-sized women" (2x03 "The Collection"). The TV ad for Enorme, a 15-second black and white sequence of Jenna being caressed by a young man in a room full of blowing curtains while she whispers "Make him chase the junk," spoofs endlessly repetitive perfume commercials. It furthermore critiques the plus-size craze as Liz interjects, "Can't plus-sized women wear regular perfume?" Jenna's newfound happiness, unfortunately, breaks her overeating habit and causes an unwelcome weight loss, which she fights as fervently (with the help of Kenneth and his experiences in fattening pigs) as she had initially fought the weight gain. Her concern, once again, lies neither with her own health or comfort, but solely with commodified product her body as a : "Everything is based on the fat! Enorme, the offer to play Ms. Pac Man in the live action Atari movie." Jenna's body thus becomes an example of how femininity is essentially constructed as masochism (Williamson 61) and how women's bodies are constructed for consumption.

In contrast, Liz's body is clearly meant to consume. She overturns the writer's table when her Mac'n Cheese has disappeared (5x20 "1001"), threatens to "cut up Kenneth's face so bad he'll have a chin" when her sandwich is stolen, and eats a caramel sundae on her treadmill (2x14 "Sandwich Day"). These scenes are placed like short sketches within the overall narrative, which makes them easily recyclable within the series itself—as when characters reminisce about the past—but also outside the series, as numerous fan-created videos dedicated to Liz's eating habits demonstrate. Liz's eating on a treadmill furthermore evokes Miss Piggy's 1980s aerobic video "Snackcercise," in which she advises women to snack their way to an attractive figure. Once again, Miss Piggy—and with her Liz Lemon—favors the "pleasure principle" (Rowe, *Unruly Woman* 29). Liz's unapologetic love of food adds to her comic second's queer persona, as her femininity is downplayed by her rejection of the masochism outlined by Jenna. Food even becomes a dating issue, when Liz does not react to a typical pick-up line ("Can I buy you a drink?") in a bar. She wonders instead whether the guy would also buy her mozzarella sticks (1x08 "The Break-Up"). On another occasion, she ends a rendezvous because her date admits to not really caring about food (1x16 "The Source Awards"), and later considers a relationship with anti-boyfriend Dennis Duffy solely because he cooks chili for her on a regular basis (5x20 "100"). The hierarchical inversion between food and romance further distances her from the postfeminist sensibility.

Both bodies and their relation to food are depicted as extreme, extreme enough at least to question their claim to normative femininity, which for both women is questionable to begin with.[28] Especially for Jenna femininity is intrinsically connected to the mediated femininity of contemporary celebrities. She is constructed as the entertainment industry's "id" and represents everything female celebrities can "do wrong" starting with, but not limited to, weight fluctuations. The status and treatment of actresses and starlets is essential to *30 Rock*'s large-scale interrogation of the entertainment industry. The female celebrity furthermore marks the cornerstone of postfeminism, as she is exemplary of a femininity constructed around the aim to please and therefore central to *30 Rock*'s construction and disruption of femininities.

5.4   Femininities

Jenna's character is acutely reflective of "the gender-based representational incongruities" Holmes and Negra discuss in their introduction to "Going Cheap? Female Celebrity in Reality, Tabloid and Scandal Genres." From her white trash background, to her allusions to sex tapes, mental breakdowns, her bitchiness towards other (attractive) women, the constant threat of her demise, and to the pleasure her co-workers and herself take in her failures, Jenna is constructed as the epitome of everything expected from contemporary female, not-quite A-list, stars, including sexual and bodily excess. In agreement with Holmes' and Negra' observations, the male counterpart in *30 Rock*, Tracy Jordan, is not ridiculed in the same way for his social transgressions (many of them drug-related), but rather pitied and helped. He, at least initially, also makes considerably more money despite Jenna's unquestionably higher degree of professionalism. Though Jenna is generally not depicted as invested in feminist issues, she complains about the double standard:

Jenna: There is no way I'm working with that guy. Do you know that he once got arrested for walking naked through La Guardia?
Liz: Yeah.

Jenna:	And that he once fell asleep on Ted Danson's roof?
Liz:	Yeah. Tracy has mental health issues.
Jenna:	He bit Dakota Fanning on the face!
Liz:	When you hear his version, she was kind of asking for it. (1x01 "Pilot")

Liz's remark highlights the absurdity of victim blaming, which trivializes male celebrities' offenses. *30 Rock* further problematizes both Tracy's behavior and Liz's reaction to it shortly after in "Jack-Tor" (1x05), when Liz falsely assumes that Tracy's refusal to read his cue cards is a result of his illiteracy rather than his airs and graces. She is called out for her patronizing attitude, a theme repeatedly picked up as *30 Rock* continues to place Liz in storylines that reveal her latent racism.[29] Over time, the series furthermore rewards Jenna with increasing success. While she never crosses over into "respectable" engagements, her film stints become more frequent, and in season six, thanks to her appearance as a judge on *America's Kidz Got Singing*, Jenna becomes, as she herself puts it enthusiastically, "officially a B-list celebrity" (6x02 "Idiots Are People Two"). This professional rise mirrors her private happiness with Paul. At this point, Jenna's story deviates from the "female stars 'in crisis'" story. Holmes and Negra argue that the "reason why stories of professionally accomplished/personally troubled female celebrities circulate so actively is that when women struggle or fail, their actions are seen to constitute 'proof' that for women the 'work/life balance' is really an impossible one." Jenna's diversion then proves the opposite and additionally elevates Jenna to a level of superiority at which mocking some of the outrageous aspects of her personality becomes enjoyable, even for audiences who sympathize with her. Rather than distancing viewers from her character, her excessive embrace of the demeaning trope of the "out of bounds" female celebrity, to use Tasker's and Negra's term, becomes her redeeming quality. As Rabinovitz argues, in "a sitcom, characters are only as attractive as their capacity for generating humor" (159), a sentiment reflected in reviews that contest audiences "never want a character like Jenna to become someone entirely human, only a more interesting cartoon" (Blake).

Part of her cartoonish quality is formed by her white trash background that—like Liz's eating habits—relates proper femininity to class. In fact, her white trash mother's obsession with beauty pageants and negligence towards her daughter due to her various affairs is presented as the root of Jenna's craving for attention. The need to be in the spotlight at all costs is illustrated by Jenna's willingness to participate in publicity stunts, no matter how degrading. When Jack asks her to do publicity for her unlicensed Janis Joplin biopic, she eagerly responds "Do you need a sex tape released?'Cause I got a weird one" (3x18 "Jackie Jormp-Jomp"). Similarly, in season one, she participates in a photo shoot in which she is seen making out with a rubber chicken (1x15 "Hard Ball"). The connection between her lower-class background and apparent lack of self-esteem, however, is qualified two seasons later. The *TGS* sketch "That's a Dealbreaker" becomes so successful that *Time Out New York* wants to feature Jenna on the cover. Liz complains about not receiving enough credit for writing that sketch and insists on joining the photo shoot. Throughout the session, Jenna gives Liz salient advice, including how to purse her lips suggestively and to never catch the ridiculous props thrown at them. After Jenna leaves, however, Liz succumbs to her own desire for fame. The final product shows middle-class college-educated Liz, with Groucho Marx glasses and a rubber chicken on a toilet. After she feigns shock at the outcome in the presence of her co-workers, a close-up reveals that Liz is giddy with joy (3x21 "Mamma Mia").

Despite moments like these, which portray Jenna in an unusually mature manner and relate her to other female characters on the show, *30 Rock* in general revels in her character's excessiveness to lay bare the postfeminist paradigms she adheres to. She regularly gives Liz relationship advice that is an absurdly twisted version of something which might appear in a women's magazine or has been said in a romantic comedy. Her bon mots include such questionable information as "Love is wearing make-up to bed and going downstairs to the Burger King to poop" (2x12 "Subway Hero") or her Woody Allen-inspired explanation that "relationships are like sharks, Liz. If you're not left with several bite marks after intercourse, then something's wrong" (5x09 "Chain Reaction of Mental Anguish").[30] The quotes illustrate how Jenna is characterized by being "too much," in this case too much of a postfeminist woman, as her entire persona functions to take some of postfeminism's stable features to their extreme or literalizing them to the point of absurdity. Jenna regularly talks about how she is going to "use her sexuality" to get her way. Her costumes for her appearances on *TGS* are either very revealing, portraying female stereotypes like "the cat lady," or completely ridiculous, as when in season five's live episode, she threatens to have a wardrobe malfunction, "to slip a nip" as she puts it, pointing at her cleavage with her character's alien monster claw.

Jenna's feminine excess reflects the excessive style of the series overall and expands from her character to the visual representation of some of her scenes, for example the incorporation of horror film music into the score, when Jenna observes Kenneth eating poisoned food (3x19 "The Ones"). This adds to *30 Rock*'s metacritical impetus insofar as "excess provides a [...] a fresh and slightly defamiliarized perspective" (Sconce 551). By embracing the artificiality of her femininity, Jenna quite literally makes a spectacle of herself—the kind of spectacle Shugart and Waggoner discuss as "entail[ing] an appropriation of the constraining conventions [...] to the end of establishing margins of resistance" ("A Bit Much" 66). They argue that such spectacles distinguish themselves from spectacular femininity more generally, which is introduced into mainstream media for voyeuristic pleasure "by a particular configuration of qualities—namely, parodic excess and juxtaposition—that foster a distinctively ironic and critical apprehension of their performances" (66). Jenna's gay entourage, her Miss Piggy references, and finally her relationship with female impersonator Paul all emphasize that her gender representation corresponds to Judith Halberstam's definition of "the spectacle of exaggerated femininity" (239) which creates a camp effect because it is based not on the female gender but the appropriation of markers of femininity by drag queens, and in Jenna's case, cartoon characters. Through Jenna's embodiment of parodic excess and often contradictory characteristics, which summarizes her camp appeal, *30 Rock* employs her character to make visible the show's own reliance on the same structures and stereotypes it critically points out. In Jenna's case, most prominently: neoliberal ideas about choice; empowered sexuality; her constant rivalry with other women (as long as they're equally pretty at least); her obsession with both beauty and raunch culture.

A crucial moment, which cements Jenna's claim to camp and incorporates her white trash background for that very purpose, occurs in season six, when she seeks a sponsor for her wedding to Paul. She initially finds one in The Southern Tourism Bureau which is willing to pay for their ceremony on an old plantation, "which is great because [their] wedding was going to be slavery themed anyway" (6x21 "The Return of Avery Jessup"). Her decade-long repression of her cheap southern roots, however, makes it impossible for her to shoot their commercial in a convincing accent. Tracy employs resident Georgian dialect expert

Kenneth to help Jenna remember and embrace her past identity. A montage of speech- and walk-training as originated in *My Fair Lady* (1964, Dir. George Cukor) depicts their endeavor. When Jenna sees her transformed, or rather reformed, self in the mirror, however, it prompts the following monologue:

> No, this isn't southern elegance. This is a dirt-bag girl I once knew.
>
> [in a thick southern accent which continuously worsens] A girl named Jae-na. She used to get into fist-fights at water parks and lost her virginity to a bait salesman on a waterbed. [in Jenna's normal voice again] That is not who I am anymore. I'm class-y […] This whole southern thing is wrong. I need to find a new wedding sponsor that's as classy as I am. I'm not this person [in southern accent again] Cause I done got rid of her!

Tracy later finds Jenna crying in her dressing room. She thought she had found a "classy new sponsor," but during the filming of the commercial for "Hubbard's Flavorless English Water Biscuits" the accent of that "girl from Toilet Swamp Cove" breaks out repeatedly and Jenna is fired. As she goes outside to clear her head, she runs into Liz attacked by several Muppet impersonators. Commenting in a thick southern accent that "Them poppets sure picked da wrong day to cross ma kin!" she hits Liz's opponents with her high heels. When she sees the pictures online later, she is unhappy about publicity for the very first time, assuming this expression of her inner "panhandle hick" ruins her chances at finding a suitable sponsor. Yet when she reads the caption beneath the photo and realizes that the press failed to notice that her shoes were not Christian Louboutins, she has an epiphany about herself:

> They didn't know that my shoes were cheap knock-offs. They thought they were fancy, even though they are secretly crap. That's it. That's who I am! I'm that knock-off designer shoe. My outside is shiny and pretty, but my inside is filled with cardboard and horse glue. I solved my identity crisis! More importantly, I know who will sponsor my wedding!

The sponsor, it turns out, will be OffBrandHeelz.com, whose paradoxical slogan, "naturally fancy," perfectly summarizes Jenna's rejection of her biological and familial roots, the celebration of her new identity, and embrace of the artificiality of both. The sheer exuberance with which Jenna accepts the idea that outside and inside can be in stark contrast, and that identity is a construct, mark her storyline in "The Return of Avery Jessup" as one of the series' most overt and prolonged camp moments.

The same episode also presents the audience with *30 Rock*'s recurring theme of engaging with gender representation not only through its female characters, but also its (straight) male protagonists, which sets the series further apart from many of its sitcom predecessors. The show's alpha-male, Jack Donaghy, for example, is obsessed with self-help models akin to those presented in women's magazines and quoted by Kathleen Rowe as exactly the kind of self-improvement through Protestant work ethics rejected by Miss Piggy and, by extension, *30 Rock*'s female leads. He would love to braid his girlfriend's hair, because "it is romantic and [he is] really good at it" (4x14 "Future Husband"), and in "The Return of Avery Jessup," he exclaims "I do, I wear the pants," just as his wife Avery enters, wearing pants. There is even a connection between *30 Rock*'s most "perfect" man and Miss Piggy's enhancement of femininity, which Rowe claims is at least partially achieved through her use of voice "by adopting a mannered, whispered French" (Rowe, *Unruly Woman* 27). While Liz adopts Miss Piggy's trademark "moi" to refer to herself in a moment of triumph (2x13 "Succession"),[31] otherwise the use of French is limited to men who live—to use Jack's term—in a "bubble" of handsomeness: his younger self and Liz's season three boyfriend Dr. Drew Baird (Jon Hamm). The treatment of male attractiveness, bordering on feminizing them, is continued in Liz's husband Criss, who is obsessed with his facial features (6x21 "The Return of Avery Jessup" and 7x12 "Hogcock"), to the point that Liz and Jenna must fight the knock-off Sesame Street characters who attack him for selling his hot dogs on "their" corner while he helplessly exclaims "Don't hurt my cheekbones." The attack happens right after both Liz and Criss have struggled with the unconventional gender roles they each inhabit in their relationship, since she earns more and he is more invested in domesticity. This prompts Liz to confide in Jenna how disappointed she is that this would still be an issue, since "feminism promised [them] two things: fatter dolls and an end to traditional gender roles!" While (post)feminism has not achieved these goals, *30 Rock* can freely discuss the issue of traditional gender roles in heterosexual relationships, because it has successfully inverted or modified them in almost all central couples—Jenna's advice, after all, is that Liz should not worry about the wage gap; she and Paul are happy despite the very same dynamics in their relationship, because role reversal "is such a turn-on. Paul keeps the house nice, and [Jenna tries] to get him pregnant." Jenna's relationship advice once again is less farcical than it is consistent, insofar as she merely takes normative notions to their logical extreme. If whoever earns more takes on the "masculine" position in a relationship (why else would Liz's and Jenna's relative wealth be perceived as emasculating), and men and women marry mainly to bear children, then Jenna, as the breadwinner, has every right to assume that "getting Paul pregnant" is part of her job description. Moreover, the show equips its (straight) male protagonists with vulnerability and androgyny that counter the "natural sexual difference" invoked by post-feminist sensibility and instead celebrates camp's preference for incongruous gender representation though its reliance on unconventional masculinities.

Conversely, masculinity, or traditionally masculine attributes are not limited to the male protagonists. The show's final interaction between Liz and her husband Criss takes place in a Central Park playground, where they meet to end a fight in person they had started anonymously online in a message board for Gotham City mothers. Upon realizing that Liz's sparring with a working mom who envies the stay-at-home status she had complained about online, was actually a discussion with her unhappy husband who could hardly resist playing with the children in his workplace' waiting area, they have the following conversation

Criss: Yeah, so, I hate work and evidently you miss it.
Liz: I know. I am a terrible mother.
Criss: Oh my God, if you were a dude, you would not even be thinking that. It's OK to wanna work. One of us has to. We just got it backwards: you're the dad.
Liz: I do like ignoring your questions while I try to watch TV. (7x12 "Hogcock")

The sentiment expressed by Criss is sweet, and to some extent certainly progressive, as he draws attention to the double standard in the treatment of male and female parents. His observation, however, still relies on a rigid gender system in which dad equals earner. What propels the scene to a camp embrace of the fluidity of gender roles is Liz's retort, which accepts the gender inversion, but not the gender conventions. Her acceptance of the dad role in their family, not because she earns more or does not want to stay at home, but because she likes ignoring her spouse's questions, underlines her relation to the comic second type of the wisecrack. Contrary to other female comedy types, like the dumb blonde, the wisecrack is allowed "conscious self-expression" which "invites us to laugh not at her, but with her—often at some of our most cherished notions" (Horowitz 133). In this scene, Liz shows awareness of her less than flattering characteristics (ignoring her spouse while watching TV), which is, however, used to ridicule not her, but rather the cherished notion that providing for the family is inevitably a dad's job, regardless of whether it is done by a man. Liz counters such rigid gender notions by providing a stereotypical, but decisively unflattering moniker of manliness, which expounds the non-naturalness of the supposedly natural correlation between manhood and being the main earner. She thus mirrors Jenna's former acceptance of her masculine role in the relationship with Paul, which similarly embraces a play with gender identities, but ridicules conservative definitions of male roles, as she extends her role as breadwinner to attempts to get him pregnant. In addition to this camp inversion of gender ideas, the scene also marks Liz's final rejection of retreatism and postfeminist prescriptions of happiness, as she returns from her short stint as a stay-at-home mom without any regret or guilt and encouraged by her husband and friends.

6   A Sitcom's Swan Song

The relevance of *30 Rock*'s finale for an analysis of its female leads exceeds Liz's happy ending. In an instance of surprising consistency and serial memory (especially for a sitcom reliant on sketch comedy), *30 Rock*'s finale picks up the pilot's intertextual reference to *The Mary Tyler Moore Show* not only to bring the narrative, but also the series' camp potential, full circle. Whereas the reference to the older show's theme song in the pilot establishes the parodic element of *30 Rock*, the finale draws on *The Mary Tyler Moore Show*'s final use of song for heightened emotion. As camp's affective potency is as essential for its effect as its critical capacity, there is no camp as the "conveyor of meaning" or critique without camp as "an expression of emotional tone" (Babuscio 21). *30 Rock* acknowledges this significance of emotion throughout the series' run by affording all its protagonists, and in particular its female leads, season-spanning story-arcs detailing their private as well as professional achievements, developments, and set-backs, and by counterbalancing the ridicule of certain character traits with sincerity in the depiction of their emotional investments, as when it mocks Jenna's obsession with herself and her looks, but never her relationship with Paul. The finale, however, stands out as one of the most emotional episodes of the series. Attention to the show's final episode is furthermore warranted, because it is still rare for sitcoms to end in planned finales, rather than just getting cancelled at any point due to low ratings, which has "elevated [the sitcom finale] to the status of cultural spectacle" (Morreale, "Sitcoms" 108). The first sitcom to end with such a "cultural spectacle" was *The Mary Tyler Moore Show*.[32] Hence, *30 Rock*'s final structural reference to this foundational text of television comedy can be understood as an homage to the lineage of (feminist) quality sitcom the series drew on for seven seasons. At least equally, if not more importantly, however, *30 Rock* also uses its parallels to the earlier series' final episode, "The Last Show," to create a finale that critics and fans alike deemed "deeply satisfying on an emotional level" (van der Werff). Among the shared strategies used to achieve the effect of emotional intensity is the unusual use of song— "The Last Show" and "Last Lunch" both end with a song performed by its cast members—in a genre in which music "is rarely employed for emotional purposes" (Mills 38). Thus marked as a singularly important moment in the series' run, *30 Rock*'s reliance on camp in the final moments of "Last Lunch" achieves particular relevance.

   30 Rock's finale follows the basic plot premise of *The Mary Tyler Moore Show*'s "The Last Show" (7x24). TGS has been cancelled, which prompts the show's main characters to say goodbye to their workplace of several years, as well as to each other. To further add to the episode's emotional intensity Jack and Liz are each faced with a life-changing decision. Liz must decide whether she can be a stay-at-home mom to her newly adopted twins, even though she misses work, and Jack must decide whether he can stay as GE's CEO, even though professional success does not make him happy anymore. Over the course of the hour-long finale all the main characters get the chance to dwell on their plans for the future (many quickly discarded, like Jenna's idea to go to Hollywood, where she is confronted with young, attractive Cerie-look-alikes, causing her to quote Liz's signature line of resignation: "Shut it down") and have heart-to-hearts about their fears of goodbyes. This lays the groundwork for an uncharacteristically sentimental atmosphere. The series nonetheless keeps its penchant for absurd situations: it places Liz and Tracy's teary-eyed confession of mutual affection in the strip-club they visited in the pilot; puts Tracy and Jenna in Hitler-drag for their goodbye; and causes Jenna's emotional breakdown by taking away her mirror. The latter has the unfortunate result that she cannot be sure whether she is actually sad, because she does not have her mirror to confirm her emotions anymore. The incongruity between underlying seriousness and superficial absurdity culminate in one final performance by Jenna, which not only confirms the series' dedication to the happiness of its protagonists, but also to camp. Jenna is allowed her ultimate satisfaction when Kenneth decides that *TGS*' final episode should end with a song sung by her. Jenna opts for the title song from the "musical adaption of the film of the novel *The Rural Juror*." The song choice reflects camp's incongruity as it is a call back to a running gag from season one, when no one could understand her film project's title. It also relates to one of Jenna's earliest moments of triumph, as Liz's condescending comments on Jenna's side project are dismissed by the writers, who for once support Jenna and congratulate her on her work. In addition to this past success, the song also confirms that Jenna will indeed be returning to her "first love, Broadway," thus ensuring the future of her career and her happiness. Within the diegesis of the finale, "Goodbye Rural Juror" furthermore fulfills the function songs usually have in a musical, which—in form of the special musical episode—is one on the few TV trends and sweeps stunts (as opposed to live episodes) *30 Rock* had not hitherto engaged in, and which is also the medium most closely connected to camp.[33] Brett Farmer argues that "the musical achieves narrative closure, not through a 'straight' diegetic event but through a grand finale number" (97). *30 Rock* supports a similar reading of "Goodbye Rural Juror," insofar as Jenna's heartfelt, yet over-the-top performance is interspersed with sentiment-laden scenes from the simultaneous event happening outside the studio, namely Jack's return and Liz's subsequent relief, as well as short flashbacks to earlier moments of happiness for the protagonists, such as Kenneth's triumphant freeze-frame fist pump (itself a quote from John Hughes's *The Breakfast Club*). During the song's last bars, the zoom to a close-up of Jenna's face dissolves into soft focus until the credits roll. Both techniques, close-up and soft focus, are commonly used to enhance romantic and heartbreaking moments in film and on TV, thus further aligning Jenna's performance with enhanced emotion. The seriousness of the situation is, however, disrupted by the nonsensical lyrics of "Goodbye Rural Juror," which bear no relation to the events of the finale other than adhering to the general theme of saying goodbye:

The Irma Luhrman-Merman murder
Turned the bird's word lurid
The whir and the purr of a twirler girl
She would the world were demurer
The insurer's allure
For valor were pure Kari Wuhrer
One fervid whirl over her turgid error
Rural juror
Rural juror
I will never forget you
Rural juror
I'll always be glad I met you
Rural juror
I will never forget you
Rural juror
I'll always be glad I met you
Rural juror, rural juror
These were the best days of my flerm

Due to its conventional pop-ballad melody, use of violins, and not least Jane Krakowski's performance, the song achieves its emotional impact, even as the lyrics mock the manipulative concept of ending a series with a random song.[34] The awareness of clichés and tropes underlined through intertextuality, combined with an embrace of sentiment exemplified in this sequence, summarizes the main aspects of *30 Rock*'s humor and its treatment of Liz and Jenna.

After the credits, Jenna's final appearance shows her at the Tony Award Ceremony, where she seemingly accepts the award for her role in *The Rural Juror*. Yet the actual winner interrupts her, prompting Jenna to leave the stage, not disappointed or angry, however, but mouthing the sounds of *TGS*' infamous fart machine and flashing her boobs. Her appearance at the Tony Ceremony might not be a conventional success, yet, given the idiosyncrasies of her character, *30 Rock* could have hardly given Jenna a more loving salute. The moment is an amalgam of everything she enjoyed (minus kinky sex with Paul): her goal in life has been to get a Tony in the category of "living theatrically in normal life" (4x14 "Future Husband"); she flashes the Empire State Building every Friday to celebrate (7x03 "Stride of Pride"); and she is excited to appear in the papers, even if it shows her passed out from alcohol, because to her any publicity is good publicity ("Oh my God. It's so embarrassing. Look how thin I look! And look how many e-mail I've gotten" in 1x02 "The Aftermath"). Similarly unconventional yet satisfying is Liz's final scene: she is directing a new comedy (even if it is one with a horrible recurring gag suggested by Kenneth); her kids are with her on the set (though as self-obsessed as their older counterparts); and she is on the phone with Jack—as it turns out, she can "have it all," as long as all does not include normativity.

Ultimately, what makes the camp effect of Liz and Jenna work is not whether their co-workers care about them, or whether they care about themselves, but whether the series cares about them. While some critics bemoaned the slightly sentimental tone of *30 Rock* in its final season, and particularly in the finale double episode, this enhanced emotionality is essential to camp and to *30 Rock*'s camping of postfeminism, as it ensures that the mocking of the postfeminist sensibility and how it manifests itself in Liz and Jenna never extends to a mocking of their characters. *30 Rock* often ignores the boundaries of political correctness and even in its final moments refrain from presenting any of its lead characters as flawless role models. At the same time, it engages more eloquently and more often than probably any other current TV show with the postfeminist sensibility—particularly the idea that there might be any right way to be a woman or a right way to be a feminist. With its hyperbolic, almost cartoonish exaggeration of postfeminist tropes, the show expresses the serious in terms of artifice and fun, and complicates the positions available to women in popular culture—which in the words of one of Liz's younger selves makes it "funny, cause it's true" (2x07 "Rosemary's Baby").

Furthermore, the affective sincerity of *30 Rock* is heightened when the show in its seventh season becomes even more explicitly meta and topical than ever before: several episodes are dedicated to the presidential election of 2012; another is specifically structured around the question of whether women can be funny (framed in a *Sex and the City*-style voiceover) revived at the time through a number of magazine spreads; Jenna parodies Lady Gaga with her summer hit "Balls, Balls, Balls" (7x02 "Governor Dunston"); Liz receives a feminist media award; and in the finale almost no scene is without reference to current events, the show's past, or TV in general. The context provided by *30 Rock*'s metaqualities, its sketch-influenced carnivalesque humor, and affection for its characters, create an environment in which Jenna can be read as an affirmative parody rather than the ridicule of a weak persona, and in which Liz

Lemon's "traditionally gendered flaws" make her a commentary on rigid gender notions rather than an unsympathetic character.

As such, *30 Rock* certainly makes fun of women—as it does of most anything (it is, after all, "the most unethical" of TV shows)—and is thus not feminist in the way *Murphy Brown* and similar shows have been. Even more poignantly, however, its humor is based in the self-reflective portrayal of our cultural expectations of women in media, thus questioning women's as well as feminism's status quo both on- and off-screen, and complicating the audience's perception of both as a meta-postfeminist text. *30 Rock* thus functions as a comment on current media products, (including itself); subversive, as Jack Babuscio has claimed for camp more generally, as "a means of illustrating [...] cultural ambiguities and contradictions" (28), eliciting through its use of feminist camp, and its rootedness in postfeminist media culture, a more critically aware media consumption in the audience. Its feminism is less about answers and models, and more about questions and invitations to "think again" about what we perceive to be normal and desirable in a postfeminist era.

Notes

1. I offer an analysis of how *30 Rock* incorporates elements of quality television usually associated with drama shows on cable TV in "*30 Rock*: Complexity, Metareferentiality and the Contemporary Quality Sitcom."
2. For the real-life connections between GE, NBC, and other companies, see Bratslavsky (10–11).
3. Linda Mizejewski similarly argues that *30 Rock* offers "a metacommentary on feminist politics and contentions." Though she does not argue in terms of camp, Mizejewski shares my conviction that there is more to feminist comedy than the uncovering and judging of good/bad stereotypes: "the gender politics of *30 Rock* can [...] be framed by theories of feminism and of comedy that veer away from the good image/bad image criticism implied by objections to particular comic tropes, stereotypes, or narratives."
4. For a history of the dumb blonde, see Horowitz (13–15).
5. A similar issue had been brought up in 1984 during the second season of *Kate & Allie* (1984–1989), a sitcom following the lives of two divorced women and best friends, who move in together to support each other and raise their children. In the episode "Landlady" Kate and Allie face a substantial rent increase, because they live in a one-family dwelling with two families. After their attempt to pass as a lesbian couple to convince

their (gay) landlady that they are, in fact, one family living in a one-family dwelling falls through, the following dialogue summarizes the episode's moral:

Landlady: This apartment is a one-family dwelling.

Kate: Sure, as long as *you* get to say what a family is.

Landlady: Everybody knows what a family is.

Kate: A lot of people wouldn't consider a gay couple a family, but you two do. And now so do we.

Allie: A family is anybody who wants to share their lives together.

Kate: Right, raise their kids together. Put up with their craziness...

Allie: It's love that defines a family. And it can be any kind of love. Your kind, our kind, theirs...

Kate: Who's to say which kind of family is the best? You of all people ought to know that.

6. For more on aspects of gender in Lily Tomlin's comedy, see Jennifer Reed's "Lily: Sold Out! The Queer Feminism of Lily Tomlin" and Susan Horowitz's *Queens of Comedy*.

7. See also Diane Negra's critique: "In general, postfeminism partners well with other conservative formulations such as a corporate culture that reinforces divergent social privileges. With its heavily classist character, postfeminism flourishes under the conditions of private wealth and public austerity that currently prevail in the US" (91).

8. For a differentiated analysis of the manifestations of sexualization see Gill, "Beyond the 'Sexualisation of Culture' Thesis" (137).

9. See also Michele Schreiber for a connection between this trope and the romance genre.

10. See for example Alex Vesey and Kristen Lambert, who cheer on "Lemon's refusal to trade in self-gratification for heterosexual romance."

11. The retreatist scenario is connected quite obviously to neoliberalism's and postfeminism's unwavering admiration for choice by Charlotte in the already mentioned episode "Time and Punishment" (4x07), yet questioned by her three friends, especially career-oriented Miranda:

Charlotte: It's my life and my choice. [....] Don't you dare hang up! I'm interviewing girls to replace me and I really need you to get behind my choice.

Miranda: You get behind your choice.

Charlotte: I am behind my choice. I choose my choice.

Miranda: I don't have time for this. I have to go to work. Some of us still have to go to work.

Charlotte: I choose my choice! I choose my choice!

12. The difference in genre-heritage is acknowledged in the *30 Rock* episode "Up All Night" (1x13), when Liz tries to avoid being seen by Jack's (ex-) wife Bianca (Isabella Rossellini), with whom she had a violent encounter at a party in the prior episode caused by Liz's claim to be engaged to Jack. As Liz tries to crawl out of Jack's office unseen, she is stopped midway by Bianca, blurting out: "This would work on *Ugly Betty*."

13. Jason Mittell refers to one example from Louis C. K.'s show *Louie* "when Louie plays with the form by having the same actress play Louie's date in one episode and his mother in another episode's flashback" (par. 10).

14. This also attests to the potential of flashbacks, and indeed of all sketch comedy elements in *30 Rock*, to be used out of context, and thus to be easily recyclable over different media formats (such as animated GIFs and YouTube videos) and diverse bases for revenue (such as smartphone apps). This strengthens the show's appeal in convergence culture, where the boundaries between old and new media and between consumers and producers are continually blurred (see Jenkins).

15. "The one-week period during which audience size figures of network program time slots are calculated for the purpose of establishing rates for commercial time" (Clemente 410).

16. This is not to imply that *30 Rock* is immune to the draw of sweeps week's stunts: both of its star-studded life-shows, for example, aired during such periods.

17. When confronted by Liz about the reasons that "made [him] think [she] was gay?" Jack points to her Converse sneakers as "definitely bi-curious" (1x03 "Blind Date").

18. Liz: "Well, I'm Liz, and obviously my philosophy is simple like a bean. I'm fixing problems in my personal life the same way I fix problems at work. I saved the show, now I'm going to save me. Because Lizbeanism means that I am a dike… against the rising waters of mediocrity." (5x22 "Everything Sunny All The Time Always")
    Elisa: I have a terrible secret. Please don't ask me what it is.
    Liz: I don't want to know what it is! … Are you a man?
    Elisa: *Really*, Lemon? That's your guess? You want to see me naked?
    Liz: Kind of. (3x19 "The Ones").

19. "I genuinely don't know," Liz comments for example in the season six episode "Idiots are People Two," when pointing out to Tracy how many of his co-workers are gay. Only in the very last episode does Lutz 'come out' as bisexual, when he refers to himself as "Dumb, old, uncool, part-Inuit, bisexual, 51-year-old Lutz."

20. *30 Rock*'s appeal to queer audiences is reflected in the show's 2011 win of a GLAAD award (*Gay and Lesbian Alliance Against Defamation*) in the category Outstanding Individual Episode (in a series without a regular LGBT character) for the season four episode "Klaus & Greta."

21. Many reviewers see their friendship in a different light and lament the lack of emotional support the two characters provide each other. See for example a review of "My Whole Life Is Thunder" which describes their friendship as an example of the series' "toxic relationships" (Arbeiter) or Kate Dailey's unfavorable comparison between Leslie Knope (*Parks and Recreation*) and Liz Lemon, which criticizes that "If Liz interacts with Jenna out of any feeling at all, these days, it's frustration and the desire to condescend."

22. Especially the first meeting, a.k.a. the "meet cute," in which it becomes instantly clear that the two protagonists are meant for each other. In Liz's case, Kat wins her over by liking the same book and facing the same issues she encountered in school, such as her deviant feminism as well as femininity:

    Kat: He's my dad. It's "Take Your Daughter to Work" day, which I object to on feminist grounds.
    Liz: It's patronizing. Like girls don't know what jobs are. [...]
    Kat: Do you think I could pull off a haircut like Scout had in the movie [*To Kill a Mockingbird*]?
    Liz: I've been there. And you should know that people are gonna assume you're ...
    Kat: I'm a lesbian. I know, I just needed to hear it.

23. Including such references as: "You soloed me! (6x12 "St. Patrick's Day") as Liz's comment on Criss' reaction to her declaration of love; the carbonite freezing of Don Geiss (4x15 "Don Geiss, America, and Hope"); the casting of Carrie Fisher (2x07 "Rosemary's Baby"); and the repeated inclusion of Princess Leia outfits in the plot and dialogue (e.g. 3x14 "Funcooker" and 6x18 "Murphy Brown lied to us").

24. Also surprisingly accurate is Jenna's comment that "Reese Witherspoon is just a likable version of me" (5x19 "I Heart Connecticut"). Rowe analyzes Witherspoon as *the* postfeminist actress because of her mixture of sex appeal and innocence, high-brow education and southern aristocratic background (*Unruly Girls* 127–8), which translates well into its negative—less likable—version as an actress with white trash southern roots and over-developed sexual confidence.

25. Among them: three-ways with two of the Backstreet Boys, and with Roseanne and Tom Arnold, as well as affairs with O.J. Simpson and (repeatedly) Mickey Rourke.

26. Cases in point are her worshipping of "radical feminist" Rosemary Howard (2x04 "Rosemary's Baby"), and her listening to riot grrrls Sleater Kinney (7x03 "Stride of Pride") and queer performer Peaches (4x14 "Future Husband").

27. This description is taken from Morreale's account of a similar scene in *Xena: Warrior Princess*: "Xena plants a long lingering kiss on the lips of Miss Artyphys. Although Miss Artyphys is a man in drag, the visual image presents two women locked in an embrace" (*"Xena"* 85).

28. While Liz and Jenna are unusual for contemporary TV texts, their bodies are, of course, not nearly as radical as, for example, John Waters' use of fat female bodies as disruptive forces in his camp films. For a discussion of how they and other fat bodies are employed, see Stukator.

29. While *30 Rock* is most often discussed in terms of feminism, its treatment of race warrants a detailed analysis, which unfortunately goes beyond the context of this book. Some preliminary remarks can be found in reviews like Te-Nehisi Coates', who claims that *30 Rock* has not received enough credit for its interrogation of whiteness, or Alyssa Rosenberg's, who argues that *30 Rock*'s "initial premise was as much a racial one as it was about gender."

30. A comment on quirky, quality romantic comedies (during the phase of the nervous romance) and their supposed wisdom about gender differences and love, this quote refers to the shark metaphor from *Annie Hall* (1977, Dir. Woody Allen): "A relationship, I think, is like a shark. You know? It has to constantly move forward or it dies. And I think what we got on our hands is a dead shark."

31. "Who's got two thumbs, speaks limited French, and hasn't cried once today, this moi!" The emphasis on her two thumbs is probably a direct reference to Miss Piggy who, indeed, does have all the other qualities mentioned by Liz, but not two thumbs.

32. The planned finale is closely connected to the show's status as the first sitcom to be recognized as "quality television" (see Feuer et al.).

33. *Crazy Ex-Girlfriend*, which started airing in 2015 on The CW, relies heavily on musical numbers—often parodies of songs or whole genres—to spoof tropes of co-dependent relationships and gender stereotypes in contemporary TV, and can thus be read as the latest addition to postfeminist camp texts on US network television.

34. *The Mary Tyler Moore Show* ends with the cast singing "It's a Long Way to Tipperary."

WORKS CITED

30 Rock. Creat. Tina Fey. NBC, 2006–2013.
Absolutely Fabulous. Creat. Jennifer Saunders and Dawn French. BBC2/BBC One, 1992–2012.
Abramovitch, Seth. "30 Rock: The New Normal." *TV.com*. 17 Feb 2012. CBS Interactive. 5 Nov 2012 http://www.tv.com/news/30-rock-the-new-normal-27867/.

All About Eve. Dir. Joseph L. Mankiewicz. 20th Century Fox, 1950.

All That Heaven Allows. Dir. Douglas Sirk. Universal Pictures, 1955.

Ally McBeal. Creat. David E. Kelley. Fox, 1997–2002.

Annie Hall. Dir. Woody Allen. United Artists, 1977.

Arbeiter, Michael. "*30 Rock*: Chronicling the Final Chapter - Week 8." *Hollywood.com.* 07 Dec 2012. 21 Feb 2013 http://www.hollywood.com/news/tv/45711083/30-rock-chronicling-the-final-chapter-week-8?page=all.

Arthurs, Jane. *Television and Sexuality: Regulation and the Politics of Taste.* Maidenhead: McGraw-Hill Education, 2004.

Attallah, Paul. "The Unworthy Discourse: Situation Comedy in Television." *Critiquing the Sitcom: A Reader.* Ed. Joanne Morreale. Syracuse: Syracuse UP, 2003. 91–115.

Babuscio, Jack. "Camp and Gay Sensibility." *Camp Grounds: Style and Homosexuality.* Ed. David Bergman. Amherst: University of Massachusetts Press, 1993. 19–37.

Baby Mama. Dir. Michael McCullers. Universal Pictures, 2008.

Bewitched. Creat. Sol Saks. ABC, 1964–1972.

Blake, Meredith. "Murphy Brown Lied to US: Review." *A.V. Club.* 19 Apr 2012. Onion. 18 June 2013 http://www.avclub.com/articles/murphy-brown-lied-to-us,72508/.

Bratslavsky, Lauren M. *Television Representing Television: How NBC's 30 Rock Parodies and Satirizes the Cultural Industries.* MSc Thesis. University of Oregon, June 2009. 10 Jul 2013 https://scholarsbank.uoregon.edu/xmlui/bitstream/handle/1794/9851/Bratslavsky_Lauren_Michelle_ms2009sp.pdf.

Bronski, Michael. *Culture Clash: The Making of Gay Sensibility.* Boston: South End, 1984.

Butler, Jeremy G. "Redesigning Discourse: Feminism, The Sitcom, and *Designing Women.*" *Journal of Film and Video* 45.1 (1993): 13–26.

Butler, Judith. *Gender Trouble: Feminism and the Subversion of Identity.* New York: Routledge, 2008.

Cashmere Mafia. Creat. Kevin Wade, co-prod. Darren Star. ABC, 2008.

CBS Los Angeles. "Not PC Enough? *30 Rock* Rated Most Unethical TV Show." 6 Jan 2011. *CBS Local Media.* 2 Nov 2011 http://losangeles.cbslocal.com/2011/01/06/not-pc-enough-30-rock-rated-most-unethical-tv-show/.

Charlie's Angels: Full Throttle. Dir. Joseph McGinty Nichol. Columbia Pictures, 2003.

Chee, Alexander. "Is "30 Rock" just "The Muppet Show" with Humans?" *Salon.com.* 4 Oct 2012. Salon Media Group. 13 Nov 2012 http://www.salon.com/2012/10/04/is_30_rock_just_the_muppet_show_with_humans/.

Clemente, Mark. N. *The Marketing Glossary: Key Terms, Concepts and Applications.* Glen Rock: Clemente, 2002.

Cleto, Fabio. "Queering the Camp." *Camp: Queer Aesthetics and the Performing Subject —A Reader.* Ed. Fabio Cleto. Edinburgh: Edinburgh University Press, 2008. 1–42.

Coates, Ta-Nehisi. "*30 Rock*'s Rejection of White Guilt." *The Atlantic*. 31 Jan 2013. The Atlantic Monthly Group. 2 Mar 2013 http://www.theatlantic.com/entertainment/archive/2013/01/-i-30-rock-i-s-rejection-of-white-guilt/272732/.

Cohan, Steven. "Queer Eye for the Straight Guise: Camp, Postfeminism, and the Fab Five's Makeovers of Masculinity." *Interrogating Postfeminism: Gender and the Politics of Popular Culture*. Eds. Yvonne Tasker and Diane Negra. Durham: Duke University Press, 2007. 176–200.

Crazy Ex-Girlfriend. Creat. Rachel Bloom and Aline Brosh McKenna. The CW, 2015–.

Critchley, Simon. *On Humour.* London, New York: Routledge, 2002.

———. "On Humor." New York, 14.05.2008. Lecture. Authors@Google.

Cybill. Creat. Chuck Lorre. CBS, 1995–1998.

Dailey, Kate. "Leslie Knope, Liz Lemon, and the Feminist Lessons of NBC's 'Parks and Recreation'." *DailyBeast*. 8 Apr 2010. Newsweek Daily Beast Company. 20 Jun 2012 http://www.newsweek.com/leslie-knope-liz-lemon-and-feminist-lessons-nbcs-parks-and-recreation-222734.

Desperate Housewives. Creat. Marc Cherry. ABC, 2004–2012.

Designing Women. Creat. Linda Bloodworth-Thomason. CBS, 1986–1993.

Dollimore, Jonathan. "Post/Modern: On the Gay Sensibility, Or the Pervert's Revenge on Authenticity." *Camp: Queer Aesthetics and the Performing Subject – A Reader.* Ed. Fabio Cleto. Edinburgh: Edinburgh University Press, 2008. 221–236.

Doty, Alexander. *Making Things Perfectly Queer: Interpreting Mass Culture*. Minneapolis: University of Minnesota Press, 1993.

Ellen. Creat. Ellen DeGeneres. Disney, 1994–1998.

Feuer, Jane, Paul Kerr, and Tise Vahimagi. *MTM: "Quality Television."* London: BFI, 1984.

Fey, Tina. *Bossypants*. Boston: Little, Brown and Company, 2011.

Genz, Stephanie. "Singled Out: Postfeminism's 'New Woman' and the Dilemma of Having It All." *The Journal of Popular Culture* 43.1: 97–119.

———. *Postfemininities in Popular Culture*. Basingstoke: Palgrave Macmillan, 2009.

Gerhard, Jane. "*Sex and The City*: Carrie Bradshaw's Queer Postfeminism." *Feminist Media Studies* 5.1 (2005): 37–49.

Gerigk, Anne. "Dis-placing Laughter in *30 Rock*: Beyond Corporate Comedy or Back to the Funny Female's Modern Roots." *Gender Forum: An Internet Journal for Gender Studies* 35 (2011).

Ghost. Dir. Jerry Zucker. Paramount Pictures, 1990.

Gill, Rosalind. "Postfeminist Media Culture: Elements of a Sensibility." *European Journal of Cultural Studies* 10.2 (2007): 147–171.

———. "Postfeminism." *The International Encyclopedia of Communication*. 2008. Blackwell. 13 Apr 2012 http://www.blackwellreference.com/subscriber/tocnode?id=g9781405131995Lchunk_g97814051319952Lss90-1.

————. "Beyond the 'Sexualization of Culture' Thesis: An Intersectional Analysis of 'Sixpacks', 'Midriffs' and 'Hot Lesbians' in Advertising." *Sexualities* 12.2 (2009): 137–160.

————. and Christina Scharff. *New Femininities: Postfeminism, Neoliberalism, and Subjectivity.* New York: Palgrave Macmillan, 2011.

Griffin, Sean. *Tinker Belles and Evil Queens: The Walt Disney Company from the Inside Out.* New York: New York University Press, 2000.

Heffernan, Virginia. "It's February; Pucker Up, TV Actresses." *New York Times.* 10 Feb 2005. The New York Times Company. 12 Sep 2012. http://www. nytimes.com/2005/02/10/arts/television/10heff.html?_r=1&pagewanted =print&position=.

Holmes, Su and Diance Negra. "Introduction: GOING CHEAP? Female Celebrity in Reality, Tabloid and Scandal Genres." *Genders* 48 (2008).

Horn, Katrin. "*30 Rock*: Complexity, Metareferentiality and the Contemporary Quality Sitcom." *Amerikanische Fernsehserien der Gegenwart: Perspektiven der American Studies und der Media Studies.* Ed. Christoph Ernst and Heike Paul. Heidelberg: transcript, 2015. 153–183.

Horowitz, Susan. *Queens of Comedy: Lucille Ball, Phyllis Diller, Carol Burnett, Joan Rivers, and the New Generation of Funny Women.* London: Routledge, 1997.

Hutcheon, Linda. *Irony's Edge: The Theory and Politics of Irony.* London: Routledge, 1994.

I Love Lucy. Creat. Jess Oppenheimer, Madelyn Davis, and Bob Carroll, Jr. CBS, 1951–1957.

Jagose, Annamarie. *Queer Theory: An Introduction.* New York City: New York University Press, 1997.

Jenkins, Henry. *Convergence Culture: Where Old and New Media Collide.* New York: New York University Press, 2008.

Kate & Allie. Creat. Sherry Coben. CBS, 1984–1989.

King, Geoff. *Film Comedy.* London, New York: Wallflower, 2002.

Laugh-In. Creat. Ed. Friendly and George Schlatter. NBC, 1967–1973.

Levy, Ariel. *Female Chauvinist Pigs: Women and the Rise of Raunch Culture.* New York: Free Press, 2006.

Lipstick Jungle. Creat. DeAnn Heline and Eileen Heisler. NBC, 2008–2009.

Lotz, Amanda D. "Postfeminist Television Criticism: Rehabilitating Critical Terms and Identifying Postfeminist Attributes." *Feminist Media Studies* 1.1 (2001): 105–121.

Maude. Creat. Norman Lear. CBS, 1972–1978.

McRobbie, Angela. "Post-Feminism and Popular Culture." *Feminist Media Studies* 4.3 (2004): 255–264.

Mean Girls. Dir. Mark Waters. Paramount Pictures, 2004.

Mildred Pierce. Dir. Michael Curtiz. Warner Bros., 1945.

Mills, Brett. *The Sitcom.* Edinburgh: Edinburgh University Press, 2009.

Mitchell, Danielle. "Straight and Crazy? Bisexual and Easy? Or Drunken Floozy? The Queer Politics of Karen Walker." *The New Queer Aesthetic on Television: Essays on Recent Programming.* Eds. James R. Keller and Leslie Stratyner. Jefferson: McFarland, 2006. 85–98.

Mittell, Jason. *Complex TV. The Poetics of Contemporary Television Storytelling.* Pre-Publication Edition. MediaCommons, 2013.

Mizejewski, Linda. "Feminism, Postfeminism, Liz Lemonism." *Genders* 55 (2012).

———. *Pretty / Funny. Women Comedians and Body Politics.* Austin: University of Texas Press, 2014.

Modern Family. Creat. Christopher Lloyd and Steven Levitan. ABC, 2009–.

Moonlighting. Creat. Glenn Gordon Caron. ABC, 1985–1989.

Monty Python's Flying Circus. Perf. Graham Chapman, John Cleese, Terry Gilliam, Eric Idle, Terry Jones, and Michael Palin. BBC, 1969–1974.

Morreale, Joanne. "*Xena: Warrior Princess* as Feminist Camp." *The Journal of Popular Culture* 32.2 (1998): 79–86.

———. "Sitcoms Say Goodbye: The Cultural Spectacle of *Seinfeld*'s Last Episode." *Journal of Popular Film and Television* 28.3 (2000): 108–115.

———. *"Do Bitches Get Stuff Done?"* *Feminist Media Studies* 10.4 (2010): 485–487.

Murphy Brown. Creat. Diane English. CBS, 1988–1998.

My Fair Lady. Dir. George Cukor. Warner Bros., 1964.

Neale, Steve and Frank Krutnik. *Popular Film and Television Comedy.* London: Routledge, 1995.

Negra, Diane. *What a Girl Wants? Fantasizing the Reclamation of Self in Postfeminism.* New York: Routledge, 2009.

Parks & Recreation. Creat. Greg Daniels and Michael Schur. NBC, 2009–2015.

Press, Andrea L. "Feminism and Media in the Post-Feminist Era." *Feminist Media Studies* 11.1 (2011): 107–113.

Rabinovitz, Lauren. "Ms-Representation: The Politics of Feminist Sitcoms." *Television, History, and American Culture: Feminist Critical Essays.* Eds. Mary Beth Havalovich and Lauren Rabinovitz. Durham: Duke University Press, 1999. 144–167.

Reed, Jennifer. "Lily: Sold Out! The Queer Feminism of Lily Tomlin." *Genders* 49 (2009).

———. "Sexual Outlaws: Queer in a Funny Way." *Women's Studies: An Inter-Disciplinary Journal* 40.6 (2011): 762–777.

Richardson, Niall. "As Kamp as Bree: The Politics of Camp reconsidered by *Desperate Housewives.*" *Feminist Media Studies* 6.2 (2006): 154–174.

Robertson, Pamela. *Guilty Pleasures: Feminist Camp from Mae West to Madonna*. London: Tauris, 1996.

Robinson, Don. "Murphy's Revenge." *The Register Guard*: 24 Sep 1992, 10A.

Roof, Judith. *All about Thelma and Eve: Sidekicks and Third Wheels*. Urbana: University of Illinois P, 2002.

Rosenberg, Alyssa. "Liz Lemon's White Guilt, The Black Crusaders, and Grizz and Dot Com: Why '30 Rock' Mattered On Race." *ThinkProgress*. 29 Jan 2013. Center for American Progress Action Fund. 2 Mar 2013 http://thinkprogress.org/alyssa/2013/01/29/1499261/black-cruasders-grizz-dot-com-30-rock/.

Rowe, Kathleen. *The Unruly Woman: Gender and the Genres of Laughter*. Austin: University of Texas Press, 1995.

———. *Unruly Girls, Unrepentant Mothers: Redefining Feminism on Screen*. Austin: University of Texas Press, 2011.

Russo, Mary J. *The Female Grotesque: Risk, Excess and Modernity*. New York: Routledge, 1995.

Saturday Night Live. Creat. Lorne Michaels. NBC, 1975–.

Schreiber, Michele. "'Misty Water-Colored Memories of the Way We Were…': Postfeminist Nostalgia in Contemporary Romance Narratives." *Reclaiming the Archive: Feminism and Film History*. Ed. Vicki Callahan. Detroit: Wayne State University Press, 2010. 364–383.

Schuyler, Michael T. "Camp for Camp's Sake: *Absolutely Fabulous*, Self-Consciousness, and the Mae West Debate." *Journal of Film and Video* 56.4 (2004): 3–20.

Sconce, Jeffrey. "'Trashing the Academy': Taste, Excess, and an Emerging Politics of Cinematic Style." *Film Theory and Criticism: Introductory Readings*. 6th ed. Eds. Leo Braudy and Marshall Cohen. New York: Oxford University Press, 2006. 534–553.

Sex and the City. Creat. Darren Star. HBO, 1998–2004.

Shugart, Helene A. and Catherine Egley Waggoner. "A Bit Much: Spectacle as Discursive Resistance." *Feminist Media Studies* 5.1 (2005): 65–81.

———. *Making Camp: Rhetorics of Transgression in U.S. Popular Culture*. Tuscaloosa: University of Alabama Press, 2008.

Starbuck. Dir. Ken Scott. Entertainment One, 2011.

Stukator, Angela. "'It's not over until the fat lady sings': Comedy, Carnivalesque, and Body Politics." *Bodies Out of Bounds: Fatness and Transgression*. Eds. Jana Evans Braziel and Kathleen LeBesco. Berkeley: University of California Press, 2001. 197–213.

Suddenly Susan. Creat. Clyde Phillips. NBC, 1996–2000.

Sweet Home Alabama. Dir. Andy Tennant. Buena Vista Pictures, 2002.

Tasker, Yvonne and Diane Negra. "In Focus: Postfeminism and Contemporary Media Studies." *Cinema Journal* 44.2 (2005): 107–110.

The Big Bang Theory. Creat. Chuck Lorre and Bill Prady. CBS, 2007–.
The Breakfast Club. Dir. John Hughes. Universal Pictures, 1985.
The Carol Burnett Show. CBS, 1967–1978.
The Golden Girls. Creat. Susan Harris. NBC, 1985–1992.
The Kermit and Piggy Story. Dir. Peter Harris. Playhouse Video, 1985.
The Kids Are All Right. Dir. Lisa Cholodenko. Focus Features, 2010.
The Mary Tyler Moore Show. Creat. James L. Brooks and Allan Burns. CBS, 1970–1977.
The Switch. Dir. Will Speck and Josh Gordon. Miramax Films, 2010.
The Stepford Wives. Dir. Frank Oz. Paramount Pictures, 2004.
Thornham, Sue. *Women, Feminism and Media.* Edinburgh: Edinburgh University Press, 2007.
Traister, Rebecca. "30 Rock takes on Feminist Hypocrisy – and its own." Salon. com. 25 Feb 2011. Salon Media Group. 4 Nov 2011 http://www.salon. com/2011/02/25/30_rock_jezebel_feminism/.
Ugly Betty. Creat. Silvio Horta. ABC, 2006–2010.
van der Werff, Todd. "How *30 Rock*'s well-plotted final season echoes *The Mary Tyler Moore Show.*" *The A.V. Club.* 31 Jan 2013. Onion. 28 Feb 2013 http://www. avclub.com/articles/how-30-rocks-wellplotted-final-season-echoes-the-m,91814/.
Vesey, Alyx and Kristen Lambert. "'I Can Have It All': Liz Lemon Negotiates Power, One Sandwich at a Time." *Flow.TV.* 24 June 2008. Flow. 9 Aug 2012 http://flowtv.org/2008/07/i-can-have-it-all-liz-lemon-negotiates-power-one-sandwich-at-a-timea-vesey-and-k-lambertflow-staff/.
Wallace, Kelsey. "*30 Rock* and Liz Lemon and Feminism - Oh Blurg!" *Bitch Magazine.* 14 May 2009. Bitch Media. 30 Oct 2011 http://bitchmagazine. org/post/30-rock-and-liz-lemon-and-feminism-oh-blurg.
Walls, Jeanette. "Boxing Gloves or Kid Gloves for Quayle?" *New York Magazine*: 2 Nov 1992, 11.
Weiner, Jonah. "I Want to GOP to There: *30 Rock*'s Weird Conservative Streak." *Slate.com.* 6 May 2009. The Slate Group. 18 June 2012 http://www.slate. com/articles/arts/culturebox/2009/05/i_want_to_gop_to_there.single. html.
Whatever Happened to Baby Jane. Dir. Robert Aldrich. Warner Bros., 1962.
White, Patricia. *UnInvited: Classical Hollywood Cinema and Lesbian Representability.* Bloomington: Indiana University Press, 1999.
White, Rose. "Funny Women." *Feminist Media Studies* 10.3 (2010): 355–358.
Who's the Boss? Creat. Martin Cohan and Blake Hunter. ABC, 1984–1992.
Will & Grace. Creat. David Kohan and Max Mutchnick. NBC, 1998–2006.
Williamson, Judith. *Consuming Passions: The Dynamics of Popular Culture.* New York: Boyars, 1986.

Wolf, Werner. "Metareference across Media: The Concept, its Transmedial Potentials and Problems, Main Forms and Functions." *Metareference Across Media: Theory and Case Studies.* Eds. Werner Wolf and Walter Bernhart. Amsterdam: Rodopi, 2009. 1–89.

Xena: The Warrior Princess. Creat. Robert G. Tapert, John Schulian. Universal Television, 1995–2001.

CHAPTER 5

Taking Pop Seriously: Lady Gaga as Camp

Even though Lady Gaga's professional career spans a mere seven years, she has not only been dubbed the "Queen of Pop," ahead of Rihanna, Taylor Swift, or Beyoncé by *Rolling Stone Magazine* (Molanphy), but has also been described as "unquestionably the most divisive cultural icon to come along in decades" (Holdship). While the former statement can easily be backed up by her singles sales, Twitter followers, and several other record-breaking numbers, the latter is probably best exemplified by an online feud between Camilla Paglia and Jack Halberstam sparked as early as 2010. While both agree on Gaga's immense influence and her heavy reliance on intertextuality, their respective evaluations of the two facts could hardly diverge more. Paglia, one of the early feminist defenders of Madonna's status as a progressive pop figure, sees in Gaga a "ruthless recycler of other people's work," "the diva of déjà vu," and finally, in a rather surprising turn in her argumentation against Gaga's artistic appropriations: "the death of sex." Halberstam counters by stating that "[m]any people have noted that Lady Gaga lives in the long shadow of Madonna but noting this is not the same as totally collapsing two performers from very different historical and cultural milieu," and voices how baffled he is "that Paglia condemns Lady Gaga for her 'poker face' when she adored Madonna's performance in 1990 in 'Justify My Love' because it confirmed that 'we are nothing but masks'" ("What's Paglia Got to Do With It?"). Reasons for the discrepancy between these two critics are probably manifold, but I venture that there are two issues that chiefly influence the contradicting evaluations of Lady Gaga's work, of

© The Author(s) 2017   193
K. Horn, *Women, Camp, and Popular Culture*,
DOI 10.1007/978-3-319-64846-0_5

which Halberstam's and Paglia's dispute is a significant, but not nearly the only example.[1]

First, Paglia's lament that "[p]erhaps the symbolic status that sex had for a century has gone kaput; that blazing trajectory is over," depends heavily on the notion that the omnipresence of sex and the sexualization of female bodies is something worthy of nostalgic longing. When she suggests that Gaga's fans do not know the difference anymore between "real" sex appeal and its lackluster substitution by something more "clinical"—and even calls this "alarming"—she presumes that Gaga's success is based on a mistake made by ignorant fans and a failure on the part of the artist. This is not to say that Paglia is wrong in her observation about the stark difference between Madonna and Gaga when it comes to the staging of sex. An interviewer for *LA Times*, for example, notes that in "the 1980s, Madonna employed bondage imagery, and it felt sexual," and continues by reflecting Paglia's sentiment, yet without her vitriol: "Gaga does it, and it looks like it hurts" (Powers). Put this way, the difference between the two performers becomes less one of the opposition between "clinical" calculation versus authentic passion, and more one of a development from enthusiasm to disenchantment. Paglia's statement is thus revealed to willfully ignore what Halberstam calls "historical and cultural milieu." In her assessment, Paglia rejects the possibility that the difference she spots between Madonna's and Gaga's renditions of sex is the result of a conscious decision based on a changed status of sex itself and that it is valued as precisely that by a generation of fans oversaturated with "sex" as the omnipresent marker of everything from transgression to marketability.

A second, even more important difference between Halberstam and Paglia is the value they attribute to repetition and artifice. Whereas Halberstam sees in Gaga the symbol of a "feminism of the phony, the unreal, and the speculative, [...] a celebration of the joining of femininity to artifice, and a refusal of the mushy sentimentalism that has been siphoned into the category of womanhood" (*Gaga* xii–xiii), Paglia dismisses Gaga as "a laminated piece of ersatz rococo furniture." Contrary as their positions are, they rely on a vocabulary that unites them in alluding to, but never naming, a concept for whose oppositional sides they are as emblematic as for Gaga's academic standing, namely camp. Paglia's contemptuous moniker "ersatz rococo furniture" evokes Sontag's famous meditation on camp, in which she gives "a pocket history of camp" that includes "the rococo churches of Munich" (280), but ultimately dismisses camp as mere surface value and therefore a-political. Halberstam in contrast relies on terms that have shaped a later, queerer examination of camp, such as Michael Bronski's statement that by "exaggerating, stylizing, and remaking what is usually thought to be average or normal, camp creates a world in which the real becomes the unreal" (42–3), or Andrew Ross' claim that camp addresses "the relation between 'artifice' and 'nature' in the construction of sexuality and gender identity" (72). That one of the most prominent early online feuds about Lady Gaga could ultimately be traced back to discussions on camp should come as no surprise given Lady Gaga's overt references to camp predecessors (Madonna, Judy Garland, Andy Warhol), objects (*The Wizard of Oz*) and styles (drag, vogue). And yet, like Halberstam and Paglia, most critics, even those who emphasize the queer aspects of her performances and persona, point to camp only in passing, if at all.[2] I therefore want to enrich the critical reception of Lady Gaga by empha-sizing and analyzing camp as an essential aspect of her artistic output, particularly during her meteoric rise to international stardom from 2009 to 2011.

Due to the density of Gaga's oeuvre and its transgression of media boundaries, and to pop's inherent conflation of person and persona, Lady Gaga invites us, even more than previous examples in television and film had done, to question the categories of the representation of differ-ence—how do we portray lesbian desire, what does a postfeminist (have to) look like?—and she more fundamentally follows Judith Butler's dic-tum that some (ontological) terms and categorizations are fundamentally laughable and that "laughter in the face of serious categories is indispen-sable for feminism." Butler claims that "[w]ithout a doubt, feminism continues to require its own forms of serious play" (*Gender Trouble* xxx). Gaga's camp provides such serious play not only in connection to femi-nist, but also to queer concerns. Whereas my analysis of lesbian camp in cinema drew fundamentally on a shared history of frustration and a search for alternative forms of pleasure—camp's affective potential—and my reading of 30 *Rock* focused primarily on concerns on metareferen-tiality—camp's critical capacity—(though both strategies are, of course, present in each example only to varying degrees), the "cumulative star image" and the performances of Lady Gaga rely on affect and critique to an equal extent. This chapter consequently connects to the broader issues discussed so far, while examining pop music's affective and critical legacy more specifically. I therefore begin my analysis of Gaga's oeuvre

and its significance as divasdetached attachment by tracing the relation between camp and pop music, particularly in regard to earlier pop
"divas" such as Madonna and Annie Lennox. Against this background,
I illustrate how Lady Gaga's performances and videos incorporate various strands of pop legacy, before analyzing her second world tour,
The Monster Ball, as a demonstration of the sincere quality of extreme
theatricality.

1   Gaga for Pop Giants: Stars, Divas, and the Intimacy of Pop

"[T]he meaning of pop is the meaning of pop stars," Simon Frith argues
in his seminal study *Performing Rites. On the Value of Popular Music*
(210). As seemingly obvious as his statement is, it goes a long way in
accounting for the distinct quality of the reception of pop music. While
popular culture in general often invites the conflation of star image and
act, popular music offers little to no distinction or distance between artifact and artist. Hence, the analysis of singular events or products in pop
music will inevitably fail to grasp their meaning—even as it accounts for
intertextual references or genre conventions—if it disregards the star's
cumulative image and how it features in a video, performance, costume,
or song.

Discussing the potential of Madonna's songs, videos, and performances as parody rather than pastiche, Ramona Curry "takes the position that meanings of any given text arise not predominantly in readers'
experience of its construction but in their discursive interactions with it
in the context of myriad associated texts" (16). She therefore (with reference to Richard Dyer's *Stars*) introduces the idea of "the star's composite image, which is an intertextual conglomerate itself" and which
provides the context in which individual texts are understood (16). The
star herself thus becomes the link in a complex communication process
spread across different media, and it is she who invites the consideration of para- and metatexts in the interpretation of singular events and
images. This focus on *performers* rather than single *performances* has
consequences for how camp relates to popular music. The breaching of
boundaries between person and persona is one crucial aspect of camp's
affinity for musical performers, as they extend the role playing beyond
the confines of, for example, a feature-length film (Madonna's several

"phases" did not only happen in her videos, just as Cher's constant rein-
ventions were not confined to new musical styles). Equally important is
the incongruous centrality of the star's physical embodiment—the dancing body, the singing voice—in a context of utter theatricality.

The function of camp in Lady Gaga's work can be viewed as a means
of creative re-signification as well as of critique and transgression. Both
strategies signify a queer surplus value. Among the most obvious tie-ins
with queer discourses in Gaga's oeuvre is the rejection of a stable gender and sexual identity. Slipping effortlessly between female and male
drag, between cone-bras and strap-ons, gay male S/M sex scenes and lesbian make-out sessions in her videos and public appearances, Lady Gaga
refuses to be defined by her sexuality. This refusal is further emphasized
by the over-the-top artificiality of her costumes, which seldom allow
for a distinction between on- and off-stage clothing, or private and star
persona, and thus evoke Sontag's claim that camp conceives of "being
as playing a role" (56). This in turn is closely connected to Babuscio's
definition of camp as "gay sensibility" (19), which develops through the
necessity of passing for straight in a hostile environment and leads to a
heightened awareness of the theatricality of everyday life.

Such an affinity towards theatricality and incongruity is already introduced into Lady Gaga's star image by her stage name. It implies an
unambiguous, even respectable gender identity through the moniker
lady, while gaga—meaning "slightly mad, typically as a result of [...]
infatuation, or excessive enthusiasm" (*Oxford Dictionaries*) and thus
establishing a context of absurdity—belies a lady's claim to respectability, creating friction between the serious and the frivolous at the heart
of camp. More specifically, her name introduces a concept of dispropor-
tionate emotional attachment (the excessive enthusiasm) and evokes a
mode of excessive femininity characteristic of the gender play performed
by Gaga's camp diva predecessors. Her stage name also introduces her
fondness for intertextuality and media reflexivity, as gaga connects her to
the band Queen and their song "Radio Ga Ga." At the time of its release
in 1984 *Radio Ga Ga* was not only one of the most elaborate and expen-
sive videos to date, but also—in an ironic twist—served as the band's
comment on popular music's historicity, mediality, and growing com-
mercialization. With its lavish production design and (seeming) discon-
nect between visual and audio content, Queen's music video emerges as
an important inspiration for Gaga's use of the format. Overall, her name

thus inscribes her equally into pop and gender discourses, and anticipates her manipulation of both.

1.1　The Queerness of Divas

Lady Gaga's appearance at the *MTV Video Music Awards* in 2010 in a dress made entirely out of raw meat provided a striking example of such manipulation and stressed the strategies of pop intertextuality and excessive femininity implied in her name. As she climbed the stairs to the stage to accept her award for *Best Video of the* Year *(Bad Romance)*, she handed her meat purse to Cher, who presented the award. Cher herself was dressed in a fishnet costume reminiscent of the one that had caused similar reactions of outrage 20 years before the media frenzy caused by the 'meat dress' in the wake of this award show. In 1989 Cher's see-through dress, coupled with strongly homoerotic imagery of sailors, led to several stations, including MTV, banning her video for "If I Could Turn Back Time." Standing side by side on stage in 2010 Cher and Lady Gaga gave a stunning visual impression of what had and had not changed in pop music over the previous decades.[3] As award shows and video productions still permanently ask for more "flesh," especially from its female stars, and "camp is a method by which the hegemony is queered, denaturalized, and thus, subverted through overarticulation" (Devitt "Girl" 32), both dresses, particularly in their combination, provided resistive camp answers to pop culture's sexist interpellation.

Cher's own rise to the status of one of the most iconic divas of US popular music has largely been the result of a constant reinvention of her star persona over her five decades-long career, which embraces pop's stigma of inauthenticity (vis-à-vis rock) as much as femininity's assumed artificiality (versus unmarked masculinity). Enhanced by bodily modifications, Cher's costumes and wigs have transcended the boundaries of a star's usual reliance on fashion and instead propelled her into the realms of feminine drag. According to Koestenbaum and Kushner's study of the relationship between (opera) divas and gay audiences, this is a central aspect of be(com)ing a diva: "divas are themselves, like drag queens' personae, distillations and exaggerations of certain feminine traits" (139–40). Their appeal lies in their offer of "lessons in the art of anger: how to fight an oppressive order by inventing a resilient self" (113). Similarly resilient selves in popular music have been fashioned, among others, by Grace Jones, Madonna, and Annie Lennox, for whom the tragic component of earlier diva worship has taken a backseat to gender play, and whose use of drag, even more than Cher's, has regularly included androgyny.[4] Queer diva worship is thus no longer shaped just by a closet logic of having to hide parts of one's identity and inventing a resilient self, but by the search for models that defy gender conventions and sexual expectations.

While popular music and its performers have often been dismissed as inauthentic, superficial, and frivolous, they have also shown an exceptional openness to gender play, prompting scholars like Sheila Whiteley to conclude that "popular music has played a significant, if often ambiguous role, in the shaping of identity and self-consciousness" of queer audiences (208). As popular music "is sold on the basis of the pop star's identity" which is "performatively constituted by the artist's expression" (Hawkins, *Settling* 12), self-fashioning has become a central (queer) aspect of its production and consumption to counter the conflation of stage personas and notions of "realness" and to qualify the potentially essentialist readings of bodies through intensified role play. From David Bowie's androgynous alter egos Ziggy Stardust and Aladdin Zane (referenced by Lady Gaga among others via the lightning bolt make-up for *The Fame*'s cover art) to Madonna's numerous guises and masquerades, popular music has provided a fascinating incongruity: seemingly endlessly changeable, often over-the-top visual images on the one hand; and on the other supposedly heartfelt, often autobiographically understood songs—"deeply personal" for creators and fans alike (Hawkins, "Dragging" 11). Even more important for popular music's central camp icons is their refusal to acknowledge this seeming contradiction (and thus the underlying value system): 'trite' songs are treated as high art; while even comically outrageous outfits are treated as everyday couture. Accordingly, Loran Marsan reads Cher as a camp icon not because she dresses outlandishly, but because she refuses to acknowledge the outlandishness of her costumes. Marsan specifically refers to a monologue from her *Do You Believe?* show in Las Vegas, in which Cher introduces her bright red wig as her "natural hair color" and describes it as "very conservative," since she is "dressing her age now" (53). The queerness of such performances results from the embrace of "what appears to be antithetical—such as age and youth, natural and artificial," which exposes the contingency of such perceived opposites and thereby "illuminat[es] the artifice and construction of the norms themselves and putting distance between them and their assumed originary nature" (Marsan 55).

Relying on similar denaturalizing strategies, another major pop star, Madonna, has established herself as the prime example of resistance to narrowly defined femininity and heteronormativity positioned at the heart of popular music. Her commercial success "facilitates her potential to cause gender trouble" rather than hinders her subversive potential, Reena Mistry claims with reference to an interview Judith Butler gave in 1994. Butler stressed that "any attempt at subversion is potentially recuperable," but that it was nonetheless possible and important to appropriate and re-channel dominant aesthetic strategies (Osborne and Segal). In her study of the relation between queer identity making and popular music Jodi Taylor similarly stressed the connection between commercial success and subversive potential as critique becomes more potent, if more people and especially more "unassuming" people are exposed to it. She considers popular performers like Lady Gaga

> especially dangerous, disturbing and subversive because they pre-empt, perform and circulate a range of new identificatory and disidentificatory possibilities that lie outside of the given codes of gender and sexual identity and pleasure [...] And they do so spectacularly and on a grand scale in the most popular and populist forms of music culture: the pop charts. (47–8)

Returning to Madonna's appeal to queer audiences, Doris Leibetseder suggests that it is further augmented by "her willingness to act as a political figure as well as a popular one and to recognize that such fraught domains as sex, religion, and family are indeed, political constructions, especially for lesbian and gay people" (117). Such a combination of the political and the popular is also central to Lady Gaga's star image, notable among others in her rallying against the military policy of "Don't Ask, Don't Tell" until its abolishment in 2011, the establishment of her "Born This Way" Foundation in 2012, or her contribution of the song "'Til it Happens to You" to the campus-rape documentary *The Hunting Ground* (2015, Dir. Kirby Dick). Such activism forms an important paratext for both a singer's popular output and influences the reception of their reliance on camp. Beyond the frivolous quality of her iconography Stan Hawkins therefore claims that Madonna's use of camp "constructs a potent statement of defiance which functions as a vehicle both for resistance and empowerment" (*Settling* 50).[5] Crucial to this effect are Madonna's "array of polished performances and chameleon-like changes in appearance" (Peñaloza 190), and "the layers of her performances that become 'falser than false'" and thus make her work "an extreme statement about the epistemological fluidity of contemporary culture" (Pisters 33–4). The superficial becomes ground for the profound, as Pamela Robertson also concedes when she—despite her overall rather ambiguous stance on Madonna's subversive value—accounts for Madonna's "cumulative image from her varied and multiple performances [...] as a kind of meta-masquerade" (125–6).

In their reliance on masquerade Cher and Madonna, like most previous camp icons, present themselves as glamorous. While to a certain extent an essential part of any kind of stardom, glamor has inherently subversive elements, as historically "glamour represented an audacious refusal to be imprisoned by norms of class and gender, or by expectations of conventional femininity" (Dyhouse 3). In keeping with this resistive stance Lady Gaga has adopted the pop diva's typical outlandish couture and intensified its effect through the increased extravagance and speed of her costume and image changes. Though Robertson relates this masquerade only to Madonna's feminist value, there is a clear connection to Judith Butler's remarks on performative subjectivity, which in turn connects to Andy Warhol's practices, which serve as crucial intertexts for Gaga's artistic output. Though approaching the question of originality from vastly different points of view, both Butler and Warhol challenge the evaluation of "original" over copy through which their queer theory and queer art are connected. Where Butler insists that "gay is to straight *not* as copy is to original, but, rather, as copy is to copy" (31, emphasis in the original), Warhol produced similar, but never identical images and portraits from ultimately devalued "originals." Ultimately these notions also resurface in pop divas' constant self-reinventions, which, like these other forms of copying, leave "a trace of difference to queer subjectivity" (J. Dyer 55). In an interview accompanying a photo shoot, in which she is seen without a bra, but with the silhouette of a strap-on visible beneath her pants, Gaga picks up this rejection of the "original" and comments on the press obsession with the "truth" about celebrities and personal identity—as if there was such a thing:

> some major magazine [is] like *[high-camp voice]*, So, the art direction of the shoot is: we want the world to see *the real you*. [...] But you don't really wanna get to know me or photograph my soul, you want to do some version of what you already think I am and then expose something that

you believe is hidden. When the truth is, me and my big fucking dick are all out there for you. (Patterson 52)

Thus elevating a sex toy to the status of identity signifier, Gaga once again articulates the "opposition between authentic subjectivity and inauthentic society" (Suárez 134) that is characteristic of her work and camp in general. She exposes the hypocrisy of accepting only a narrow range of gender expressions, personal styles, and identificatory strategies as authentic and true (original), while those falling outside this spectrum are accused of pretense (copy or lie). Put another way, Gaga rejects the notion that putting on a show is tantamount to hiding something in favor of locating the authentic expression in the "show" itself. Toying with gender parody, identity politics, and artistic integrity, Lady Gaga's camp becomes both a mode of making room for queer humor, and subsequently pleasure, as well as a critique of those discourses that oppress alternate models of meaning making and which fail to grasp the sincerity of her—and others'—playfulness. Her refusal of conventional sex appeal through clothes that hide or distort her body, that feature spikes and armor to counter the availability of the female body, or that reveal so much they deny the special status awarded to slim female figures, her negation of conventional star narratives by insisting on the primacy of her public persona to the point of negating a private one, or her revision of tropes of musical expression of love and romance, therefore need to be understood not as negative refusal, but as productive creation generating at the heart of pop culture spaces for queer identification and pleasure and investing surfaces with affective surplus value. Lady Gaga uses camp as both a means of creative re-signification and of critique and transgression. While camp achieves—as it had done for her diva predecessors—the defamiliarization of the familiar, rendering the seemingly normal and natural unnatural, as "it constantly draws attention to the artifices attendant on the construction of images of what is natural" (Dyer, "Culture" 42), this is not an end in itself. More importantly, camp's inversion of values and norms privileges the status of the opposite, namely the deviant. Though not always comic in nature, Lady Gaga's oeuvre nonetheless provides the "rebellious type of pleasure" Ken Feil associates with queer comedy and its reliance on camp, which cheers on "the triumph of queerness against the limitations of the social world" (484).

The centrality of visual markers in the critical reception of Madonna, Gaga, and other pop divas notwithstanding, their resistive potential rests not solely on those. Rather, as Stan Hawkins remarks in his analysis of Madonna's "Music," camp qualities can also be located in "the subtleties and excesses of musical treatment" ("Dragging" 8–9). Richard Middleton offers a diachronic analysis of Madonna's vocal role play, ranging from "a coquettish sex-kitten," to "sexually ruthless woman-of-the-world," and "the more traditional role of torch-song protagonist" that supports her queer star image (37–8). Non-visual aspects are also important in accounting for the incongruous performances and affective power of other pop divas. The embrace of serious artificiality represented in the costumes of such stars as Cher or Annie Lennox can also be found in their vocal performances. Cher, for example, popularized auto-tune effects on her album *Believe* (1998), which toy with the "central pop gesture, the sung note" (Frith 210). Frith stresses the relevance of voices to our understanding of pop as both artificial and intimate, when he argues for the voice as "the most taken-for-granted indication of the person, the guarantor of the coherent subject" at the same time as he acknowledges that popular music "uses the voice as something artificial, posed, its sound determined by the music." Enhanced through technology in both its intimacy (voices sound as if they were sung just for us) and distance (they can sound almost non-human), the "authenticity or 'sincerity' of the voice," Frith stresses, "becomes the recurring pop question" (210). Against this backdrop, Cher's altered voice on "Believe" becomes particularly glaring in its disregard for common pop standards. Kay Dickinson emphasizes how the track's vocal arrangement expresses a "delight in the inauthentic, in things which are obviously pretending to be what they are not and which might, to some degree, speak of the difficulties of existing within an ill-fitting public façade" (344). This delight in the inauthentic is contrasted with the song's lyrics which evoke classic themes of "the triumph and liberation of the downtrodden and unloved" (344). Concerning Madonna's voice, Stan Hawkins argues in a similar vein regarding the queer effect of "Music," in which the vocoded parts, together with the guitar riff, "metamorphose into something alluringly beautiful, quirky, and flamboyant, the effect of which is camp" ("Dragging" 9).

Technological alterations are not the only way to "queer'" vocal performances. Long before, Dusty Springfield, for example, cemented her status as a 1960s iconoclast through her duet with herself for the song "Mockingbird." Here, Springfield—whose visual effect has been described as expressing "her own unspeakable queerness through an elaborate camp masquerade that metaphorically and artistically transformed a nice white girl into a black woman and a femme gay man, often simultaneously" (Smith, "You Don't" 106)—sings both the male and female parts of a love song. She thus forces audiences to either accept her "naturally" masculine voice as such (despite supposedly "knowing" her female gender) or hearing the song as sung by same-sex lovers. Annie Lennox has produced similar effects in songs like "Sweet Dreams" by lowering her voice beneath even her speaking voice during some parts, while belting opera-like high notes in others. Such vocal role play has become a regular component of Lady Gaga's songs and, as an ethnographic study among gay fans of Lady Gaga suggests, "fans identify Gaga's use of her low register and chest voice as key to her vocal appeal" (Jennex 354). Such a masquerade of the gendered voice is often intensified by foreign languages or accents (Spanish in "Alejandro" and "Americano," German in "Scheiße," and French in "Bad Romance"[6]) or the "imitation" of well-known vocal tropes, such as the rhythmic speaking in "Dance in the Dark" that produces a sonic connection to Madonna's "Vogue."[7] The same track also contains breathing, sighing, and screaming—all rather unusual vocal sounds on pop tracks—and furthermore relies heavily on echo effects and technological distortions of the voice for its eerie impression, which amounts to the audio equivalent of a house of mirrors. The same album, *The Fame Monster*, also contains such songs as "Speechless," which Lady Gaga sings with a slightly raspy voice and a little vibrato that marks this song as a rock ballad, and "Monster," in which two distinct vocal personas emerge from the over-dubbing: Gaga's heavily autotuned, teenaged voice ("he ate my heart"); and another more mature, seemingly less artificial voice.[8] *The Fame Monster* thus presents a stark deviation from her prior pop- and dance-oriented material on *The Fame*, as her voice exposes a closer connection to the body through a higher degree of raspiness and breathiness at the same time as it is ornamented with even more technological effects and distortions that stress its artificial character as just one instrument (or sign) among many. As *The Fame Monster* is furthermore characterized by glaring vocal differences between its different tracks and a darker tone overall than prior productions, its audio qualities support the more open embrace of serious topics after Lady Gaga's initial success in 2008 and 2009 and the intensification of Lady Gaga's visual masquerade. This additional manipulation of a supposedly natural, bodily property, the voice, adds crucially to her embrace of theatricality, while enhancing her song's emotional impact.

Another way in which pop songs have fostered queer affect has been sexual ambiguity on the level of lyrics, as exemplified by Cher's "The Way of Love" (1971). The use of pronouns subtly introduces queer romance into the otherwise relatively unmarked song; Cher is left for a man, which marks her and/or her ex-lover, to whom the song is addressed, as bisexual. In a similar manner, the classic "Son of a Preacher Man" (1969) by Dusty Springfield is either a song about a woman who only loved once, or about the only affair with a man the queer song persona ever had. Judy Garland's "Over the Rainbow" (1939) leaves its interpretation similarly open to its audiences. Its queerness depends on the willingness to read "rainbow" figuratively rather than literally. In recent years "gay" lyrics have become less subtextual, particularly through the influence of lesbian chic, which may have become most apparent in Katy Perry's first hit, "I Kissed a Girl" from 2008, in which she famously did as the title of the song implies and then hoped her "boyfriend don't mind it." In 2010 Rihanna delivered a similar message with her song "Te Amo," in which she recounts another woman's attraction to her. She must refuse, however, because she "doesn't feel that way," claiming that while they can dance, the other woman "would have to watch her hands." Such toying with lesbian imagery (and sound bites) securely framed by the heterosexuality of both singer and song personas, however, has little to offer in terms of the queer spaces of identification provided by the more subtextual, yet more serious embrace of queer sexual expressions in the older song examples. For Lady Gaga, the lyrical embrace of non-normative sexuality can be traced from comparatively subtle hints via the use of pronouns in her debut album ("Pokerface") to the explicit mention of LGBT concerns on later albums such as "Americano" (about gay marriage) and "Born This Way." Tongue-in-cheek double entendres offer an additional way to reference queerness: "I want your psycho / Your vertigo shtick / Want you in my rear window" from "Bad Romance" or "Come to me / with all your subtext and fantasy / Just do that thing that you do / In a perverse hue" from "Artpop" and the gender confusing wordplay "I want to be that G.U.Y." from "G.U.Y." in which the abbreviation ostensibly stands for girl under you, but is pronounced guy. As interesting as the presence of queer undertones in her lyrics is the lack of any song that celebrates traditional, heteronormative relationships. This focus on unfulfilled, complicated, overly sexual, queer, and overall non-normative expressions of love underlines her refusal to support the values usually associated with pop love songs.

Another way to inscribe oneself into a different set of values and foster camp incongruity in popular music has been the embrace of what Mark Booth describes as the strategy's central feature, "being committed to the marginal with a commitment greater than the marginal merits" (69). One telling example is Dusty Springfield's song "You don't have to say you love me" (1966). Described by Smith as adding "sheer tragedy and queen melodrama" to Springfield's persona, Springfield herself called the song "commercial," resulting in a contradiction that summarizes the camp dichotomy of Springfield's success. Smith adds "what set it apart from pure kitsch is that [Springfield], like any grand diva, treated this work of somewhat dubious artistic merit with the integrity and creative energy one would bestow upon an aria" ("You Don't" 114). Aria-like integrity for a pop song has also been credited to Judy Garland and her (and camp's) signature song "Over the Rainbow." The song's and Garland's appeal have been summarized by John Clum as "brilliant singing" and a "captivating [...] belief in what she's doing," which makes her performance "refreshingly honest, more honest sometimes than the parts call for" (150). Such sonic incongruity was reiterated by Lady Gaga early in her career, when she performed her dance track "Pokerface" in a deeply emotional piano version for *AOL Music Sessions* in 2009. Here she added growls to her vocal performance and exhibited a higher dynamic in volume, and a larger range than on the album version. These changes enhanced the song's emotional effect at the same time as they mocked the supposed "artlessness" of pop and dance tracks by presenting it as "serious" music. A classical instrument like the piano, which received an additional edge through her playing some notes with the heel of her pumps, intensified this effect. In other renditions of the song the clash between content and form was further enhanced by her costume, which consisted of a Burlesque-inspired see-through bubble dress, under which she was wearing a Madonna-like flesh-colored cone bra for her 2009 concert tour, or a planetary head piece for the introduction to the song on *The Ellen Degeneres Show*. Taking her songs and fans seriously, but not the distinction between high and low art (classical music and pop), or between natural and deviant gender (biological sex and drag), such moments place Lady Gaga in line with the aforementioned pop divas.

What distinguishes her, however, from this legacy, is her increased and increasingly blatant engagement with queerness through the choice of her intertexts, as I explore below, as well as changes in her reliance on media that expand the possibilities used by her predecessors and infuses them with overtly metareferential qualities.

1.2   The Technology of Pop

Among the pop divas who have consciously used the medium of music videos to define their image and sharpen their critique of the music industry's treatment of women has been Annie Lennox. She thus emerges as a particularly enlightening intertext for Lady Gaga's use of this—now primarily digital—medium.

Annie Lennox's use of cross-media storytelling to confound audiences about her gender and sexuality is especially noteworthy. In the 1983 video for the Eurythmics song "Who's That Girl" Lennox, for the most part, is dressed as a nightclub singer with long blonde wig and pink lipstick. Towards the end of the video, however, she appears as another character, this time as a male audience member in a black suit and slicked back black hair. The video ends with a still image of both her characters just shy of kissing. At the 1984 *Grammy Award* show, Lennox resurrected the male character from *Who's That Girl*. By adding sideburns and Elvis-type mannerisms she performed "Sweet Dreams" in a huskier voice than usual to enhance her performance of masculinity. Lennox's cumulative star image influences the reading of these two instances of cross-dressing insofar as the Eurythmics had already flirted with scandal in 1982 with their single "Love is a Stranger." The accompanying video showed Lennox in two very different female outfits—1980s leather chic and Marilyn Monroe wig with fur coat—both of which she discarded with a gesture that typically ends performances by female impersonators: the dramatic removal of the wig to expose the short hair underneath and thus, supposedly the performer's "true" (male) gender. Adding to this multi-layered performance was Lennox's first outfit in *Love is a Stranger*, fur coat and sparkly earrings, reminiscent of Julie Andrew's costume in *Victor/Victoria* (1982, Dir. Blake Edwards). Andrews plays a down on her luck female performer who pretends to be a male female impersonator, including the big wig removal cum "gender reveal" at the end of the performance, through which "Victor/Victoria collapses these generic gender conventions of short hair and removal of the wig to 'expose' her (male) disguise as real" (Straayer 421–22). Allusions to drag are carried over into Lennox's solo career, though they take on a different quality as other critics have remarked upon. Starting with Eurythmics' *Savage* (1988), whose cover art shows her once again wearing an unnaturally blonde wig, Lennox turned away from primarily relying on androgyny to resist the public consumption of her body and "to find alternative ways of distancing herself from the characters she assumes" (Rodger 25). The cover art for her debut solo album *Diva* (1992) shows her in high female drag with colorful make-up and a feathered head piece, and the music video for the song "Why" from the same album reverses the former "revealing" story through a narrative (and visuals) of "putting on a mask." *Why* begins with a scene typical for depictions of cross-dressing in Hollywood Cinema. Lennox is sitting in front of a large mirror, applying her heavy make-up (to the point of changing the contours of her face) and putting on costume and wig. The performance of femininity and the effort that goes with it are put front and center to highlight the artificiality of mediated gender ideals. Stressing the mask of femininity is, of course, central to Robertson's argument on female camp's deconstructive quality, based on Russo's dictum that "To put on femininity with a vengeance suggests the power of taking it off" (70). Lennox in particular wielded this kind of power in earlier media representations, which only added to the evocativeness of her later "female female impersonation." In her analysis of the "array of female guises" used in Lennox's music videos Gillian Rodger thus concluded that Lennox consciously used a medium which generally serves as a marketing device to withhold her body and reject its objectification and sexualization (21–2; see also Hawkins, *Settling* 127).

E. Ann Kaplan's "Gender Address and the Gaze" insightfully addressed the music video's centrality to both the exploitation of female pop performers and their emancipation. Kaplan claims that the music video "constructs several different kinds of gender address and modes of representing sexuality, several different positions for the spectator to take up in relation to sexual difference" (89). She elaborates that cinematic theories of the gaze are complicated in music videos, because there is no clear diegesis that creates a firm subject position. Kaplan names "arbitrariness of the images," "lack of limitations spatially," "frequently extremely rapid montage-style editing," and "precise relationship" of sound and image as reasons for the music video's "unique" way of addressing the audience (124). For Andrew Goodwin, this uniqueness stems from the "aural address of the pop singer," which results in "a direct address to the listener/viewer in which the personality of the storyteller usually overwhelms characterization within the story" (76). Focusing on Madonna's video for *Material Girl* (1984), Kaplan describes this effect as "Madonna, as historical star subject, break[ing] through her narrative positions" and thus using the music video not only to promote her new single, but also to add another layer to fans' and critics' understanding of her star persona at the same time as her star persona influences the way the video's material girl is read as an intervention in conventional portrayals of women in music videos (126). Similarly, Gillian Gaar claims that the Eurythmics and Annie Lennox, rather than using "their videos as just another promotional tool, [...] used the medium as another venue of artistic expression, learning to manipulate their image instead of being manipulated by their image" (264). As these examples illustrate, music videos lend themselves particularly well to such manipulation as they are immutably bound to a performer's song (and thus their voice and persona), but little else—not to narrative logic, nor spatial boundaries, and so on. Hence, music videos have historically provided a plethora of intertextual references and superficially disconnected images only bound by loose associations or aesthetic concerns. Additionally, music videos are produced to "withstand repeated viewings," which Goodwin connects to their fast-moving imagery, as the medium is generally intended to be "difficult to decode on one viewing" (61). Through these exuberant aesthetic qualities music videos have provided fruitful ground for camp.

For Lady Gaga, the potential for producing and shaping her image via music videos has dramatically increased through online promotion. No longer restricted by the format of music television, Lady Gaga has produced music videos that appear on TV in shortened versions, while the full videos (13:51 minutes in the case of *Marry The Night;* 8:44 minutes for *Alejandro;* 9:31 minutes for *Telephone,* and often for long parts without music) are only available online. Digital media, however, not only allow for new forms and content of the music video, but also allow artists to take their videos out of the "linear flow of relatively short text-segments of different kinds inherent to the televisual apparatus" (Kaplan 90). To a certain extent artist and fans are thus able to produce their own context for the "repeated viewings" still central to the experience of music video audiences (Goodwin 61). Hence, the creation of aesthetic and narrative connections between music videos and across different media is enhanced through digital distribution. This in turn leads to new creative freedom and additional control in the shaping of star images.

The role of formerly ephemeral live performances has changed most drastically through the internet's memory effect; every (professionally or privately) taped performance now has the potential to be viewed on demand and to thus add to the star image and the narration of stories and identities across media boundaries. Prime examples of recorded live performances that have become essential to star images are Judy Garland's *Judy at Carnegie Hall* (1961) and Bette Midler's *Art or Bust* (1984). Garland's performances especially have received scholarly attention for their role in the development of her cult status and their production of "complex emotions" (see Jennings 92). The significant difference today lies in the almost instantaneous and usually free online accessibility of live performances, which enhances their chances of becoming a recognizable part of the star's oeuvre. When considering the status of the live performance as "one of the recurring pleasures of popular culture," a "spectacular act" whose liveness results in a "sense of risk, danger, triumph, virtuosity" (Frith 207), now paradoxically combined with widespread access and longevity, it should come as no surprise that Lady Gaga's critical breakthrough (almost a year after her commercial breakthrough) and one of her signature performances that combined camp's metareferential and affective capacities, was a live performance.

2   INTERNET KILLED THE VIDEO STAR: NARRATING METAREFERENTIALITY ACROSS MEDIA

2.1   Paparazzi: *Rewinding Warhol*

Werner Wolf conceptualized metareferentiality as the result of 'metaization': "the movement from a first cognitive or communicative level to a higher one on which [...] all the means and the media used for such utterances, self-reflexively become objects of reflection and communication in their own right" (3). Metareferences thus make it possible to turn the form and medium of the object in question into its content, and it has become one major component in contemporary popular culture through which audiences and producers can distance themselves from and think critically about the framework (whether capitalist, sexist, racist, or heteronormative) of their production and consumption. Such a "meta-concern" for the music industry is, as mentioned in the beginning of this chapter, inscribed in Stephanie Germanotta's stage name, and further highlighted through the constant allusions to sex, money, and fame in her songs—as on her debut album *The Fame*. Apart from referring to Andy Warhol's famous quote on everyone's "15 minutes of fame," which in the age of YouTube has become its own truism, Lady Gaga also revives Warhol's concept of homemade superstars. In a combination of the gay subcultural practice of "voguing" and the participants' so-called houses and Warhol's factory, Lady Gaga has assembled the "Haus of Gaga," which is creating her in turn—by providing her stage costumes and accessories, and producing some of her songs and her short films.

Among the earliest of these short films are those that served as openers for different parts of her first concert tour, in which Lady Gaga was sometimes depicted as her alter ego "Candy Warhol" (a combination Andy Warhol and one of his "superstars," the transsexual actor Candy Darling)—who is musing about her relationship to the "big beautiful monster" that is pop. Through these alter egos and her outrageous costumes Lady Gaga constantly draws attention to the highly performative nature of pop music and pop stars. By highlighting the mechanisms of the historic, economic, and generic framework of pop music—or at least making it hard to ignore them—through her videos, shows, and music, she adds another layer to her music and by doing so, contributes to Candy Warhol's motto that "Pop will never be low brow." Lady Gaga's appearance at the *MTV Video Music Awards* 2009 marked an early culmination of her depiction of a rather ambiguous relationship to pop music fame (Paparazzi [Live Performance @ VMA 2009]).

Starting with a few notes of her breakthrough hit "Poker Face," the performance not only recreates her own, short history of fame, but also reframes the hitherto sexually connoted lyrics "He can't read my Pokerface" (when the song persona fantasizes about women) in a much darker context as masking her fear. "Amidst all of these flashing lights I pray / the fame won't take my life" Lady Gaga, lying on the floor, adds pleadingly to the original song lyrics as the "Pokerface" intro fades into the opening string section of "Paparazzi." The stage performance seems to set in immediately after her fall depicted at the beginning of her *Paparazzi* music video, as she needs the help of her backup dancers to get on her feet. In a scene reminiscent of *Phantom of the Opera* (1986, Comp. Andrew Lloyd Webber), through the giant chandelier crashed on the stage floor, and *Sunset Boulevard* (1950, Dir.

Billy Wilder), through the iconic, domineering staircase—both iconic pop-cultural texts about the detrimental effects of fame—Lady Gaga proceeds to perform "Paparazzi" in a radically different manner to the song's released version. While her voice on the album version is notably higher and more youthful, taking on the role of the adoring teenage fan, the voice during the live performance reflects an overall somber mood through its lower register and darker timbre, harder onsets, a more intense vibrato, and noticeable breathing, which give the vocal performance an urgent undercurrent. During the chorus the contrasting vocal arrangements are particularly striking in their difference between naïve celebration and desperate pleading; whereas in the single version Lady Gaga sings several notes in her head voice and tends to sing high notes towards phrase endings ("Papa-paparazzi"), in the live version she lowers her voice at this point and adds an almost growled, raspy "oh yeah," which evokes a spontaneous and emotional quality absent from the polished single. The differences between single and live versions also extend to the musical accompaniment. Whereas the single version is dominated by the rhythmic phrasing provided by a drum machine, the live version builds much of its emotional intensity via the staccato-like string arrangement, which pushes the performance forward and adds a menacing ambience. After the more speech-like section ("Real good, we dance in the studio / Snap-snap, to that shit on the radio / Don't stop for anyone")—which in both "Paparazzi" versions ends on the near-shouted Warhol reference "We're plastic, but we still have fun"—the live version proceeds with a frenetic piano interlude. Its last notes blend with the piercing strings, as Lady Gaga stands up to walk back from the piano to the now empty center of the stage. Synchronized with her distressed interpretation of the chorus' final repetition, fake blood starts streaming down her naked mid-section, contrasting sharply with the otherwise completely white costumes and stage props. The increasingly dramatic musical and vocal performance is further enhanced by both the singer's and the background dancers' contorted movements and manic facial expressions throughout the performance. Especially Lady Gaga's movements become even less natural and more tense shortly before her final breakdown, as the dancers return to gawk at her bleeding body. Finally, after her vocal performance culminates in a guttural scream which fades into sobbing, her lifeless body is pulled up above the stage—the drama of the performance contrasting sharply with the figure of the dead singer suspended mid-air with the gesture of a shrug, seemingly accepting her expected fate. Meanwhile the dancers surround and applaud her, as a fusillade of flashing lights ends the scene.

The performance presents itself as a sharp critique of the cannibalistic relationship of performer and paparazzi/public. At the same, the performance consciously provokes a scandal and thus ensures exactly this kind of public/paparazzi attention. Lady Gaga thus refuses to position herself as an 'outsider looking in.' Instead—like Lennox's and other divas' reclamation of the music video as a medium of withholding—she uses a standard promotional tool not to (primarily) promote her product, but rather to cultivate her resistive star image. Essential to this image is the blending of art (as fake/lie) and reality, which becomes particularly obvious when the flashing lights that are part of the show mix with the flashing lights from reporters and fans. While many aspects of this performance underline its sincerity (particularly the musical accompaniment with strings, the dramatic gestures, and the emotional vocal performance), others ensure that it stays connected to its pop and entertainment context and does not speak from a removed outsider perspective.[9] The intertexts, for example, are decidedly not high art but rather examples of what one might refer to as hand-me-down formats. Rather than referring to an opera, Lady Gaga references a musical *about* an opera. Similarly, she chooses a film noir *about* silent film rather than a silent film per se as her intertext. The parallels between *Sunset Boulevard* and *Phantom of the Opera* extend beyond their main characters' obsession with fame and their hand-me-down character to the motif of striving for one final masterpiece (a consciously odd choice for an up-and-coming star that points to the often short-lived careers of pop singers) and longing for the affection of a younger lover (which adds a melodramatic, kitschy component). Even more glaringly than these intertexts the fake blood stands out as a stagy effect that belies the dramatic intensity and artistic virtuosity of the preceding piano interlude. A similar contrast arises between the soulful vocal interpretation, Gaga's grand gestures, and the song's blatantly mindless lyrics, such as "loving you is cherry pie" ("Paparazzi"). The performance thus works on several levels: as eye-catching entertainment; as highly emotional musical expression; and as metacommentary. Meanwhile it stresses rather than smooths over the tensions between these vastly different approaches to popular music. Laying bare the devices of the music industry through the performance's metareferences, in which the performance of the consequences of fame become the basis for the establishment of fame, the show simultaneously embraces the over-the-top emotionality of this dramatic reinterpretation of a hitherto rather standard pop song. The performance furthermore infuses future encounters with the song's album version with an additional critical (through its metacommentary) as well as affective edge (through its heightened emotionality), as social media and video platforms ensure this alternate version's entrance to and continued presence in the public consciousness. Lady Gaga's performance at the 2009 *MTV Video Music Awards* thus establishes itself as an evocative cue for the singer's increasing reliance on camp's estranging, yet compelling mode of embracing the surface to change the message. It also stands as an important indicator for the many instances of cross-media narration the singer weaves into her oeuvre.

The *Paparazzi* music video had already introduced many of the above-mentioned themes through its mise en scène and intertextual references. It garnered additional meaning in the context of cross-media narration when the later video for *Telephone* (a collaboration with Beyoncé from the extended album, *The Fame Monster*) was designed as its sequel, and it stands as the first of many music videos whose length and narrative content exceeds that of the respective songs (and conventional music videos). Reintroducing through a non-musical prologue the diegetic framework Kaplan had defined as atypical for the medium, Paparazzi, and several other Lady Gaga videos, limit the "arbitrariness of the images" and narrow the "different positions for the spectator to take up in relation to sexual difference" (Kaplan 89), usually in favor of queer subject positions. In the case of *Paparazzi*, the actual song begins only three minutes into the video, coinciding with Lady Gaga's emergence from the limousine for her comeback (awaited by the eponymous paparazzi) after the near-fatal fall from her balcony. Up until this point the video, directed by Jonas Åkerlund and co-starring Alexander Skarsgård, is accompanied only by a piano whose hesitant, often interrupted, overall non-melodic sound establishes an atmosphere of impending doom. Between snapshots of markers of the main character's fame, such as dollar notes with her face, which are interspersed with symbols of Lady Gaga's non-fictional fame via product placement, the video tells the story of a gold-digging lover who eventually pushes Lady Gaga over a balcony, when she refuses his sexual advances in front of prying paparazzi. Her fall is presented as a *Vertigo*-like (1958, Dir. Alfred Hitchcock) fantasy sequence: her body, in slow-motion free fall, posing, showing off her ring (studded diamonds spelling Dior), to the soundtrack of her heavy breathing as the black and white vortex in the background swirls increasingly fast until it swallows her body. A self-consciously outdated editing effect, an iris wipe in shape of her body, rather than a cut, moves the video to the scene of her mutilated body sprawled on the floor, where antique cameras used by the intradiegetic paparazzi and headlines, which swirl into the picture to summarize the fallout of the events, correspond to the "classical" theme. As soon as the song's first notes set in, the video reverts to modern editing techniques characteristic of music videos. Accordingly, the theme of the macabre and the menacing behind beautiful façades is translated from Hitchcockian devices into contemporary images.

As indicated, the lyrics pay homage to Andy Warhol through the line "We're plastic, but we still have fun," which answers his comment on celebrity culture: "I love Hollywood. They're beautiful. Everybody's plastic, but I love plastic. I want to be plastic" (Heylin 13). Beyond this connection, the integration of Hollywood iconography as the hallmark of celebrity, fame, and glamor is as paramount in Gaga's work (and the Paparazzi video), as it had been in Warhol's, whose iconography "reveals something tragic and real [...] presenting images which force viewers seriously to consider what happens beneath the iconography of commodity fetishism" (J. Dyer 34). In keeping with this theme, the video consists of several close-ups of commonly fetishized female body parts (lips, hair, legs), which in full shots are revealed as belonging to the corpses of murdered women scattered around a mansion. Here—the parallel editing implies—a party, which is stylized to look like more conventional pop music videos, is contemporaneously ongoing. Telling the story of Lady Gaga's return to the spotlight, the video ends by returning to the seemingly reunited couple. Wearing a yellow Mickey Mouse costume, which mocks the infantilizing tendencies of pop culture, and drinking her signature tea, a symbol of both aristocracy and aloofness, Lady Gaga gets up to mix her boyfriend a drink. Rather than ending the narrative here, however, the beat (though not the song) goes on, as Gaga proceeds to poison him. In a voice-over following old telephone sounds her disengaged voice informs the police, "I just killed my boyfriend." After a short intermission during which only intradiegetic sounds can be heard, the song starts again but serves only as background music for the flashing lights and police sirens that dominate the soundtrack. Once again swirling headlines inform the audience of Gaga's fate: the murder makes her an even bigger star. The sonic effect of keeping the original song's volume at a minimum stresses how the video privileges its narrative over that of the original song. The original song persona had fulfilled the typically female role of adoring groupie. The video positions her instead as self-sufficient, self-confident, and successful in her own right, while it emphasizes the public's sordid appetite for star scandals. Overall *Paparazzi*, as well as subsequent videos by Lady Gaga, challenge normative readings of her songs by either foregrounding the already existing tensions in the lyrics or by providing strong counter-narratives through their visualization. They thus add productively to the "debate about whether or not the video image triumphs over the song" (Goodwin 86). In analyzing Madonna's video, Susan McClary claims that no matter how memorable a video's images the music remains "responsible for the narrative continuity and the affective quality in the resultant work" (161). With videos as visually and narratively complex and as thematically removed from the songs they are 'based' on as Lady Gaga's music videos, the overwhelming impact of music in this medium needs to be reconsidered and the affective potential of images and narrative stressed.

2.2   Telephone: Lesploitation After Lesbian Chic

One year later Lady Gaga continued the story of *Paparazzi* in her video collaboration with Beyoncé in *Telephone* (whose lyrics and music bear no relation to "Paparazzi"). Shifting her focus to the representation of gender and sexuality rather than an inquiry into stardom and fame, the *Telephone* video is intertextually complex and narratively even more removed from the song it is based on than *Paparazzi*. *Telephone* is designed as a remake of lesploitation films, drawing on the clichéd and sexualized images of "girls behind bars" B-movies.[10] Like other exploitation films, most prominently the genres blaxploitation and sexploitation, lesploitation films were constructed around minority issues and fringe topics and meant for the viewing pleasure of straight white men. The lesploitation genre stressed the objectification of women's bodies and female—especially lesbian—sexuality, the trivialization of violence against women, and the impossibility of meaningful bonding between women.

These features still define current pop culture, which makes this theme's combination with the collaboration of two of the most successful and influential contemporary female pop artists so revealing. With lesploitation, the creative team behind *Telephone* furthermore chose a theme that had already been reappropriated by queer, namely lesbian, audiences. The process is comparable to the ongoing cult success of 1950s gay and lesbian pulp novels, whose colorful and sensationalistic covers serve as an inspiration for the sets and costumes of *Telephone*. Their cultural significance as camp, however, stems from the interaction between the attention-grabbing covers, shallow literary quality, and dark themes, as well as their incongruous effects on queer audiences. The texts were equally "instrumental in creating certain stereotypes" as "their very lack of respectability allowed them to perform the iconoclastic function of presenting, if only obliquely, subversively positive images" (Smith, "Icons" xxi). By portraying the lesbian femme whose image was made popular in mainstream culture by exactly these pulp novels, Lady Gaga furthermore adds another significant component to the ever-growing array of gender performances expressed in her photo shoots, on stage, and in videos, ranging from hyper-femininity to androgyny, and conflating lesbian femme, drag queen, and stud.[11]

Complementing the recurring habit of gender parody in Gaga's oeuvre the *Telephone* video emphasizes the potential for queer pleasure in the genre in several ways: it casts butch performance artist Heather Cassils as the genre and cultural norms defying object of the protagonist's desire; it installs two female bodybuilders as guards, who are not portrayed as sadistic or lonely outsiders in contrast to their counterparts in the original movies; it brings the female gaze into the foreground via the insertion of shots of female onlookers; and adds the lesbian happy ending these films normally lack when Gaga and Beyoncé drive off into the sunset together.[12] In this innovative approach to the genre, as Tavia Nyong'o calls it, the video "upend[s] the heterosexual fantasies that underpinned [...] the archive of mainstream representation." Another important source for queer audiences' "rebellious type of pleasure" lies in the video's over-the-top visual design, which at times can produce a narrative that counteracts, or at least complicates, the genre's plot and the stereotypes it employs. Having Lady Gaga arrive in a low-cut latex suit, for example, sporting stripes otherwise known from early prison uniforms, undercuts the supposed innocence and naiveté of the "new girl," which the normative "girls behind bars" storyline asks for. In another significant difference from the original plot and its cliché of the new inmate, through her prison garment-like clothing Lady Gaga is not only implied to be, but actually *known* to be not innocent. The video's audience has seen the character's cold-blooded murder of her abusive boyfriend in the *Paparazzi* video to which *Telephone* serves as sequel.

Whereas the lesploitation film tries to uphold the image of the ultimately available and seemingly—at least in the beginning—tamable young girl, *Telephone* starts with Lady Gaga as an established criminal.

In other scenes the video does not contradict, but rather exaggerates, what the lesploitation genre accepts as a given: the glamorization and sexualization of life behind bars. The effect, however, is everything but reassuring for the originally implied straight male viewer, as exemplified by the video's cage dance sequence. This is one of only three dance sequences in the ten-minute Telephone film and thus resembles a dance number in film musicals, which provides a spectacle that interrupts the narrative flow—usually in favor of a utopian transgression of boundaries and differences. In a rather dystopian manner, Gaga dances seductively together with her scantily clad, conventionally attractive female backup dancers in the prison hallway. Their movements are interrupted by scenes depicting Lady Gaga as the victim of a crime—or rather her body as a living crime scene as she is wrapped in "crime scene, do not cross" barrier tape—whose limbs still move rhythmically to the music, which results in the visual clash of battering and glamor already shown in Paparazzi. This unsettling combination of violence against the female body and its objectification is repeated in the other two dance sequences, once when Gaga and Beyoncé dance in a pool of dead bodies, and again when Lady Gaga prepares poison for a mass murder. In all three scenes, Gaga represents a stereotype of women's conventional presentation in the media: sexy stripper; devoted housewife; chaste Wonder Woman. All three figures are constituted through costume, hair, setting, and make-up in a way that underlines their constructedness and, via their close connection to violence in the video, their inherently oppressive nature. While thus subverting the allure of conventional ideas about gender identity and desire, at the same time the video makes room for positive depictions of queer desires and gender performances, which the genre—and by extension today's media—usually tries to repress. The genre of the lesploitation film lends itself especially well to the discussion of gender expressions femme and women's depiction in popular media, because "[d]ifferences between women are stressed, as if to take the place usually occupied by gender: differences between butch and personas, differences in age, [...] physical differences" (Mayne 127). In *Telephone* men accordingly appear only in minor roles as backup dancers, dinner guests, and another abusive boyfriend, this time Beyoncé's, who is quickly killed off. Women, in contrast, are represented in all shapes and sizes, and several constellations of power, antagonism, friendship, and desire without being devalued or played off against each other. Rather than, for example, using the wardens' non-conforming bodybuilder physiques to divert from Lady Gaga's own rumored sex deviation, the video stresses the connection between these different kinds of women as gender outlaws. At the same time, the video portrays as attractive what heteronormative culture would reject, such as muscular Heather Cassils or curvy women of color in the prison yard, while placing conventionally attractive women, such as Gaga's female dancers or even Beyoncé herself in contexts that problematize their sexual allure. Thus, *Telephone* flips the power dynamics of media reception, where the empowering queer reading of such products as lesploitation films are relegated as "readings against the grain," or appropriations. Here, by contrast, any straight reading would be forced to justify itself as a valid reappropriation. This is especially visible, if "Telephone" is compared to the preceding collaboration between these performers, namely Beyoncé's "Video Phone." The lyrics for "Video Phone" on the one and "Telephone" on the other hand can be positioned as opposing treatments of the supposed availability of women.

> Press record I'll let you film me [...] If you want me, you can watch me on your video phone [...] (Beyoncé, "Video Phone")

> Call all you want, but there's no one home, and you're not gonna reach my telephone! (Lady Gaga, "Telephone")

The videos mirror the attitudes conveyed in the respective lyrics, as *Video Phone* consists almost exclusively of dance sequences by either Beyoncé alone or supported by Lady Gaga, whose male onlookers, albeit slightly abstracted through their heads merging with cameras, feature prominently in the video. There is hence no question for whose viewing pleasure the choreography is designed. *Telephone*, in turn, complicates questions of the gaze, in part by adding a narrative in which women are the driving force rather than ornamental accessories. The only intra-diegetic video of Gaga is furthermore produced by the prison's cameras, which are operated by women. The other "recordings" are Polaroid pictures Gaga takes of herself and Beyoncé. Besides offering a blatant advertisement for a product Gaga is commercially affiliated with and thereby underscoring her status as powerful business woman even within the video's narrative, the Polaroid pictures serve as a powerful point of reference to another iconic, if unusual, road movie, *Thelma & Louise* (1991, Dir. Ridley Scott). As such, the pictures of Gaga and Beyoncé are not meant to be seen primarily by men—even if found by men, they would merely serve to tease those following them in vain. The pictures are taken instead to capture a moment of female bonding, as the reference to *Thelma & Louise* underscores. But whereas a picture is all that remains of the heroines in the original road movie, in *Telephone* they serve to capture the fleetingness and spontaneity of a moment, which, in contrast to *Thelma & Louise*, does not stand for defiance through self-annihilation, but for triumph over that which used to repress the two female protagonists. *Telephone* thereby pays homage to a watershed story of a 1990s progressive "girl power" culture through a positive retelling, while the video distances itself from the film's depiction of women as victims and their limited access to freedom and mobility.

A similar method is used in the video's treatment of another film that also combines the genres of rape revenge and road movie, both of which are—despite frequent attempts—flawed in their usefulness for creating filmic spaces for women. Quentin Tarantino's *Kill Bill* series (2003–2004) is referenced not only through the story of an abused woman who goes on a killing spree, but also through the iconic Pussy Wagon. Yet *Telephone* brings the Pussy Wagon closer again to its original meaning as a ridiculous, but ultimately endearing, "chick magnet" from the musical *Grease* than the negative connotations it took on in Tarantino's film, where it serves a visual reminder of the female protagonist's sexual exploitation.[13] While Tarantino used the Pussy Wagon as a cynical joke at women's expense, *Telephone* makes the car exemplify freedom, mobility, and unity between the female couple. This re-signification is further underscored visually, as the pink and yellow pick-up with huge flame ornaments in *Kill Bill* is a comment on the owner's lack of taste and a kind of comic relief. In the stylized, brightly colored aesthetics of *Telephone*, however, the car blends right in—its literalized purpose written on the car perfectly complementing Gaga's and Beyoncé's figurative costumes.

The reclaiming of the car as a feminist space, or rather the subversion of the car as a predominantly masculine space in film and popular media, is additionally achieved via Lady Gaga's wearing of an otherwise out of context leopard-print catsuit. The costume evokes the one worn by Shania Twain in the video *That Don't Impress Me Much* (1997), another take on the independent woman favored by 1990s pop culture. Whereas Shania Twain's progressive image of modern womanhood depended on her free choice of which ride to take as a hitchhiker, *Telephone* has Lady Gaga dance in front of a pick-up truck—next to guns, the most phallic symbol of American manhood—that is either her own or Honey B's. By connecting *Telephone* aesthetically to these references, the queer subtext of the narration is further strengthened and ties in with the significance of Beyoncé's ethnic marking as correlating to lesploitation's treatment of race. Mayne suggests that in this genre "the opposition of black women and white women is eroticized" in lieu of gender differences (138). Thus, Beyoncé is not only linked to Pam Grier as a central star of the exploitation genre, but also to the queerness of several of Grier's roles (such as in *The Big Doll House*, 1971, Dir. Jack Hill). *Telephone*, however, does not limit itself to a lesbian reading, but stresses the queer performativity of gender and sexuality by tying in the lesbian couple with Gore Vidal's most famous literary (and later filmic) creation, the transsexual character Myra Breckinridge. *Myra Breckinridge* (1970, Dir. Mike Sarne), according to Dennis Altman "was part of a major cultural assault on the assumed norms of gender and sexuality which swept the Western world in the late 1960s and early 1970s" (132). *Telephone* introduces its iconography via the title character's stars and stripes bikini revived by Gaga's and Beyoncé's costumes in the third dance sequence. Especially given Gaga's own (then) precarious status as a cisgender woman, the reference is both daring and funny, as it creates a string of gender deferrals: Lady Gaga poses as a hermaphrodite, who passes as a woman, who is playing a lesbian mimicking a transsexual man, who passes as a woman modeled on the asexual Wonder Woman. A reading of *Myra Breckinridge* concludes that "through its camp conventions the novel queers these heterosexual acts, reminding us of the queers who exist in its margins—and who must be erased by the end" (Eisner 267). Yet the contemporary performance of Myra, as well as of numerous other icons, figures, and characters from the above-mentioned films and texts, lack any tragic components, specifically a tragic ending, which entirely changes their function. Gender deviants in *Telephone* no longer serve as foils against which to posit the "healthy" alternative, a heteronormative lifestyle. Rather, they are represented as the alternative themselves, when what dominant discourses with much media support have deemed "good" and "normal" is exposed as artificial and/or oppressive. In outrageous costumes, wigs, and masks, the video's protagonists, above all Gaga herself, enact the significance of camp

> as a "queer performativity", through which a subjectivity is enacted that takes not the heterosexist imperatives [...] as its exemplary performative act [...], but rather the queer deviation, and demystification, of those very imperatives. (Cleto 32)

By reveling in the seemingly shallow and stereotypical, by exaggerating known forms and conventions, and by taking sexism and objectification to its extreme, Lady Gaga's work places an ironic, demystifying parody at the heart of pop culture. Via camp, her videos and performances reappropriate mainstream discourses and make room for the unsettling, disturbing, and in turn, empowering and queer. Just as the *Telephone* video's "prison for bitches" cannot contain its transgressive inmates, so mainstream media discourse is unable to hold its inherent queer potential at bay, as the video, and Gaga's artistic output more generally, show.

2.3   Yoü and I: *Postfeminism for Mermaids*

An escalation of gender confusion and an exploration of queer potentiality shaped the promotion campaign for the song "You and I" from the 2011 album *Born This Way*. The campaign also presented what might be one of the most elaborate uses of the possibilities of the digital age in Lady Gaga's oeuvre. Its reliance on cross-media storytelling and social media served as a means of addressing and building an interpretative community (interviews and Twitter messages, e.g., "Beware of strange oddities. The more he tries to fix me, the more magical I become," served to initiate fans into the video's intertextual references and explored themes), and supported the creation of a *Gesamtkunstwerk*, as the accompanying videos and performances were presented for contextualized viewing and its themes were developed across several different media. One of the campaign's protagonists, Jo Calderone, first appeared as a model in the Japanese *Vogue Homme* in September 2010. It was later revealed that the male model Jo Calderone was Lady Gaga in drag, who also posed for an alternative cover of the same *Vogue Homme* issue in a modified version of the meat dress worn at the *MTV Video Music Awards* 2010. Jo Calderone was later featured on the cover of the single release of "You and I," starred in its music video, and performed the song at the *MTV Video Music Awards* 2011.

The song's campaign and its focus on "strange oddities" is particularly striking as "You and I" is among Lady Gaga's most conventional songs. Described by music critics as "torchy, retro-classic, all-American power ballad" (Copsey), "country ballad" (Mason) and "cheesy, high-gloss, pop rock for the mainstream middle" (McCormick), the song tells a similarly cheesy story about the song persona's feelings for her all-American ex-lover, "Nebraska guy." Precisely through this proximity to normative discourses, the *Yoü and I* video became powerful as an act of appropriation, "by which traditional and/or culturally popular stories [...] that advance a traditional, oppressive ideology of gender are referenced clearly in such a way that the messages apparent in the new text challenge those traditional notions of gender" (Shugart 211). In the case of *Yoü and I*, one of the discourses dismantled is postfeminism's celebration of retreatism, the professional woman's supposedly empowering decision to withdraw "from the workforce (and symbolically from the public sphere) to devote herself to husband and family" (Tasker and Negra 108), which *30 Rock* also addressed extensively. The video's premise, *Billboard* claims based on a Lady Gaga interview, is that she has walked all the way from New York to Nebraska to get her boyfriend back (Mapes). While this narrative is not only closely linked to the retreatist scenario, but also to masochistic conventions of postfeminist representations more generally, a reading in tune with such notions is complicated by the video's disharmonic and fragmented imagery, which counters the song's content and romanticized ideals of submissive femininity.

The video's opening shot depicts the blurry outlines of a female figure, dressed in black, walking down a road between corn fields. While the Bride, as the accompanying Twitter messages have identified her, comes slowly into focus, exposing her veil, cyborg arms, and large glasses, the video cuts to a couple dressed completely in white. He kneels before her and caresses her thigh in what seems to be the anticipation of their wedding night. In quick succession, the audience is then confronted with close-ups of the black bride's bleeding feet, the white bride's youthful face, the black bride's broken nails, and surgical equipment pointing to further storylines and scenarios. While in one storyline the black bride breaks down before a truck, in another a different female figure convulses to the sound of electrical shocks. Next, an extreme close-up shows ice-cream dripping from an older man's dirty hands, then his laughing face while he strangles a doll, and finally the black bride caressing the very same doll in anticipation of the lyrics "I'd give anything to be your baby doll," which are tainted by association in threatening ways. While all three vignettes are advanced with close-ups and medium shots in which different items block the audience's view and enhance the feeling of disorientation, one shot hints at the introduction of a mermaid into the story, when the video cuts to fins splashing in a bathtub. Silence dominates the soundtrack, only interrupted by the chirping of crickets, footsteps on gravel, electric buzzing, and the muted screams of the convulsing woman. Accompanied by the chitter of birds, an establishing shot of the rural ideal comes next: corn fields, trees, a barn, and a small house all bathed in sunlight. To this image, at 0:46, the song begins.

The first lines of *You and I*, which describe her return to a town long left behind, are sung by the black bride. The song's "homecoming" theme is therefore disrupted by the visual clash between her avant-gardist robe, including a voluminous hat and extreme high heels, and her "natural" rural surroundings. The striking black figure among sunlit fields is less reminiscent of a prodigal daughter returning to where she belongs, than of the protagonists of *The Adventures of Priscilla—Queen of the Desert* (1994, Dir. Stephan Elliott), two drag queens and a transsexual woman stranded in the hostile territory of the Australian outback as symbols of seemingly irreconcilable cultural differences. The stark contrast between nature and culture continues the themes established in the album's first single "Born This Way," that is, the freeing potential of constant reinvention through dissociation from the "the natural" in favor of a turn to artificiality.[14] The oppressive manner in which the video depicts the countryside supports a positive reading of the bride's ill-fitting clothes in contrast to the rural background. The resilient self of drag queen and pop star symbolized by the black bride are established as a necessary reaction to a non-nurturing environment marked by the traces of violence, poverty, and decay.

These themes are carried over into the video's next section which is, in contrast to the harshly lit open landscapes of dirt roads and corn fields, dominated by much darker images from inside the barn. Here, the man introduced as the husband of the white couple is shown as a Frankenstein-like figure experimenting on different women and on the mermaid known via Twitter as Yüyi. The continuation of the baby-doll theme through these images of him literally creating women to please himself in a powerless doll-like manner distances the video from the song's supposedly romantic words and hints at the violence underlying the white couple's marriage. The video thereby rejects its superficial happy ending. The wedding is further denied its status as a positive outcome through the ghostlike cross-dissolve that colors its final images as simultaneously flimsy and scary. The bride's mixing of mourning clothes and bridal moniker adds to the impression of a less than ideal outcome to the song's longed-for union with "Nebraska guy."

The only woman to emerge from the video's ordeal unfazed is Yüyi, whose name, through its pun on you/I, points to the hybrid nature of the mermaid as a creature on the border between self and other, between human and fish. Besides transformation and hybridity, the most important associations evoked by the figure of the mermaid revolve around sexuality. A symbol of voracious female sexuality in traditional folklore, modern adaptations have rendered her almost asexual, a symbol instead of "impossible love, erotic potential, and impotent desire" (Johnson 77). The mermaid thus serves as a particularly potent metaphor for the contemporary pop star as the perpetual object to be desired, but not as a subject supposed to express desire herself. A further troubling aspect of the mermaid myth in this regard is the glorification of masochism through the self-mutilation that accompanies the mermaid's transformation and the willing abdication of her once-powerful voice (Jarvis 621). The video emphasizes the latter aspect through several scenes in which the different female figures embodied by Lady Gaga at first sing the lyrics in a manner typical for music videos, but then stop lip-synching while the song's vocal track continues. The effect not only shatters the illusion of the music video as a diegetic entity, but also relates the interactions between the video's couples to the silencing of women. While the original song thus presents the lyrics "I'd rather die without you and I" with the rock ballad's typical enthusiasm, the video refuses to be compliant with such romanticizing of dependency and instead focuses on the destructiveness of this feminine ideal of self-sacrifice. *You and I* instead celebrates the mermaid's freakish hybridity and her queer sexuality. Rather than aiming for conformity by becoming human, Yüyi stays in her hybrid form until the end of the video, where she is last seen embracing the human lover who succumbs to her demands—rather than the other way around—by joining her in the water and caressing her fins and gills. Yüyi's exceptional status among the women kept in the barn is further emphasized through her role in the "Haus of Ü ft." video series which was released online after *Yoü and I*. Here Yüyi is the only one of the five protagonists to be shown in the role of star through images of her trailer on set and her entourage. A final indicator to her special status among the video's alter egos is her position on the director's chair, where she seems quite at home posing confidently in sunglasses and smoking a cigarette, presumably still holding on to the source of her allure and power, her voice.

Rather than using *Yoü and I* to produce a video echoing the song's conventional sentiment and relying on the supposedly "most honest Gaga song to date" (Sullivan) to create similarly "honest" images, Lady Gaga turns both ideas on their head and creates a video that refuses the primacy of stars' private lives as meaningful intertexts and exposes the reactionary undertones of love ballads to which "You and I" refers musically. The video *Yoü and I* also expands the song's original focus on heterosexual romance not only through Yüyi's interspecies romance but also particularly through the prominent status of Jo Calderone. His character in many ways builds on Annie Lennox's male drag, but goes much farther in terms of queering his persona and performance. In the video he is singing the lyrics and he is sung to by Nymph, the last female character played by Lady Gaga, thus becoming "Nebraska guy" himself, which makes Gaga's alter ego the object of her affection as well as the (male) song persona singing about another guy. The video also finally delivers on the sexual component only hinted at but ultimately withheld in Eurythmics' *Who's that Girl*, as Lady Gaga as Jo and Lady Gaga as Nymph kiss passionately. The "Haus of Ü ft." videos further connect him to the figure of the Bride, as she takes off her wig and swings her blazer over her shoulder, echoing his movements. Their shared mannerisms point to the potential that one of the two is the other in Butlerdrag—yet never revealing who is original and who is copy in another instance of derailing this question in a -inspired manner.

Jo Calderone's queerest and simultaneously most metareferential moment, however, occurred outside of several videos associated with "You and I," when he substituted for Lady Gaga in the "You and I" performance at the *MTV Video Music Awards* 2011 ("Lady Gaga – Speech + Yoü And I"). The result was a mise en abyme of scandalous(ly queer) live performances created through references to Queen (via Brian Ferry), Annie Lennox, and Madonna. The performance also offered a keen critique of media reactions to Lady Gaga's star persona through Jo's opening monologue in which he acts as a kind of devil's advocate.

Introducing himself as Gaga's boyfriend, Jo quickly starts to reveal supposedly private details about their relationship. Gaga thereby picks up
the recurring theme of critiquing media's obsession with looking behind
the façade, particularly when Jo reveals that there is indeed no such
thing, as he voices his irritation that Gaga keeps her heels on even when
she showers. His bafflement at her outrageous make-up and hair—"at
first it was sexy, but now I'm confused"—similarly mirrors the media's
waiting for the final revealing of the artist's "true self." Yet they, like Jo
himself, are perpetually denied this revelation as Jo is informed by Gaga
in a typically camp elevation of role play: "You and I, we are just the
rehearsal."

Jo then takes to the stage and starts to perform "You and I," without
changing any of the lyrics to fit his gender and presumed heterosexuality. Reminiscent of Annie Lennox's appearance as Elvis Presley at the
Grammy Award ceremony in 1984, Gaga as Jo sings in a notably lower,
huskier timbre, foregoes the head voice Gaga uses on the album version
and adds growls, raspiness, and sharper onsets which make the song, in
tune with Jo's gestures and facial expressions, with the stronger reliance
on electric guitars, overall more aggressive. Some notes are sung so low
that Jo uses vocal fry, a technique which further enhances the song's
connection to rock and country as well as Jo's masculinity.

Successfully passing as Jo not only added to Gaga's large array of
gender performance, but constituted the re-enactment of yet another
iconic award show performance by a female artist, Madonna's "Like a
Virgin" at the 2003 *MTV Video Music Awards*. In one of the most discussed moments of lesbian chic, Madonna ended this trio with Britney
Spears and Christina Aguilera by kissing both younger singers. For the
performance, Aguilera and Spears dressed in white dresses modeled
after Madonna's costume for the "Like a Virgin" video (1984)—evoking naiveté and stressing their status as successors—while Madonna
herself dressed in a stylized tight tuxedo, which served the purpose of
visually setting her apart, rather than making her appear masculine or
even androgynous. Framed—and made safe—as the choreographed element of a dance performance, the kiss is part symbolic act (the Queen
of Pop bestowing her "power" to her successors), part voyeuristic
spectacle (cashing in on lesbian chic), and wholly un-queer as all participants embody "hegemonic femininity," while "the representation
of desire" between the women involved is suppressed in congruence
with Ann Ciasullo's definition of the desexualization and objectification

characteristic of lesbian chic (578). In 2011, tasked with presenting an award to Britney Spears, Gaga as Jo changed this script entirely when he presented himself as a fan of Britney Spears, mentioned his younger self's (and thus implying Gaga's younger self's) sexual fantasies of Spears, and proceeded to flirt with her. Out bisexual Lady Gaga as Jo Calderone—aggressively masculine rather than sexily androgynous—coming on to Britney Spears in an unrehearsed manner lacked the safety nets offered by Madonna's choreographed smooch and for all the involved masquerade and showmanship proved 'too real' for Spears (and several commentators).[15] She refused Jo's advances by claiming "I've done this already." While the earlier Madonna kiss emptied of content and context not only happened, but became iconic, the one infused with queer desire was thereby denied its moment in the spotlight. Spears' rejection thus only helped to emphasize the differences between the two (almost) kisses and how "this" had not been done already.

From opening monologue, to performance, to award ceremony, Jo's appearance added several layers of gender play to the conglomerate of "You and I" texts and furthermore enhanced the critique of conventional ideas of artistic integrity established in the video and earlier examples of Gaga's work. Gaga as Calderone also exploited the untapped potential for queer pleasure of prior performances by other pop divas, while simultaneously making a powerful statement about media's continued double standards in terms of gay/straight as well as male/female. As symbolic places for the music industry and its production of both artistic and commercial value, award shows are uniquely suited to such metareferential performances and appearances as Lady Gaga offered at the *MTV Video Music Awards* in 2009, 2010, and 2011 via "Paparazzi," the meat dress, and Jo Calderone. Aimed at the broad audience of such shows, as well as critics and journalists, however, award show performances are limited in their capability to produce the affective intensity usually associated with live musical performances. Wade Jennings for example argues that "cult stardom is most manifest when those in the group act as one to the star's public performance" (93). Similarly, Lady Gaga's camp effect is never more apparent than during her concerts as the epitome of fan–artist interaction, artistic accomplishment, and "authentic" musical expression—the latter here not understood in rock-inspired terms of the "integrity" or biographical "realness" of the respective performers, but by what Moore defines as the "ability to articulate for its listeners a place of belonging" (219).[16] *The Monster Ball*, Lady Gaga's second world tour (2009–2011), offered precisely that via a performance consciously structured to speak to and enhance the cohesion of an in-group of fans through camp strategies.

3   "FOLLOW THE GLITTER WAY": *THE MONSTER BALL* AND CAMP LIVE IN CONCERT

3.1   *Dancing and Feeling: The Pop Concert as Utopia*

For Simon Frith, music has the capacity to "intensify" and "collectivise" feelings (36), particularly during those special occasions, out of the flow of the everyday, as provided by pop concerts. Investigating this idea of the concert's collectivizing power more closely, Georgina Born suggested that such live performances offer "a compensatory or utopian social space" which "may enact alternatives to [...] wider forms of hierarchical and stratified social relations" (380). Even beyond the specific event, Born also claimed "music's capacity to animate imagined communities" (381). Finally, she arrived at the conclusion

> that music—given its hyper-connotative, hyper-affective propensities—promotes a formation of social bonds [...]. Moreover, rhythm, dance, bodily proximity and corporeal experience [...] promote the intensification of affect and the creation of affective associations. (384)

Particularly for minorities this utopian space of affective association has historically held great value as a temporary safe space, an "excuse" to be their true selves in a community created by a shared object of adoration and what that object stands for. Judy Garland concerts, for example, "particularly the wild shows of adoration for Garland, were more about the audience than the performer in that they allowed gay men a communal presence forbidden elsewhere," John Clum argues and proceeds to cite David Harris' insistence that "Fandom, in other words, was an emphatic political assertion of ethnic camaraderie" (152–53). Dyer complements this observation by stressing the camp component of artist–fan interaction at Garland's concerts as characterized (using Babuscio's term) by a "gay sensibility" that holds together "intensity and irony, a fierce assertion of extreme feeling with a deprecating sense of its absurdity" ("Judy" 163).

This legacy of diva performances as well as the concert's status as a privileged space of group cohesion and social utopia, are reflected in several aspects of Lady Gaga's second world tour, from name to narrative, from intertexts to interludes. Alluding to voguing balls in its name (and thus to alternative forms of queer kinship) and to *The Wizard of Oz* (1939, Dir. Victor Fleming) in its narrative (and thus queer media history), the concerts of Lady Gaga's second world tour tell the story of a group of gender misfits who are looking for the magical Monster Ball, which promises to be a place where they will finally be "set free." "And to get to *The Monster Ball* all you got to do is follow the Glitter Way," Lady Gaga tells the audience. On several occasions throughout the concert Lady Gaga addresses her audiences as her "little monsters," refers to her fans' queerness, and the "bad bitches" who have served as her role models, while describing those "outside" as "freaks," thereby stressing the insider/outsider reversal central to camp's inversion of hierarchies of value and its connection to the social utopia of the concert space. Basing this creation of a momentary utopia in *The Wizard of Oz* imagery through "the glitter way" as a glamorized reference to the yellow brick road Dorothy must follow with her cohort of social pariahs, Gaga once again relied on a specifically queer pop-cultural ancestry, when she invoked not only the film text per se, but its affective potential, its reception history, and its status as the epitome of camp and queer appropriation in US pop culture. By furthermore placing the reference within a decidedly queer context and adding to the original's aesthetic excess on several levels *The Monster Ball* continued Lady Gaga's strategy of relying on intertextuality, not only to refer to camp texts of a different era, but also to update them and produce a camp text with critical and affective value for contemporary audiences.

During *The Monster Ball* the evocation of community, kinship, and non-biological family ties of the freaks and outsiders through Gaga's dialogue with the audience and her dancers were interspersed in a lavishly extravagant show, which created the paradox effect Dyer attests to camp appreciation: emotional intensity and a sense of its absurdity. Isherwood's seminal definition of camp as the expression of serious issues in terms of artifice and fun frames this antithetical quality narratively with the story of isolation felt by the gay character in a rural area. The novel thereby stresses "the communal empowerment that the strategy enforces" (Denisoff 135). *The Monster Ball* picked up this theme of communal empowerment and thus became one of the most notable examples of the strategic use of camp in Lady Gaga's oeuvre to achieve queer pleasure. Divided into four acts set in New York, titled City, Subway, Forest, and Monster Ball, the story of *The Monster Ball* show was ripe with over-the-top imagery.[17] Each of the four parts was introduced with a short video that, in stark contrast to the colorful live act itself, was in either black and white or unsaturated colors. Only jarring visual effects, such as a gush of turquoise from performance artist Millie Brown's mouth on to Lady Gaga's dress or dark red blood pouring from a heart Lady Gaga seems to be eating, disrupt the otherwise sterile aesthetic of the interludes. The contrasting effect between these interludes and the playful live show was further emphasized by staccato-like editing which made the body of Lady Gaga and other protagonists in the clips rhythmically match their house/electro score, which further distanced the interludes from the pop-centric live show. The bodies in these interludes were disjointed or merged into the backgrounds to become inseparable from their environment and unrecognizable as humans. They functioned as mere stand-ins for lifeless fashion mannequins and as ornamental features for the already highly abstract imagery. Against this extremely artificial and cool background, the live parts of the show, characterized by overtly emotional confessions, highly sexualized bodies, and intertextual references to both queer-coded and nostalgic cultural artifacts, became even more clearly legible as a camp spectacular due to a signature "mischievous incongruity" (Medhurst 158).

Furthermore, masquerade was employed throughout the performance to show that "gender should be a game, something we play at," which becomes possible through camp as it "allows us to not take ourselves too seriously while exposing the violence and oppression implicit in all gender enforcement" (Eisner 262). The motif of violence was introduced via the interludes, which were not only stylistically set apart from the rest of the show, but also through their tone: the short clips were full of aggression directed at bodies and restrictions against free movement and expression; whereas the live show featured playful feminine and queer masquerades that reveled in exaggerated stereotypes and the artificiality of gender roles. Many of the parodied roles were borrowed from musicals, which is especially noteworthy because of "the open acknowledgement in musicals that masculinity and femininity are equally performative, and that this performativity has spectacle as its intent" (Cohan xvi) and of musicals' presentation of femininity as "not an innate quality guaranteed to women but instead a special effect available to anyone with the proper skill and accessories" (Whitesell 273). From the *Sunset Boulevard*-evoking entrance to "Dance in the Dark" and the *Grease*-inspired costumes and stage design for the song "Just Dance," *The Monster Ball* developed into a distorted *The Wizard of Oz* tribute; distorted, because the destination was not Auntie Em's farmhouse or another stand-in for a traditional home, but the Monster Ball, which was closer to the freak-populated Emerald City than to rural, familiar Kansas. For Niall Richardson *The Wizard of Oz* emerged as a camp icon because gay men, like Dorothy, felt marginalized from mainstream domesticity and therefore enjoy the fantasy of returning to, and gaining acceptance within, traditional culture (56). Yet, as camp's function in popular culture has taken on more queer than gay connotations, a camp retelling of Dorothy's adventures must also change the moral of the story—the crucial difference being that "queers resist the regimes of the normal [...] we no longer fight intolerance but resist normalization" (Escoffier 175). Where *The Wizard of Oz* aimed for acceptance and inclusion by whatever was deemed to be normal, the story and style of *The Monster Ball* did not look to any kind of traditional home but headed for a place where the goal was to be free in the company of kindred spirits, rather than being accepted into the heteronormative fold.

3.2   The Monster Ball's *Guide to Camp*

The show opens dramatically with a guttural scream by Lady Gaga from the song "Dance in the Dark." As the opening video fades and the neon signs of the city scenery are unveiled, Lady Gaga is only visible as a shadow on the top of a staircase. The scenery is reminiscent of a run-down former amusement area, a Times Square for has-beens so to speak, where instead of fashionable consumer products, whiplashings, death cases, and car accidents are advertised in bold letters. BBQs and "good food" are on an equal footing with liquor and drugs, as are sedation, implants, and dentistry, which all seem to be available at the same place right around the corner of "Hotel (T)Hass."[18] Pop culture's obsession with both decay and beauty, or more precisely the decay of beauty—a recurring theme in Lady Gaga's work—is thus written into *The Monster Ball* from the very beginning. The opening number "Dance in the Dark" picks up this thematic emphasis, as the song is dedicated to several mainly female celebrities (except for legendary Las Vegas entertainer Liberace) who were crushed by their star image and the expectations that came with it. Lady Di, Marilyn Monroe, Sylvia Plath, child beauty pageant participant JonBenét Ramsey, and Judy Garland, all died tragically before their time, either by suicide, murder, or fame-related complications such as substance abuse. A repressive society forced them to live a double life, where personal struggles such as bulimia, drug addiction, or homosexuality, and public persona had to be kept separate at all costs. Susan McClary even calls Marilyn Monroe "the quintessential female victim of commercial culture" (158), the prime example of the "desired, sexual [woman] simultaneously idolized and castigated, and finally sacrificed to patriarchal standards of behavior" (155). Through the lyrics—"Marilyn, Judy, Sylvia, tellem' how you feel girl! Work your blonde (Jean) Benet Ramsey, we'll haunt like Liberace, find your freedom in the music"—those icons are likened and asked to speak to the central figure of the song, a woman made to feel ashamed by her domineering boyfriend and therefore only "dancing in the dark," her freedom of movement and expression thus also "sacrificed," to use McClary's terms, to misogynistic "standards of behavior." The song's musical arrangement supports this dichotomy via the computerized male voice, whose sampled singing of the word "dance" is replayed in a staccato-like fashion, which makes it the song's rhythmic structure as well as a menacing echo to Gaga's emotional performance of the lyrics.

Matching both the dark subject of the song and the atmosphere of stage design, Lady Gaga is, for most of the song, only seen as a motionless shadow behind a gauze screen. When at the end of the song she descends a staircase with handrails made of "silicone, saline, poison" injection needles in a pants-less purple costume with giant shoulder pads, the scene both evokes and parodies a common show business trope, the classical diva entrance as perfected by Norma Desmond, *Sunset Boulevard*'s aging star.[19] "Dance in the Dark" furthermore connects its commentary on fame and social pressure with a more general examination of women's potentially destructive body image. Low self-esteem due to a lack of positive role models and isolation, as well as condescending and judgmental messages from a misogynistic environment, leave women feeling either unattractive ("a mess") or slutty ("tramp"/"vamp"). This sexy/ugly divide is not only literally stated in the scenery as another neon sign, but also manifested in the song succession, which places the bleak "Dance in the Dark" back to back with Lady Gaga's disco anthem "Just Dance." Positioning Lady Gaga as both the vulnerable protagonist of "Dance in the Dark" as well as the careless partygoer of "Just Dance,"

The Monster Ball rejects the rigid distinction between these female arche-types. Additionally, this constellation inflicts "Just Dance," which as a dance track belongs to the musical genre "most closely associated with physical motion" and in the mind/body divide "decisively on the side of the 'feminine' body" and therefore commonly "dismissed by music critics" (McClary 153), with additional meaning. Here the song—and with it the act of dancing described in it as well as the dancing resulting from it at *The Monster Ball*—rises from the seemingly shallow to a sign of empowerment, inviting camp's excessive affective attachment to super-ficial, marginal, or frivolous cultural objects. It also pays tribute to the liberating effects clubs, and dance more generally (for example through voguing), have historically held for queer minorities.

"Just Dance" is referenced once more, when Lady Gaga performs another rather dark track from *The Fame Monster*, namely the song "Monster" whose lyrics include the line "I wanna just dance / but he took me home instead."[20] The song's literal meaning veers between the relationship with a "bad guy" ("We French kissed on a subway train / He tore my clothes right off") and the disturbing implication of date rape ("We might've fucked / not really sure, don't quite recall"). The lines "he ate my heart / and then he ate my brain," however, also point to a more metaphorical meaning by connecting the song to the *Crevette Films* of Lady Gaga's first concert tour, *The Fame Ball*, in 2009. Here, her character Candy Warhol explains "Pop ate my heart, and then he swallowed my brain," which leaves her only one thing to live for: "the fame" ("Lady GaGa—The Brain"). This metareferential connection is made even clearer in the live performance as Lady Gaga ends the song's performance during *The Monster Ball* in a blonde wig and smeared with blood, thus creating a visual image similar to the 2009 "Paparazzi" per-formance. Yet, rather than ending once more with a sacrificial tableau vivant, Lady Gaga "survives" the renewed attack and transitions swiftly into one of her longer dialogues with the audience, for which she fur-thermore assumes one of the most clearly marked roles in *The Monster Ball*, that of Tinker Bell, the fairy from J. M. Barrie's *Peter Pan*, who was made famous by the Disney animated movie and who, like Dorothy in Oz, in the meantime has gained equally queer[21] and "family-friendly," nostalgic[22] connotations. As Lady Gaga is lying on the stage in a black leather outfit and with fake blood smeared over her throat and arms, she turns to the audience and says:

Do you think I'm sexy? 'Cause I think you're sexy.
I don't believe you. Do you think I'm sexy? You know I'm kinda like
Tinker Bell. If you don't clap for her, she dies.
Do you want me to die?
Scream for me! (*The Monster Ball*)

In contrast to the Disney version, Gaga's reincarnation of Tinker Bell speaks for herself and actively solicits the attention and validation she needs to survive. The incongruous combination of the sweet and mute fairy's background with Gaga's sex-positive and outspoken rendition is both a dismissive comment on the child-woman ideal Tinker Bell represents, and a symptomatic one on Gaga's status as a star: the gesture puts the power into the clapping hands of fans and offers a more positive interpretation of fame than the two intertexts had provided.[23] The episode thus further strengthens the communal aspect of the show. Simultaneously, it redefines the boundaries of sexiness queerly, as Gaga in her blood-smeared bondage get-up is cheered on by the crowd after the question "do you think I'm sexy" and then breaks out into one of the most overtly sexual songs in her repertoire, "Teeth," a three-and-a-half-minute long request for cunnilingus.

Despite these new connotations *The Monster Ball* does not completely do away with the image of the winged fairy and stays true to Isherwood's dictum that "you can't camp about something you don't take seriously" (110). Fulfilling the expectation raised by the "glitter way" reference to The Wizard of Oz's yellow brick road in the beginning, the concert features the film's iconic twister in the form of a giant tube of screens, which is lowered on to the stage, as Gaga comments:

Oh, what's that thing way up in the sky? It's very beautiful but very strange.
Is it a rainbow? No. Ohh, I don't feel so well. Little Monster… I'm feeling very strange.
Oh no, it's a twister! (*The Monster Ball*)

Gaga takes on the role of the naïve, childlike woman once more, strengthening her connection to Dorothy, while also referencing Judy Garland and her signature gay anthem "Over the Rainbow." Yet, when Gaga re-emerges from the eye of the storm, her outfit does not resemble Dorothy's dull dress. Rather, it is an extravagant take on the fairy-like

Glinda, good witch of the North, in the form of the so-called Living Dress. Inspired by Hussein Chalayan and designed by Vin Burnham, the dress earns its name from a system of mechanical components that can be remotely controlled to move different parts of the dress, head-piece, and wings. During the song "So Happy I Could Die," Lady Gaga merges the two characters, lost Dorothy and savior Glinda, who is not only a mighty sorceress, but also the key figure who lets Dorothy know about her own powers and how she can use them (even if it is only to get home). The episode thus ties in with the overall story arc of being self-sufficient on one's way to freedom and personal growth, while it delivers the most awe-inspiring and show-stopping sight of the evening with Lady Gaga on a rising pedestal in a dress moving seemingly of its own accord; as Isherwood ended his definition of camp, "you're expressing what's basically serious to you in terms of fun and artifice and elegance" (110). Most striking about *The Monster Ball* is hence not its frequent recourse to cultural artifacts with an inherent gay appeal, but the show's underlying seriousness despite its superficial flamboyance and visual extravagance. Following Hutcheon's argument on irony and ambiguity as opposites rather than connected (33), *The Monster Ball* is never ambiguous in its artistic or its political messages. While some dialogue, like Tinker Bell's musings on her hatred towards "the truth," only vaguely supports the theme of repositioning notions of authenticity, other utterances are quite overtly connected to Gaga's activism and thus stress the connectivity between the politics of camp and politics proper.

During her performance of "Alejandro," for example, rather than demanding her audience "dance" or "put your paws" as she does during other dance sequences, Lady Gaga screams "Put your hands up for equal rights!" Through this gesture Lady Gaga stresses her willingness to commit herself to political causes, a characteristic already crucial to Madonna's appeal to gay and lesbian audiences (Leibetseder 117). The video establishes the song's association with Gaga's commitment to the abolishment of the military policy of Don't Ask, Don't Tell, while the song itself is an ode to one of the "lowest" forms of popular music, Euro-Pop, through its sonic citations of Abba's "Fernando" (1986) and Ace of Base's "Don't Turn Around" (1988). The video clashes with these light, popular evocations by introducing an extremely dark scenario that references queer underground director Kenneth Anger's *Inauguration of the Pleasure Dome* (1954) and the fascism represented in *Cabaret* (1972, Dir. Bob Fosse).[24] The song's violin introduction based on Vittorio Monti's "Csárdás"—which not only hints sonically at the incongruity that the visuals will later intensify, but also adds a musical gravitas not usually associated with popular music—provides the only musical connection to the video's darkness. The song's musical make-up thereby rejects the distinction between high art and pop culture and instead equates the emotional resonance of both cultural spheres.[25] The accompanying video, directed by Steve Klein, similarly adds gravitas to unusual images, when it inserts an homage to Madonna's *Vogue*, recreated, however, by men in military regalia and thus—like many scenes in *Alejandro*—highlighting the homoerotic component of the military. Allusions to Anger's *Inauguration* include: the indistinct, wind-like noises that provide the sonic background to the respective opening credits; several costumes; the sexual eruption bordering on destruction in which, however, Gaga steps in for Anger's original male blonde beau: the procession elements; and maybe most overtly, the swallowing of a rosary (though for Gaga the swallowing is shown in reverse). In addition to being an early example of "reworkings of mass cultural products [...] informed by gay identifications and desires" (Suárez xvii), *Inauguration*'s significance as an intertext specifically in the context of criticizing Don't Ask, Don't Tell stems from the film's investment in the private pleasures of queerness. As Matthew Tinkcom summarizes, *Inauguration*—like many of Anger's films—focuses on "moments in which separate figures costume themselves and subsequently enter the spaces of spectacle, where their dress becomes the occasion for them to have special powers" (138). Similarly, *The Monster Ball* provides a "space of spectacle" in which elaborate costuming affords at least the special appreciation by one's peers, if not "special powers." Yet Anger's film more specifically reflects its pre-Stonewall cultural (and legal) environment, which in the military extended to 2010, by presenting these figures "as allegories for the pleasures of enforced privacy among queers" (139). In the video, however, such pleasures clash with the privacy-denying nascent fascism of *Cabaret*. In contrasting the two iconographies and their intertexts the video stresses the oppressive and destructive nature of the privacy enforced through Don't Ask, Don't Tell.

This video and its meaning-laden and unabashedly queer intertexts are recreated during *The Monster Ball* through costume, dance moves, and stage design, thus emphasizing the song's serious undertones over its comparatively frivolous music and lyrics. During *The Monster Ball*, the song's final image intensifies this discrepancy as it ends on two male dancers kissing alone in the spotlight. The rest of the stage remains dark, the music is slowly muted, and even Gaga has left the stage to make room for this toned-down image that interrupts the show's visual exuberance and thus gains additional emotional resonance as a symbolic act of civil disobedience.

In keeping with such moments of sincerity, the show takes a firm stand on what is to be expected at the end of the glitter way, freedom from (sexual) constraints. The show expresses its serious appreciation of the "monstrous" community not despite its frivolity but precisely because of its frequent tongue-in-cheek moments and humorous components. This rejection of any normalizing authority regarding gender, sexuality, and morals is never compromised, which relates queer Lady Gaga to gay Judy Garland, who was

> likely to share the insider jokes [...]. The one thing Garland never kidded, however, was *Over the Rainbow*. She knew the complex and highly personal associations the song had for many in her audience, and she never distanced herself from those emotions. (Jennings 100)

Lady Gaga follows a similarly appreciative rationale and thus a crucial camp dictum—to mock "the solemnities of our culture," but never to "discard the seriousness of a thing or individual" (Babuscio 28)—throughout her concert in which she mocks many things, but never the music that has come to mean so much to her fans. This music she performs, like Garland, "more honest[ly] than the parts call for" (Clum 150). Fittingly, she ends the concert with "Bad Romance" whose lyrics, particularly in this live context, work on two levels. First, the song functions as a description of a universal topic, romantic love, nonetheless particularly resonant with the gay and lesbian youth who make up a large portion of her fan base through the line "I don't wanna be friends," which evokes the issue of falling for one's (straight) best friend. Second, the song works as working through Gaga's "bad romance" with fame and fortune, which has provided a common thread throughout *The Monster Ball*. Here Gaga's emphatic plea for "all your lovers' revenge" might be understood to refer her fans' prior idols, and "I want your love" becomes the musical equivalent of Tinker Bell's "clap for me." Gaga emphasizes the song's affective resonance by singing almost the entire first verse a cappella, significantly slowed down and with a comparatively breathy and notable vibrato on final syllables absent from the recorded version. Stepping out of the choreography, jumping when she asks her fans to jump, and relying on the purposefully ungraceful and unsexy "monster claw" (as the deformed version of the usual "put your hands in the air") to cheer on her fans as they cheer her on, the performance of "Bad Romance" stresses the communal experience of "rhythm, dance, bodily proximity and corporeal experience" through which concerts are able to deepen affective intensity and create "affective associations" (Born 384). The final show element before "Bad Romance" is the destruction of the Fame Monster with the help of her fans. "Bad Romance" thus presents the plot's conclusion now that Gaga (and the audience with her) has followed the glitter way to its end and finally reached the mythic Monster Ball. This narrative device frames the song not as the traditional encore the performer adds as a thank you to their fans, but rather as a joint celebration of the community of deviants: a "free bitch" (which the song persona in "Bad Romance" calls herself proudly) and her little monsters. To accept then Gaga's earlier invitation to follow the glitter way extended to those in attendance at *The Monster Ball* means to follow and acknowledge pop's equally glamorous, entertaining, and subversive predecessors, as well as to open oneself to new spaces for artistically and politically authentic expression, and immerse oneself in the community created by its "hyper-affective" (Born 384).

4   GROTESQUELY SERIOUS

For later versions of *The Monster Ball* (such as the one taped for Lady Gaga's HBO special) in 2011, another song was added after "Bad Romance," "Born This Way," Lady Gaga's addition to the string of gay anthems (Katy Perry's "Firework," Ke$ha's "We R Who We R," or Pink's "Raise Your Glass") produced in the wake of the *It Gets Better* campaign in 2010. Among these, "Born This Way" was the only song to feature the words that make up the LGBT acronym in any explicit form or variety ("whether gay straight or bi / lesbian transgender life"), thus intervening in the commodification of queerness as decor without identity or community. While the song therefore, in many ways, continued the themes already present in prior works—her devotion to queer fans and political rallying for equality—its video marked a step in a new (or at least newly prominent) aesthetic direction, the grotesque. For female performers, the grotesque—like camp—gains its critical edge from the defamiliarization of feminine iconographies. Yet, where camp succeeds through exaggeration, the grotesque mode is one of turning to what is conventionally coded as "ugly and aberrant" (Covino). Through this turn to the "ugly," the female performer "refuses the imperative that she stays beautiful and domesticated, and seeks the heights of self-fashioning with reference to a body that does not obey prescribed limits" (Covino). Such a spectacular, out-of-bounds femininity is at the center of the *Born This Way* video. During the three-minute intro, Gaga stages herself as the birthing Mother Monster, with images evoking the horror genre's privileged specter of abjection, the "monstrous feminine" in the form of archaic mother, monstrous womb, and deadly female (see Barbara Creed's study). The abject boundary breaching of Mother Monster is articulated through psychedelic mirror effects, seemingly infinite numbers of doppelgängers, and clones of dismembered heads in wax-like, melting shells in different stages of development and regression. The video's liquid, fluctuating, hyper-organic qualities are complemented by vaginal rather than phallic symbols and shapes. When finally Gaga's own body emerges from the shadows in unusually conventional "sexy" clothes— black bra and glittering panties—it is disfigured through shoulder and cheek implants. Towards the end of the video, Gaga is shown less and less as a distinct star body when she merges with the orgy-like combined bodies of her dancers and finally bathes with them in a primordial ooze in which she—like the intro's Mother Monster specifically and the grotesque body in general—is no longer "separated from the rest of the world" (Russo 8). Basing her arguments on Mikhail Bakhtin's *Rabelais and His World*, Mary Russo stresses the grotesque female body's "association with degradation, filth, death, and rebirth." Whereas the "classical body" is "closed, static, self-contained," Russo defines the grotesque body as "open, protruding, irregular, secreting, multiple, and changing" and therefore connected to "social transformation" (8).

Such bodies played a role in Gaga's masquerade much earlier through her costumes, which denied the distinction between thing and being, and videos like *Bad Romance*, whose Matthew Barney-inspired iconography created literally monstrous bodies.[26] *Born This Way* increased the prominence of the grotesque through its use of the imagery of sexless, non-binary reproduction like mitosis and parthenogenesis. Bodies in a constant state of mutability reject any deterministic conclusion one might draw from the song's title. Stressing the ongoing, infinite qualities of a metaphorical birth, the technical aspects of cloning, and mythical images of rebirthing, the video's grotesqueness portrays a decisively anti-essentialist version of "Born This Way." More generally, the visuals point to the political implications of the grotesque body through its relation to the carnivalesque. Crucially, Russo argues, the stepping out of sanctified forms of presentation functions as not "merely oppositional and reactive," but becomes "a site of insurgency, and not merely withdrawal" (64). This productive rather than evasive aspect of the grotesque, which gained relevance in Gaga's videos and performances during the *Born This Way* era—to make room for the deviant instead of hiding it—ties in with the camp strategies that preceded it and continue to exist alongside it. As such, the increasing prevalence of the grotesque does not present a break with the earlier mode, but rather a continued deployment of excess as a form of participatory critique. In fact, grotesque and camp can inform each other, as when in *Born This Way* the ugly, aberrant, leaking bodies visually clash with the more visually pleasing symbols of queer reappropriation (such as pink triangles, rainbows, and unicorns), to create an incongruous conglomerate of serious and playful, deep and shallow, deviant and celebratory references. Even in this turn to a darker version of camp there remains Gaga's focus on active and productive (rather than negative and passive) intervention in regimes of presentation through the stylistic surplus of elaborate surfaces. Combined with the highly affective and communal nature of her star image and performance strategies, Gaga therefore continues to present a contemporary answer to Sedgwick's plea to understand camp as "reparative" rather than "paranoid" (149). Insisting on camp's "loving" aspect, Sedgwick rejects its presentation as a "paranoid" notion solely focused on "denaturalizing [...] elements of a dominant culture," and demands its inclusion and even a focus on its "reparative" potentiality. This aspect's definition is worth quoting at length, not only for Sedgwick's ever-exuberant rhetoric, but for its intricate connections to Lady Gaga's aesthetic and affective qualities:

> The desire of a reparative impulse [...] wants to assemble and confer plenitude on an object that will then have resources to offer to an inchoate self. To view camp as, among other things, the communal, historically dense exploration of a variety of reparative practices is to do better justice to many of the defining elements of classic camp performance: the startling, juicy displays of excess erudition, for example; the passionate, often hilarious antiquarianism, the prodigal production of alternative historiographies;

the "over"-attachment to fragmentary, marginal, waste or leftover products; the rich, highly interruptive affective variety; the irrepressible fascina-
tion with ventriloquistic experimentation; the disorienting juxtapositions of
present with past, and popular with high culture. (149–50)

As such a reparative impulse Lady Gaga's camp provides an intervention
in pop-cultural discourses of gender and sexuality by pointing out current deficiencies and limits or by parodying hypocrisy and stereotypes.
The intervention comes as the result of exchanging the ever-present
monikers of hip gayness, which mostly, however, bear no relation to
queer contents, with frivolous, playful, and exuberant images that invite
Sedgwick's "perverse angle" on popular music and the subsequent "*what
if?*" of queer communality.

NOTES

1. Critic Jonah Weiner, for example, refers to her as "Pop's most pretentious
   starlet," while *Spin*'s Chuck Eddy simply observes that "Lady Gaga's pur-
   portedly transgressive persona [...] relentlessly dares you to despise her."
2. Exceptions include Jen Hutton's "visual reading of Lady Gaga" and Stan
   Hawkins' analysis of the song "Judas" ("I'll Bring You Down").
3. Diane Negra on Cher's choice of dress for the Oscars one year prior: "The
   effect of the costume was to de-naturalize the ensembles worn by other
   celebrities, the excess of Cher's outfit [...] working against the pleasurable perception of reality that inspires such close scrutiny of star bodies
   and clothing at the event" (*Off-White* 175–6).
4. Cher has, like Lennox, impersonated Elvis, see the music video for
   Walking in Memphis (1995).
5. I keep my consideration of Madonna brief, since her subversive potential
   has been sufficiently discussed, see e.g., Fouz-Hernández and Jarman-
   Ivens; Mistry; McClary; Curry.
6. Keith Harvey has argued that it "is typical in English camp for a speaker
   to sprinkle his/her speech with elements of the French language" (251).
   French is also picked up during monologues of *The Monster Ball*.
7. All quoted songs are listed under Lady Gaga (plus song title) in the works
   cited list, e.g., Lady Gaga. "Paparazzi." Music videos and live performances are listed under their respective title, e.g. *Paparazzi*.
8. For a detailed discussion of autotune effects in recent popular music, see
   Brøvig-Hanssen and Danielsen. They discuss Lady Gaga's "Starstruck" as
   one example of the use of the autotuned voice to block access to stars'
   private personas (128).

9. This marks an important difference between Gaga's metareferentiality and that of more rock-oriented performers as discussed by Martin Butler, for whom a critique of the pop industry is a question of circumstances sung about in the third person. In contrast, Lady Gaga is a metareferential signifier herself without any distance between her act and the critique of the very system she uses for her success.
10. Early examples date as far back as *Paid* (1931, Dir. Sam Wood), starring Joan Crawford; *Godless Girl* (1928, Dir. Cecil B. DeMille); and *Prisoners* (1929, Dir. Dir. William A. Seiter). Judith Mayne traces the "periods of ebb and flow of the popularity of the women-in-prison film" from the 1950s (which produced the "prototype of the genre": *Caged*) to the 1990s, noting that "one finds an interesting tension between the respectable, social problem film and the exploitative B-movie" (116–19).
11. For a summary of the history and contemporary uses of the term lesbian femme, see Rachel Devitt (*Girl* 5).
12. One notable exception is *Caged Heat* (1974, Dir. Jonathan Demme), which Mayne discusses in terms of "the coexistence of exploitation with feminism-sisterhood" and which anticipates the positive ending in *Telephone*, "with the women successfully riding off into the sunset and the villains dead" (136).
13. "You know that I ain't braggin', she's a real pussy wagon": lyrics from "Greased Lightning" from *Grease* (1978, Dir. Randal Kleiser).
14. My article in *kjl&m* provides more detailed reading of the *Born This Way* video (only available in German).
15. Hollie McKay gathers comments from several sources whose claims range from "Gaga's persistence as 'Jo Calderone' degraded an otherwise enjoyable VMAs" to "stepping outside the more comfortable vixen role" might hurt Gaga's career.
16. Lady Gaga has been furthermore discussed as remarkably adept at using social media to connect with her fans and help fans connect with each other (see Bennett). Particularly interesting, though beyond the scope of this chapter, are the ways in which fans use online representations of *The Monster Ball* to stitch together the performance's "contemporary moment" and its "conditional we" (Román 1), and thus keep "live" the utopian moment of the concert's shared presence. I address these concerns in more detail in a project I work on as part of the research group "Cultural Performance in Transnational American Studies" (funded by the German Research Council).
17. Descriptions refer to the second version of *The Monster Ball* world tour, performed from 2010 until the end of the tour in 2011. The first leg of the tour had a different stage design, other interludes, and slightly different costumes.

18. The name of the Hotel is written in a way that allows for both a reading as "thass," derogatory noun for the body part between thigh and ass, as well as "Hass," the German word for hate, reflecting Lady Gaga's tendency to incorporate European languages into her work.

19. Lyrics to "Dance in the Dark" include the line "Silicone, Saline, Poison, inject me. Baby, I'm a free bitch" (Written by: Lady Gaga, Fernando Garibay).

20. A break before "Just Dance" puts the song title out of the lyrical flow, thereby highlighting the reference.

21. Fairy used to be a pejorative term for gay. Tinker Bell's connection to gayness is so well established that Sean Griffin titled his monograph on the relationship between the Walt Disney Company and LGBT fans and employees *Tinker Belles and Evil Queens*.

22. According to the Library of Congress "[…] *The Wonderful Wizard of Oz* has become America's greatest and best-loved homegrown fairytale."

23. This idea is even more overtly expressed in "Applause," the first single from her 2013 album *Artpop*: "I live for the applause-plause, live for the applause-plause / Live for the way that you cheer and scream for me."

24. *Cabaret* is based on the autobiographical novel *Goodbye to Berlin* (1939) by Christopher Isherwood.

25. Other uses of classical music include the intro to *Bad Romance*, which is adapted from a Bach fugue, and the reliance on Beethoven's "Piano Sonata No. 8" in the five-minute intro to the *Marry the Night* video, which otherwise mainly references Madonna, thereby once again refusing the distinction between low and high culture.

26. For more on Gaga's reliance on grotesque imagery, see Annandale's "Rabelais Meets Vogue."

WORKS CITED

Alejandro. Dir. Steven Klein. Interscope Records, 2010. *Vevo.* 13 April 2017.

Altman, Dennis. *Gore Vidal's America.* Cambridge: Polity, 2005.

Annandale, David. "Rabelais Meets Vogue: The Construction of Carnival, Beauty and Grotesque." *The Performance Identities of Lady Gaga: Critical Essays.* Ed. Richard J. Gray. Jefferson: McFarland, 2012. 142–159.

Babuscio, Jack. "Camp and Gay Sensibility." *Camp Grounds: Style and Homosexuality.* Ed. David Bergman. Amherst: University of Massachusetts Press, 1993. 19–37.

Bad Romance. Dir. Francis Lawrence. Interscope Records. 2009. Vevo. 26 June 2017.

Bakhtin, Mikhail. *Rabelais and His World.* Trans. Helene Iswolsky. Bloomington: Indiana University Press, 1984.

Bennett, Lucy. "Fan/Celebrity Interactions and Social Media: Connectivity and Engagement in Lady Gaga Fandom." *The Ashgate Research Companion to Fan Cultures*. Ed. Linda Duits, Koos Zwann, and Stijn Reijnders. New York: Ashgate, 2014. 109–120.

Beyoncé. "Video Phone." *I Am... Sasha Fierce*. Columbia. 2008.

Booth, Mark. "CAMPE-TOI! On the Origins and Definitions of Camp." *Camp: Queer Aesthetics and the Performing Subject – A Reader*. Ed. Fabio Cleto. Edinburgh: Edinburgh University Press, 2008. 66–79.

Born, Georgina. "Music and the Materialization of Identities." *Journal of Material Culture* 16.4 (2011): 376–388.

Born This Way. Dir. Nick Knight. Perf. Lady Gaga. Oil Factory Inc., 2011. *Vevo*. 13 April 2017.

Bronski, Michael. *Culture Clash: The Making of Gay Sensibility*. Boston: South End, 1984.

Brøvig-Hanssen, Ragnhild, and Anna Danielsen. *Digital Signatures: The Impact of Digitization on Popular Music Sound*. Cambridge: MIT Press, 2016.

Butler, Judith. *Gender Trouble: Feminism and the Subversion of Identity*. New York: Routledge, 2008.

Butler, Martin. "'It's All About the Music, Baby!' Making Sense of the Metareferential Momentum in Contemporary Popular Songs." Karl-Franzens-University, Graz, 03 Oct 2009. Lecture. *The Metareferential Turn in Contemporary Arts and Media: Forms, Functions, Attempts at Explanation*.

Cabaret. Dir. Bob Fosse. Allied Artists, 1972.

Caged. Dir. John Cromwell. Warner Bros., 1950.

Caged Heat. Dir. Jonathan Demme. Artists Entertainment Complex, 1974.

Cher. *Believe*. WEA, 1998.

———. "The Way of Love." *Gypsys, Tramps & Thieves*. MCA Records, 1971.

Ciasullo, Ann M. "Making Her (In)Visible: Cultural Representations of Lesbianism and the Lesbian Body in the 1990s." *Feminist Studies* 27.3 (2001): 577–608.

Cleto, Fabio. "Queering the Camp." *Camp: Queer Aesthetics and the Performing Subject – A Reader*. Ed. Fabio Cleto. Edinburgh: Edinburgh University Press, 2008. 1–42.

Clum, John M. *Something for the Boys: Musical Theater and Gay Culture*. New York: St. Martin's, 1999.

Cohan, Steven. *Masked Men: Masculinity and the Movies in the Fifties*. Bloomington: Indiana University Press, 1997.

Copsey, Robert. "Lady Gaga: 'Yoü and I'-Single Review." 9 Sep 2011. *Digital Spy*. Hearst Magazines. 30 Oct 2014. http://www.digitalspy.co.uk/music/review/a339580/lady-gaga-you-and-i-single-review.html.

Covino, Deborah Caslav. "Abject Criticism." *Genders* 32 (2000). 20 Oct 2014. http://www.genders.org/g32/g32_covino.html.

Creed, Barbara. *The Monstrous-Feminine: Film, Feminism, Psychoanalysis.* New York, Routledge, 1993.

Curry, Ramona. "Madonna from Marilyn to Marlene: Pastiche or Parody." *Journal of Film and Video* 42.2 (1990): 15–30.

Devitt, Rachel E. *Girl on Girl: Passing, Ambivalence, and Queer Musical Time in Gender Performative Negotiations of Popular Music.* PhD Thesis. Diss. University of Washington, Seattle: 2009. ProQuest.

———. "Girl on Girl: Fat Femmes, Bio-Queens, and Redefining Drag." *Queering the Popular Pitch.* Eds. Sheila Whiteley and Jennifer Rycenga. New York: Routledge, 2006. 27–39.

Denisoff, Dennis. *Aestheticism and Sexual Parody: 1840–1940.* Cambridge: Cambridge University Press, 2001.

Dickinson, Kay. "'Believe'? Vocoders, Digitalised Female Identity and Camp." *Popular Music* 20.3 (2001): 333–347.

Dyer, Jennifer. "The Metaphysics of the Mundane: Understanding Andy Warhol's Serial Imagery." *Artibus et Historiae* 25.49 (2004): 33–47.

Dyer, Richard. *Stars.* London: BFI, 1979.

———. "It's so camp as keeps us going." *The Culture of Queers.* Ed. Richard Dyer. London: Routledge, 2002. 49–63.

———. "Judy Garland and Gay Men." *Queer Cinema: The Film Reader.* Ed. Harry M. Benshoff. New York: Routledge, 2005. 153–65.

Dyhouse, Carol. *Glamour: History, Women, Feminism.* London: Zed, 2010.

Eddy, Chuck. "MYTH No. 3: Lady Gaga Is All Style, No Substance." *Spin. com.* 9 November 2009. Billboard-Hollywood Reporter Media Group. 12 February 2009. http://www.spin.com/2009/11/myth-no-3-lady-gaga-all-style-no-substance/.

Eisner, Douglas. "*Myra Breckinridge* and the Pathology of Heterosexuality." *The Queer Sixties.* Ed. Patricia Juliana Smith. New York: Routledge, 1999. 255–270.

Escoffier, Jeffrey. *American Homo: Community and Perversity.* Berkeley: University of California Press, 1998.

Eurythmics. *Savage.* RCA Records, 1987.

———. Sweet Dreams." *Sweet Dreams.* RCA Records, 1983.

Feil, Ken. "Queer Comedy." *Comedy: A Geographic and Historical Guide.* Ed. Maurice Charney. Westport: Praeger, 2005. 477492.

Frith, Simon. *Performing Rites: On the Value of Popular Music.* Cambridge: Harvard University Press, 1999.

Fouz-Hernández, Santiago, and Freya Jarman-Ivens (eds.). *Madonna's Drowned Worlds: New Approaches to Her Cultural Transformations; 1983–2003.* Aldershot: Ashgate, 2004.

Gaar, Gillian G. *She's a Rebel: The History of Women in Rock & Roll.* 2nd ed. New York: Seal, 2002.

"gaga." *Oxford Dictionaries.* April 2010. OUP 13 Feb 2012. http://oxforddic-tionaries.com/definition/gaga?q=gaga.

Geller, Theresa L. "Trans/Affect, Monstrous Masculinities, and the Sublime Art of Lady Gaga." *Lady Gaga and Popular Music: Performing Gender, Fashion, and Culture.* Eds. Martin Iddon and Melanie Marshall. New York: Routledge, 2015. 209–230.

Godless Girl. Dir. Cecil B. DeMille. Pathé Exchange, 1929.

Goodwin, Andrew. *Dancing in the Distraction Factory: Music Television and Popular Culture.* Minneapolis: University of Minnesota Press, 1992.

Grease. Dir. Randal Kleiser. Paramount Pictures, 1978.

Griffin, Sean. *Tinker Belles and Evil Queens: The Walt Disney Company from the Inside Out.* New York: New York University Press, 2000.

Halberstam, Jack. "What's Paglia Got to Do With It?" *Bully Bloggers.* 14 Sep 2010. Ed. Lisa Duggan et al. 6 Feb 2012. http://bullybloggers.wordpress.com/2010/09/14/whats-paglia-got-to-do-with-it/.

———. *Gaga Feminism: Sex, Gender, and the End of Normal.* Boston: Beacon, 2012.

Harvey, Keith. "Describing Camp Talk: Language/Pragmatics/Politics." *Language and Literature* 9.3 (2000): 240–260.

"HAUS OF Ü ft. BRIDE." 13 Sep 2011. Youtube. 26 June 2017.

"HAUS OF Ü ft. JO." 6 März 2012. Youtube. 26 June 2017.

"HAUS OF Ü ft. YÜYI." 20 Sep 2011. Youtube. 26 June 2017.

Hawkins, Stan. *Settling the Pop Score: Pop Texts and Identity Politics.* Aldershot: Ashgate, 2002.

———. "Dragging Out Camp: Narrative Agendas in Madonna's Musical Production." *Madonna's Drowned Worlds: New Approaches to Her Cultural Transformations; 1983–2003.* Ed. Santiago Fouz-Hernández and Freya Jarman-Ivens. Aldershot: Ashgate, 2004. 3–21.

———. "'I'll Bring You Down, Down, Down.' Lady Gaga's Performance in Judas." *Lady Gaga and Popular Music. Performing Gender, Fashion, and Culture.* Ed. Martin Iddon and Melanie. L. Marshal. New York: Routledge, 2014. 9–26.

Heylin, Clinton, ed. *All Yesterday's Parties: The Velvet Underground in Print, 1966—1971.* Cambridge: Da Capo, 2006.

Holdship, Bill. "In Defense of Gaga." *MetroTimes.* 08 June 2011. 09 Feb 2012. http://metrotimes.com/music/in-defense-of-gaga-1.1158482.

Horn, Katrin. "Lady Gaga: Pop als Maske, Weiblichkeit als Maskerade." *kjl&m – Kinder-/Jugendliteratur und Medien in Forschung, Schule und Bibliothek* 12.4 (2012): 38–45.

Hutcheon, Linda. *Irony's Edge: The Theory and Politics of Irony.* London: Routledge, 1994.

Hutton, Jen. "God and the 'Gaze': A Visual Reading of Lady Gaga." *C: International Contemporary Art* 104 (2009): 5–8.

Inauguration of the Pleasure Dome. Dir. Kenneth Anger. Mystic Fire Video, 1954.

Isherwood, Christopher. *The World in the Evening.* Minneapolis: University of Minnesota Press, 1999.

Jarvis, Shawn C. "Mermaid." *The Greenwood Encyclopedia of Folktales and Fairy Tales.* Ed. Donald Haase. Westport: Greenwood, 2007. 619–621.

Jennings, Wade. "The Star as Cult Icon: Judy Garland." *The Cult Film Experience: Beyond All Reason.* Ed. Jay P. Telotte. Austin: University of Texas Press, 1991. 90–105.

Jennex, Craig. "Diva Worship and the Sonic Search for Queer Utopia." *Popular Music and Society* 36.3 (2013): 343–359.

Kaplan, E. Ann. *Rocking Around the Clock: Music Television, Postmodernism, and Consumer Culture.* New York: Routledge, 1988.

Kill Bill: Volume One and *Kill Bill: Volume Two.* Dir. Quentin Tarantino. Miramax Films, 2003/2004.

Klinger, Barbara. *Melodrama and Meaning: History, Culture, and the Films of Douglas Sirk.* Bloomington: Indiana University Press, 1994.

Koestenbaum, Wayne, and Tony Kushner. *The Queen's Throat: Opera, Homosexuality, and the Mystery of Desire.* New York: Da Capo, 2001.

Lady Gaga. "Alejandro." *The Fame Monster.* Interscope Records, 2009.

———. "Americano." *Born This Way.* Interscope Records, 2011.

———. "Artpop." *Artpop.* Interscope Records, 2013.

———. "Bad Romance." *The Fame Monster.* Interscope Records, 2009.

———. *Born This Way.* Interscope Records, 2011.

———. "Born This Way." *Born This Way.* Interscope Records, 2011.

———. "Dance in the Dark." *The Fame Monster.* Interscope Records, 2009.

———. "G.U.Y." *Artpop.* Interscope Records, 2013.

———. "Monster." *The Fame Monster.* Interscope Records, 2009.

———. "Pokerface." *The Fame.* Interscope Records, 2008.

———. "Scheiße." *Born This Way.* Interscope Records, 2011.

———. "Speechless." *The Fame Monster.* Interscope Records, 2009.

———. "Telephone." *The Fame Monster.* Interscope Records, 2009.

"Lady GaGa - The Brain (DL link - FINAL VERSION - The Crevette Films - Tour backdrop intro video." Perf. Lady Gaga. 26 Feb 2009. Youtube. 26 June 2017.

"Lady Gaga - Speech + Yoü And I (as Jo Calderone) Live @ 2011 The MTV VMAs [HD]." Perf. Lady Gaga. 5 November 2011. Vimeo. 26 June 2017.

Leibetseder, Doris. *Queere Tracks: Subversive Strategien in der Rock- und Popmusik.* Bielefeld: transcript, 2010.

Lennox, Annie. *Diva.* RCA Records. 1992.

Library of Congress. "The Wizard of Oz: An American Fairy Tale." *Loc.gov*. 27 July 2010. 10 Dec 2010. http://www.loc.gov/exhibits/oz/.

Love is a Stranger. Dir. Jon Roseman. Perf. Annie Lennox. Sony, 1987. *Vevo*. 13 April 2017.

Mapes, Jillian. "Lady Gaga's You And I Video Leaks." *Billboard.com*. 16 Aug 2011. Prometheus Global Media. 13 Feb 2012 http://www.billboard.com/news/lady-gaga-s-you-and-i-video-leaks-watch-1005317862.story.

Marry The Night. Dir. Lady Gaga. Perf. Lady Gaga. Interscope Records, 2011. *Vevo*. 13 April 2017.

Marsan, Loran. "Cher-ing/Sharing Across Boundaries." *Visual Culture & Gender*.5 (2010): 49–64.

Mason, Kerri. "Lady Gaga 'Born This Way': Track-By-Track Review." *Billboard.com*. 23 May 2011. Prometheus Global Media. 30 Oct 2014. http://www.billboard.com/articles/news/471176/lady-gaga-born-this-way-track-by-track-review.

Material Girl. Dir. Mary Lambert. Perf. Madonna. Sire Records, 1984. *Vevo*.13 April 2017.

Mayne, Judith. *Framed: Lesbians, Feminists, and Media Culture*. Minneapolis: University of Minnesota Press, 2000.

McClary, Susan. *Feminine Endings: Music, Gender, and Sexuality*. Minneapolis: University of Minnesota Press, 2002.

McCormick, Neil. "Lady Gaga: icon or just eye-candy?" *Telegraph.co.uk*. 20 May 2011. Telegraph Media Group. 30 Oct 2014. http://www.telegraph.co.uk/culture/music/rockandpopfeatures/8523660/Lady-Gaga-icon-or-just-eye-candy.html.

McKay, Hollie. "Lady Gaga Took Male Alter-Ego to the Limit By Using Male Restrooms." *FoxNews.com*. 29 Aug 2011. Fox News Network. 30 Oct 2014. http://www.foxnews.com/entertainment/2011/08/29/exclusive-lady-gaga-took-male-alter-ego-to-limit-by-using-male-restrooms/.

Medhurst, Andy. "Batman, Deviance and Camp." *The Many Lives of the Batman: Critical Approaches to a Superhero and his Media*. Ed. Roberta E. Pearson. New York: Routledge, 1991. 149–163.

Middleton, Richard. "Rock Singing." *The Cambridge Companion to Singing*. Ed. John Potter. Cambridge: CUP, 2000. 28–41.

Mistry, Reena. "Madonna and *Gender Trouble*." *theory.org.uk*, Jan 2000. Communications and Media Research Institute (CAMRI), University of Westminster. Ed. David Gauntlett. 8 Oct 2010. http://www.theory.org.uk/madonna.htm.

Molanphy, Chris. "Introducing the Queen of Pop." *RollingStone.com*. 29 June 2010. Rolling Stone. 6 Feb 2012 http://www.rollingstone.com/music/news/introducing-the-queen-of-pop-20110629.

Moore, Allan. "Authenticity as Authenticication." *Popular Music* 21.2 (2002): 209–223.

Myra Breckinridge. Dir. Michael Sarne. 20th Century Fox, 1970.

Negra, Diane. *Off-White Hollywood: American Culture and Ethnic Female Stardom*. New York: Routledge, 2001.

Nyong'o, Tavia. "Iphone, U-Phone...Or Is Gaga the new Dada?... Or Roll Over Andy Warhol..." *Bully Bloggers*. 22 March 2010. Ed. Lisa Duggan et al. 20 March 2011. https://bullybloggers.wordpress.com/2010/03/22/iphone-u-phone...or-is-gaga-the-new-dada...or-roll-over-andy-warhol.../.

Osborne, Peter, and Lynne Segal. "Extracts from *Gender as Performance: An Interview with Judith Butler*." *Theory.org*. 1997. Communications and Media Research Institute (CAMRI), University of Westminster. 13 Feb 2012. http://www.theory.org.uk/but-int1.htm.

Paglia, Camille. "Lady Gaga and the Death of Sex." *Sunday Times Magazine*. 12 Sep 2010. Times Newspapers. 6 Feb 2012. http://www.thesundaytimes.co.uk/sto/public/magazine/article389697.ece.

Paid. Dir. Sam Wood. MGM, 1931.

Paparazzi. Dir. Jonas Akerlund. Perf. Lady Gaga. Interscope Records, 2009. *Vevo*.13 April 2017.

"Paparazzi (Live Performance @ VMA 2009)." Perf. Lady Gaga. 7 April 2013. Youtube. 28 June 2017.

Patterson, Sylvia. "She's the Man." *Q Magazine* April 2010: 44–52.

Peñaloza, Lisa. "Consuming Madonna Then and Now: An Examination of the Dynamics and structuring of Celebrity Consumption." *Madonna's Drowned Worlds: New Approaches to Her Cultural Transformations; 1983–2003*. Ed. Santiago Fouz-Hernández and Freya Jarman-Ivens. Aldershot: Ashgate, 2004. 176–192.

Peter Pan. Dir. Clyde Geronimi et al., Disney, 1953. Film.

The Phantom of the Opera. Music: Andrew Lloyd Webber. 1986.

Pisters, Patricia. "Madonna's Girls the Mix: Performance of Femininity Beyond the Beautiful." *Madonna's Drowned Worlds: New Approaches to Her Cultural Transformations; 1983–2003*. Ed. Santiago Fouz-Hernández and Freya Jarman-Ivens. Aldershot: Ashgate, 2004. 23–35.

Powers, Ann. "Frank talk with Lady Gaga." *LATimes.com*. 28 Mar 2010. Tribune Interactive. 28 Mar 2010. http://www.latimes.com/entertainment/news/music/la-ca-lady-gaga13-2009dec13,1,1933920,full.story.

Prisoners. Dir. William A. Seiter. Warner Bros., 1929.

Radio Ga Ga. Dir. David Mallet. Perf. Queen. EMI Records, 1984. *Youtube*. 13 April 2017.

Richardson, Niall. *The Queer Cinema of Derek Jarman: Critical and Cultural Readings*. London: Tauris, 2009.

Rihanna. "Te Amo." *Rated R*. Def Jam Recordings, 2009.

Robertson, Pamela. *Guilty Pleasures: Feminist Camp from Mae West to Madonna*. London: Tauris, 1996.

Rodger, Gillian. "Drag, Camp and Gender Subversion in the Music and Videos of Annie Lennox." *Popular Music* 23.1 (2004): 17–29.

Román, David. *Performance in America: Contemporary U.S. Culture and the Performing Arts*. Durham: Duke UP, 2005.

Ross, Andrew. "Uses of Camp." *Camp Grounds: Style and Homosexuality*. Ed. David Bergman. Amherst: University of Massachusetts Press, 1993. 54–77.

Russo, Mary J. *The Female Grotesque: Risk, Excess and Modernity*. New York: Routledge, 1995.

Sedgwick, Eve Kosofsky. *Touching Feeling: Affect, Pedagogy, Performativity*. Durham: Duke University Press, 2003.

Shugart, Helene A. "Counterhegemonic Acts: Appropriation as a Feminist Rhetorical Strategy." *Quarterly Journal of Speech* 83 (1997): 210–29.

———. "'You don't have to say you love me': The Camp Masquerades of Dusty Springfield." *The Queer Sixties*. Ed. Patricia Juliana Smith. New York: Routledge, 1999. 105–126.

Smith, Patricia J. "Icons and Iconoclasts: Figments of Sixties Queer Culture." *The Queer Sixties*. Ed. Patricia J. Smith. New York: Routledge, 1999. xii–xxvi.

Sontag, Susan. "Notes on Camp." *Against Interpretation, and Other Essays*. New York: Picador, 2001. 275–292.

Springfield, Dusty. "Son of a Preacher Man." *Dusty in Memphis*. Atlantic Records, 1969.

———. "You Don't Have to Say You Love Me." *You Don't Have to Say You Love Me*. Philips, 1966.

Straayer, Chris. "Redressing the 'Natural': The Temporary Transvestite Film." *The Film Genre Reader III*. Ed. Barry Keith Grant. Austin: University of Texas Press. 2003. 417–442.

Suárez, Juan Antonio. *Bike Boys, Drag Queens & Superstars: Avant-garde, Mass Culture, and Gay Identities in the 1960s Underground Cinema*. Bloomington: Indiana University Press, 1996.

Sullivan, Kate. "Gaga delivers on hype with 'Way'." *TheDartmouth.com*. 26 May 2011. The Dartmouth. 5 June 2011. http://thedartmouth.com/2011/05/26/arts/gaga.

Sunset Boulevard. Dir. Billy Wilder. Paramount Pictures, 1950.

Sweet Home Alabama. Dir. Andy Tennant. Buena Vista Pictures, 2002.

Tasker, Yvonne, and Diane Negra. "In Focus: Postfeminism and Contemporary Media Studies." *Cinema Journal* 44.2 (2005): 107–110.

Taylor, Jodie. *Playing it Queer: Popular Music, Identity and Queer World-Making*. Bern: Peter Lang, 2012.

Telephone. Dir. Jonas Akerlund. Perf. Lady Gaga. Interscope Records, 2010. *Vevo*. 13 April 2017.

That Don't Impress Me Much. Dir. Paul Boyd. Perf. Shania Twain. Mercury Records, 1998. *Vevo.* 13 April 2017.

The Adventures of Priscilla – Queen of the Desert. Dir. Stephan Elliott. Gramercy, 1994.

The Big Doll House. Dir. Jack Hill. New World Pictures, 1971.

The Devil Wears Prada. Dir. David Frankel. 20th Century Fox, 2006.

The Hunting Ground. Dir. Kirby Dick. The Weinstein Company, 2015.

The Monster Ball. Dir. Arthur Fogel, Matthew "Dada" Williams, and Willo Perron. Hartford, 16 Sep 2010.

Thelma & Louise. Dir. Ridley Scott. MGM, 1991.

The Stepford Wives. Dir. Frank Oz. DreamWorks, 2004.

The Wizard of Oz. Dir. Victor Fleming. MGM, 1939.

Vertigo. Dir. Alfred Hitchcock. Universal, 1958.

Victor/Victoria. Dir. Blake Edwards. MGM, 1982.

Video Phone. Dir. Hype Williams. Perf. Beyoncé and Lady Gaga. Columbia Records, 2009. *Vimeo.* 13 April 2017.

Vogue. Dir. David Fincher. Perf. Madonna. Sire Records, 1990. *Vevo.* 13 April 2017.

Walking in Memphis. Dir. Marcus Nispel. Perf. Cher. Warner Bros. Records, 1995. *Youtube.* 13 April 2017.

Weiner, Jonah. "How Smart Is Lady Gaga? Pop's Most Pretentious Starlet." *Slate.* 16 June 2009. Slate Group. 12 February 2010. http://www.slate.com/articles/arts/music_box/2009/06/how_smart_is_lady_gaga.html.

Whiteley, Sheila. "Who Are You? Research Strategies of the Unruly Feminine." *The Ashgate Research Companion to Popular Musicology.* Ed. Derek B. Scott. Farnham. Surrey: Ashgate, 2009. 205–220.

Whitesell, Lloyd. "Trans Glam: Gender Magic in the Film Musical." *Queering the Popular Pitch.* Ed. Sheila Whiteley and Jennifer Rycenga. New York: Routledge, 2006. 263–277.

Who's That Girl. Dir. Duncan Gibbons. Perf. Annie Lennox. Sony, 1983. *Vevo.* 13 April 2017.

Why. Dir. Sophie Muller. Perf. Annie Lennox. RCA Records, 1992. *Youtube.* 13 April 2017.

Wolf, Werner. "Metareference across Media: The Concept, its Transmedial Potentials and Problems, Main Forms and Functions." *Metareference Across Media: Theory and Case Studies.* Eds. Werner Wolf and Walter Bernhart. Amsterdam: Rodopi, 2009. 1–89.

You and I. Dir. Laurieann Gibson. Streamline. 2011. Vevo. 26 June 2017.

CHAPTER 6

Camp: A New, More Complex Relation to the Serious

Even if a camp perspective on popular culture is thoroughly concerned with contemporary sensibilities it nonetheless invites a new perspective on past artifacts, a re-evaluation of disavowed stereotypes, and a refreshed enjoyment of images previously condemned as reactionary. How fitting then that I found my estimation of Susan Sontag's "Notes on Camp" similarly altered by a newer, queerer notion of camp than the one she herself had proposed in 1964. Like the rejected conclusion proposed in classical Hollywood cinema that the queer villain is repulsive and evil, rather than the sexy and exciting creature contemporary readings might find in the same iconography, Sontag's conviction that she describes an a-political and superficial sensibility is repudiated, or at least complicated, by her own words. In note 41 of her 58 "Notes on Camp," Sontag muses about camp's relation to the serious. She jumps from the insistence that it is "anti-serious" to the claim that camp "involves a new, more complex relation to 'the serious'" before finally settling on the conditional "it *can* be serious" (288, emphasis added). Sontag's assertion is vague not only because of the partially contradictory three-part definition, but also due to the quotation marks around "the serious." While she herself famously argued that "camp sees everything in quotation marks" (290), to dispense with them (at least in this instance) makes for a sharper, surprisingly current formulation of camp: a "new, more complex relation to the serious."

Camp's intervention in pop-cultural discourses of gender and sexuality results precisely from relating in a new way (namely in a distancing

© The Author(s) 2017   253
K. Horn, *Women, Camp, and Popular Culture*,
DOI 10.1007/978-3-319-64846-0_6

manner) to what is usually considered a serious matter (notions of personal authenticity and originality, the heteronormativity of relationships and gender identity, etc.) and conversely arriving at a more complex idea of what it is worth being serious about: a critique—in Sedgwick's words—that is not paranoid, but reparative (*Touching* 149–50). To think of camp as detached attachment to contemporary culture is to conceive of camp as a mode of enhancing the pleasures of popular media through a lens that is aware of, and accentuates, its deficiencies. Such a perception is the result of several "new, complex relations," not only between the frivolous and the serious, but also between producer and audience, artifact and canon, affect and critique, and finally, camp and contemporary sensibilities.

Camp therefore both *results* from a more complex relation to popular culture, which stresses its incongruities and undermines its so-called truths and norms, and it *creates* a more complex relation to popular culture that combines critical awareness and affect. As such, camp's point is not to produce literal meanings, depict progressive politics, or envision alternative realities. Instead, camp arises in the interaction between said and unsaid, depicted and hinted at, parodied and referenced, to create spaces of alternative identification and pleasure. This relationality, which is often misconstrued as evasiveness, is the reason camp—despite numerous claims to the contrary—is still not dead, but perpetually alive to changing sensibilities. Its excessive aesthetics, accordingly, can rewrite the history of lesbian representation in Hollywood cinema by bringing into conversation vastly different forms of problematic gay visibility—old movie stereotypes, lesbian chic, and New Queer Cinema—to create new forms of cinematic pleasure. It can support a sitcom's carnivalesque framing and offer humorous entertainment enmeshed in a serious critique of contemporary gender ideology, while enhancing the audience's attachment to ostensibly farcical characters and stories. Supported by digital media formats, camp can furthermore enhance its potential to disrupt exploitative conventions and address new audiences. It can thus rewrite the scripts of pop music's commodification of feminist and LGBT images to evoke a utopian space of communal affect nurtured by an otherwise neglected queer canon.

Finally, camp can fashion a new, reparative relation to popular culture for contemporary marginalized audiences beyond the contexts fleshed out in this book. In recent years performers like Nicki Minaj and Mykki Blanco have drawn attention to the camp possibilities for performers and audiences of color, and in 2017 camp was highlighted courtesy of a black actor referencing Beyoncé's most political and most personal work to date. In season 3 of the Netflix-sitcom *Unbreakable Kimmy Schmidt* (2015–), Titus Andromedon (Titus Burgess)—an African American character on an overwhelmingly white show who constantly calls out the "white nonsense" that surrounds him—steps out of the role of supporting character (and TV cliché of Black Best Friend), as he works through the pain of an impending break-up by doing what "any reasonable person would do in this situation […] Lemonade-ing." In three carefully crafted parodies of songs and videos that simultaneously pay homage to *Lemonade*, Titus follows the visual album's emotional journey from anger to acceptance. This development towards personal maturity is presented in the show's trademark combination of the absurd and the hilarious—Titus' trash-aesthetic re-enactments of Beyoncé's elaborate videos reflected in his nonsensical interpretations of her poetic lyrics— and yet results in his most emotionally charged performances and one of the show's most poignant scenes. Whether he struts down the street in a dress made of curtains and wonders "what's worse/being heartbroke or roach-bit," muses about the afterlife in a Cleopatra-headpiece ("What will you say at my funeral now that you've killed me/here lies Titus, stepmother to my lizards, both living and dead? His heaven will be a grand piano full of baked potatoes"), or wanders through roof-top gardens in a costume made of his "afro-centric bedspreads" to finally decide to set his lover free, the episode's aesthetics and narrative arc encapsulate his character's general camp appeal. His excessive persona rejects stereotypical representations of gay men (via overarticulation) and black masculinity (through queering), and reverses the assimilationist tendencies of minority characters in overwhelmingly white shows more generally. His serious excess, however, is also a source of humor and pleasure, and thus the embodiment of detached attachment that expands camp's often limited racial dynamics.

In all these cases, camp presents a participatory critique that both disrupts the cultural consensus and creates new webs of affinity, whereby it invites audiences to reflect on *what* they enjoy and to enjoy *that* they reflect (be it ethnic clichés or gender tropes). Not everyone will get such an invitation nor will everyone accept it; for some, Titus will remain a colorful addition to *Unbreakable Kimmy Schmidt*'s array of "weirdos," while others will recognize themselves and their cultural legacy in his diva-worshipping rejection of the status quo. Camp therefore retains its quality as an in-group humor, even in the popular mass media whose texts are produced to appeal to as many people as possible. Consuming or even enjoying such products is not tantamount to "getting" their camp value. This is reserved for specific discursive communities even in contemporary culture supposedly saturated with camp(y) aesthetics. Camp only fully unfolds its critique and its pleasure through a close examination of the images, stereotypes, and narratives (as well as their origins) that are questioned through their repetition with stylistic exaggeration in a different affective context. Such a close examination will reveal that—in contrast to recent uses of camp as an umbrella-term for the merely excessively stylized—camp films, sitcoms, videos, and performances appear sillier, more frivolous, and less engaged if read "straight." The more audiences are accustomed to camp's excessive qualities, alert to the text's many incongruities, and immersed in their specific canons, the more these texts unfold as complex interventions into representational systems. In short, camp makes their excess serious.

WORKS CITED

Sedgwick, Eve Kosofsky. *Touching Feeling: Affect, Pedagogy, Performativity.* Durham: Duke UP, 2003.

Sontag, Susan. "Notes on Camp." *Against Interpretation, and Other Essays.* New York: Picador, 2001. 275–292.

Unbreakable Kimmy Schmidt. Creat. Tina Fey and Robert Carlock. Netflix, 2015.

INDEX

© The Editor(s) (if applicable) and The Author(s) 2017

K. Horn, *Women, Camp, and Popular Culture*,

DOI 10.1007/978-3-319-64846-0

CPSIA information can be obtained
at www.ICGtesting.com
Printed in the USA
LVHW021613091122
732728LV00010B/545